CIVIL WAR JOURNALISM

**Recent Titles in
Reflections on the Civil War Era**

CIVIL WAR JOURNALISM

FORD RISLEY

Reflections on the Civil War Era
John David Smith, Series Editor

PRAEGER

AN IMPRINT OF ABC-CLIO, LLC
Santa Barbara, California • Denver, Colorado • Oxford, England

Copyright 2012 by Ford Risley

All rights reserved. No part of this publication may be reproduced,
stored in a retrieval system, or transmitted, in any form or by any means,
electronic, mechanical, photocopying, recording, or otherwise, except for
the inclusion of brief quotations in a review, without prior permission
in writing from the publisher.

Library of Congress Cataloging-in-Publication Data

Risley, Ford.
   Civil War journalism / Ford Risley.
      p. cm. — (Reflections on the Civil War era)
   Includes bibliographical references and index.
    ISBN 978-0-313-34727-6 (hardcopy : alk. paper) — ISBN 978-0-313-34728-3
(e-book)   1. United States—History—Civil War, 1861–1865—Press coverage.
2. United States—History—Civil War, 1861–1865—Journalists.   3. Press
and politics—United States—History—19th century.   4. Journalism—United
States—History—19th century.   I. Title.
   E609.R57   2012
   070.4'499737—dc23   2012019595

ISBN: 978-0-313-34727-6
EISBN: 978-0-313-34728-3

16   15   14   13   12   1   2   3   4   5

This book is also available on the World Wide Web as an eBook.
Visit www.abc-clio.com for details.

Praeger
An Imprint of ABC-CLIO, LLC

ABC-CLIO, LLC
130 Cremona Drive, P.O. Box 1911
Santa Barbara, California 93116-1911

This book is printed on acid-free paper ∞

Manufactured in the United States of America

For Mary

CONTENTS

SERIES FOREWORD

"Like Ol' Man River," the distinguished Civil War historian Peter J. Parish wrote in 1998, "Civil War historiography just keeps rolling along. It changes course occasionally, leaving behind bayous of stagnant argument, while it carves out new lines of inquiry and debate."

Since Confederate General Robert E. Lee's men stacked their guns at Appomattox Court House in April 1865, historians and partisans have been fighting a war of words over the causes, battles, results, and broad meaning of the internecine conflict that cost more than 620,000 American lives. Writers have contributed between 50,000 and 60,000 books and pamphlets on the topic. Viewed in terms of defining American freedom and nationalism, western expansion, and economic development, the Civil War quite literally launched modern America. "The Civil War," Kentucky poet, novelist, and literary critic Robert Penn Warren explained, "is for the American imagination, the great single event of our history. Without too much wrenching, it may, in fact, be said to be American history."

The books in Praeger's *Reflections on the Civil War Era* series examine pivotal aspects of the American Civil War. Topics range from examinations of military campaigns and local conditions, to analyses of institutional, intellectual, and social history. Questions of class, gender, and race run through each volume in the series. Authors, veteran experts in their respective fields, provide concise, informed, and readable syntheses—fresh looks at familiar topics with new source material and original arguments.

"Like all great conflicts," Parish noted in 1999, "the American Civil War reflected the society and the age in which it was fought." Books in *Reflections on the Civil War Era* interpret the war as a salient event in the hammering out and understanding of American identity before, during, and after the secession crisis of 1860–1861. Readers will find the volumes valuable guides as they chart the troubled waters of mid-19th-century American life.

John David Smith
Charles H. Stone Distinguished Professor of American History
The University of North Carolina at Charlotte

PREFACE AND ACKNOWLEDGMENTS

In 1861, two armies began waging a war that forever changed the United States. During the next four years, Americans fought against Americans at Fort Sumter, Bull Run, Shiloh, Antietam, Fredericksburg, Chancellorsville, Vicksburg, Gettysburg, Chattanooga, and Petersburg, as well as Ball's Bluff, Newbern, Perryville, Bethesda Church, St. Charles, and Kennesaw Mountain. At all these places—and many others—journalists from the North and South chronicled the fighting in words, illustrations, and photographs. Back at their offices, editorial writers and cartoonists expressed their opinions on how the war was being waged, the reasons for fighting, the quality of leadership, and many other subjects. All the while, the governments of the Union and Confederacy used censorship and suppression to reign in what, in their view, was too often a reckless and irresponsible press.

This book examines the journalism of the North and South during the Civil War. Various works have been written about the war press. But most have focused on a particular aspect of the journalism practiced, usually from the perspective of one side or the other. No account has chronicled the reporting and editorializing, the photography and illustrations, the press censorship and suppression, as well as the impact of the war on both sides in a comprehensive manner. This book does that.

The Civil War is unquestionably one of the most significant—some would argue the most significant—events in American history. The war settled two fundamental issues that had confronted the United States since its founding: whether the country was to be a nation with a strong central government or a loose confederation of states, and whether a country dedicated to the principles of freedom was to continue as the largest slaveholding nation in the world. Tragically, more than 620,000 soldiers from the Union and Confederacy died to settle the issues.

The Civil War also is one of the most important episodes in American journalism history. As the source of news and opinion, the press had grown to occupy an increasingly important role in American society during the first half of the 19th century. Newspapers and magazines had modernized to better report news and information, while still maintaining the editorial role they had always cherished. Illustrations and photography were becoming an increasingly important means to provide a visual record of events.

I want to thank John David Smith, editor of the *Reflections on the Civil War Era* series, for his editorial guidance. Bill Huntzicker, Jeffery Smith, and Debra van Tuyll read chapters and provided insightful feedback that improved each considerably. My graduate assistants at Penn State, Kirstie Hettinga and Cristina Mislan, were a great help in finding stories, editorials, letters, and government documents used in the book. I am also grateful for the encouragement of my colleagues in the College of Communications at Penn State, especially in the Department of Journalism.

Special thanks go to my wife, Mary, and our daughters, Emily and Megan. They have always supported my work in ways both big and small. Mary, in particular, has encouraged my research since the days when we lived near a Civil War battlefield, and I first began to think about how newsmen from the North and South reported the fighting that took place there. This book is dedicated to her.

INTRODUCTION

On the eve of the Civil War the U.S. press was a political, social, and economic force. The country's 3,725 newspapers were twice the number published in Britain and about one-third of all the broadsheets in the entire world. Moreover, the circulation per capita of America's newspapers was far greater than any other country. The majority of publications in the United States were small weeklies. But virtually every community of any size had at least one or two newspapers, and many cities had 3, 4, or more. New York City alone had 11 daily newspapers, not including those in Brooklyn. There were 12 newspapers published in Philadelphia, 11 in Chicago, and 10 in St. Louis.[1]

Newspapers "were the daily fare of nearly meal in almost every family; so cheap and common, that, like air and water, its uses are undervalued," author Charles Ingersoll observed. A visitor from Europe marveled at the popularity of the press. "Which is more astonishing," he asked, "the great speed at which these newspapers are produced, or the excited curiosity with which the otherwise phlegmatic Americans storm the newspapers' offices at the appointed hour and gobble up the produce of the presses the minute before it sees the light of day?" He noted the central role that newspapers played in the growing nation. "You meet newspaper readers everywhere; and in the evening the whole city knows what lay twenty-four ago on the newswriters' desks," he wrote. "The few who cannot read can hear news discussed or read aloud in ale-and-oyster houses."[2]

Magazines also were becoming increasingly popular, in particular a new breed of illustrated weekly publications, which had readerships that rivaled, and in some cases exceeded, the largest newspapers. Seizing on the popularity of elaborately made illustrations, the magazines packed each issue with pictures on a variety of subjects. Delighted readers snapped them up. Thus it was hardly surprising that the director of the U.S. Census of 1860 said that newspapers and periodicals "furnish nearly the whole of the reading which the greater number, whether from inclination or necessity, permit themselves to enjoy."[3]

Certainly the press benefited from America's rapid growth in the mid-19th century. Millions of new immigrants, primarily from Northern and Western Europe but also from Asia, settled on the East and West coasts. Between 1840 and 1860, the country's population jumped 84 percent from 17,069,000 to 31,443,000. Seven new states were added during the two decades (California, Florida, Iowa, Minnesota, Oregon, Texas, and Wisconsin), and three more were poised to join the Union (Kansas, Nebraska, and Nevada).[4]

Changes in journalistic and business practices also made a significant impact on the country's press, particularly in the country's major metropolitan areas. The introduction of the so-called penny press, inexpensive publications aimed at a mass audience, forever changed newspapers, which for decades had largely been editorial tools of the country's political parties. Newspapers that generally had waited for the news to come to them—clipping and printing material provided through an exchange system—aggressively covered the news for the first time using reporters. Led by two new broadsheets in New York, the *Sun* and *Herald*, editors recognized that readers craved news—news that was essential but also news that would entertain and excite. Publications in other big cities soon followed the penny press model.[5]

At the same time, a technological revolution helped make the press into a truly mass medium. The telegraph, invented in 1844, meant that newspapers for the first time could gather and report news in a timely manner. By 1852, 17,000 miles of telegraph lines were in use and linked all of the nation's major cities except San Francisco. The demands on the telegraph were so great, in fact, that some cities were connected by multiwire lines. There were 14 lines between New York and Philadelphia, and 7 lines linking New York to Baltimore and Washington, D.C. Newspaper editors and publishers embraced the telegraph. "The events of yesterday throughout the entire land will be given, as we now give the occurrences at home," said the *Philadelphia North American.* And the *Springfield Republican* proclaimed, "Nothing can be more evident to the public, and nothing certainly more evident to publishers of newspapers than there is a great deal more news nowadays than there used to be. . . . The increase of facilities for transmission of news brought in a new era." The usefulness of the telegraph led to the development of the Associated Press, the first cooperative news gathering organization.[6]

The invention of new steam-powered cylinder presses made it possible for newspapers and magazines to reach a far larger audience. The Hoe Rotary Lightning Press allowed printers to place separate sheets of paper into revolving cylinders that printed two pages side by side. Once dry, the printed pages were fed in again to print two pages on the other side. The sheets then were inserted into machines that folded them to make four pages. Five to ten thousand copies of a four-page newspaper could be turned out in an hour. And thanks to the growth of the railroad, which by mid-century linked the north and south, east and west, newspapers could be distributed more easily across the country. The *New York Tribune*'s weekly national edition had an eye-popping circulation of more than 200,000.[7]

As the circulation of newspapers and magazines grew in the mid-1800s, advertising became a more attractive way for businesses to reach customers and an important source of income. On the eve of the war, it was not unusual for advertising to comprise half or more of many newspapers. Advertisements were found throughout publications, including the front page. Advertising also had gradually become more sophisticated by the time war began. Not only had the size of advertisements grown, particularly in magazines, but many featured illustrations, creative layouts, and varied type sizes to attract the attention of readers.[8]

The growth of the press in the decade before the war was fueled in part by the debate over slavery. Countless editors started publications because they believed they could help shape the public mind on key issues: the Kansas-Nebraska Act, the emergence of the Republican Party, the Dred Scott Supreme Court decision, the Lincoln-Douglas debates, the raid on Harpers Ferry, and Abraham Lincoln's election as president. "If we fail to notice the appearance of any new paper it is not from an intentional discourtesy, but simply because we can scarcely keep up with the list, they increase so fast," a Georgia editor remarked. Newspapers were springing up as "thick in hops," according to a North Carolina journal, with every village having one publication, courthouse towns two or three, and some "where there were neither towns nor villages."[9]

With a larger population and more big cities, the North had far more publications with a greater circulation than the South. About three-fourths of America's broadsheets were published in the North and they accounted for seven-eighths of the country's circulation. The greatest contrast was between the 11 states that would make up the Confederacy and the more urban states of the North. In fact, the circulation of newspapers in the state of New York alone was more than that of all the future Confederate states combined. And the largest newspapers in the North had far more readers than their counterparts in the South. The largest daily newspaper in the North, the *New York Herald,* had a daily circulation of about 77,000. In contrast, no newspaper in the South had a circulation of more than 10,000.[10]

As readers turned to the press for news, the handling of news became more sophisticated. At the large metropolitan dailies, full-time correspondents were used to aggressively report the news for the first time. Moreover, news increasingly was distinguished from opinion on the pages of newspapers. That did not mean the reporting was always fair, balanced, or objective; in fact, often it was not. Only the most rudimentary journalistic standards existed in the mid-1800s. However, editors consistently argued for the public's right to know information and promoted the role of the press in supplying it. Moreover, they maintained the press had a duty to watch over society's institutions and expose problems in order to protect the citizenry.[11]

As the main source of news and information, newspapers and magazines helped shaped antebellum public opinion, although exactly how much is impossible to know. What is clear is that many editors published their views with seemingly little sense of the high stakes involved for the nation. Throughout the 1850s, the press of the North and South increasingly engaged in an editorial war of words, often portraying the opposing side in the most virulent and disparaging terms. Hatred begot hatred on the pages of the press.[12]

Most believed that the editorial debate in the press was essential in a democracy. But others argued that it exacerbated the growing divisions between the North and South. "How can two sections of the country ever hope to be at peace so long as the journals of the country continue to make such flings at them?" an Arkansas newspaper asked. "We cannot censure the Northern press only, for we, unfortunately, have many of the same factious spirits in the South. And it is from such sources we have most to fear." The *National Intelligencer* decried "the spirit of rancor and intolerance with which honest differences of opinion are treated by political opponents. . . . The vocabulary of abuse has been exhausted in order to furnish invective for the gratification of partisan spite and animosity."[13]

This was the American press poised to report and editorialize on the Civil War. It was a growing, but still maturing press, in many ways. During a war of unprecedented carnage and destruction—with the future of the country at stake—it came of age.

ONE

REPORTING THE WAR

When Confederate cannons opened fire on Fort Sumter early in the morning of April 12, 1861, readers across the United States already knew plenty about the stronghold guarding Charleston harbor and the Federal garrison assigned to it. Since South Carolina seceded from the Union in December, newspapers across the North and South had been chronicling the worsening secession crisis daily. By April, more than a dozen newsmen were in Charleston.

For the next four years, correspondents on both sides reported the war to an extent never seen before. The press of the Union and Confederacy published millions of words on every aspect of the conflict. Many of the accounts honestly and faithfully chronicled the war. Tireless newsmen went to great lengths to report stories on deadline and displayed considerable enterprise to describe the war in all its facets. However, other accounts mistakenly and, in some cases, irresponsibly reported the conflict. Reporters less concerned with the facts and more interested in rushing stories into print wrote damaging stories that hurt their side.

Hundreds of reporters, both full-time and soldier correspondents, chronicled the fighting on land and at sea. Others reported news from the capitals of Washington, D.C., and Richmond, Virginia. In many instances they overcame numerous challenges, including uncooperative sources and the difficulty of getting stories back to their newspaper. In the field, correspondents endured hardships and dangers. Several newsmen were killed covering the fighting and others were captured.

No standards existed for what constituted sound, thorough, and responsible journalism on the eve of the war. The special correspondents—"specials" as they were frequently known—were guided by their backgrounds, education, talent, and morals. Certainly they were a diverse group. While some reporters had previous journalism experience, others included lawyers, teachers, clerks, bookkeepers, ministers, and at least one poet. Some were college educated and their ranks included graduates of Harvard, Yale, Columbia, Amherst, University of Pennsylvania, University of Virginia, and University of Georgia. Others had only rudimentary schooling. The majority were in their twenties or thirties, although several were in their teens and some in their forties. Not surprisingly, the overwhelming majority of correspondents were white men. A handful of women reported during the war. Only one black man is known to have been a correspondent for a daily newspaper.[1]

Correspondents went in to the field equipped with notebooks, pencils, field glasses, clothing, blankets, personal items, and, in some cases, a revolver. Some sought to look their best and wore fancy vests, knee-high boots, and wide-brimmed hats. Most quickly found that the niceties were of little good. Writing from Virginia in 1862, a *New York Times* reporter told his editor, "If you send out any more correspondents, don't provide them with anything. The best outfit will get scattered in a week. Of my horse, bridle, saddle, blankets and other accoutrements, I have but one spur remaining, and I expect to miss that tomorrow morning."[2]

In the field, reporters got around any way they could, be it by horseback, wagon, train, ship, or foot. The travel often was arduous. The *Philadelphia Inquirer*'s correspondent at Fortress Monroe complained about the difficulty of finding a horse to cover the fighting. "You cannot get a horse here for love or money," he wrote. "I have hired a horse twice since I have been here—but it is gone. . . . I will walk some 20 miles to-day." The best newsmen learned to be resourceful. Peter W. Alexander of the *Savannah Republican* had to travel to Mississippi in 1862. However, the train he needed to take was full, so Alexander made the acquaintance of the engineer who agreed to let him ride in the tender if he kept the fire stoked. After being soaked in a rainstorm, Alexander spent the night in the home of a one-legged man. The other guests included "one idiot, two pigs, a man with a freshly broken arm, and a number of sick, weary soldiers."[3]

Working conditions could be extraordinarily difficult. Correspondents wrote their stories whenever and wherever they could. One newsman closed a story by writing, "Your readers must pardon a short letter. No man can write in a happy vein or style while minnie [*sic*] balls are flying uncomfortably close to his head." Confederate reporter Felix G. de Fontaine wrote his account of the battle of Shiloh while sitting on the floor of a hotel that had been converted into an army hospital.

> While I write I am sitting on the floor of one of the corridors, with the bodies of the living and the dead ranged on either side and opposite as far as the eye can reach. Groans fill the air, surgeons are busy at work by candlelight, a few women are ministering to the wants of the suffering, the atmosphere is fetid with the stench of wounds, and the rain is pouring down.[4]

In the field, specials often lived like soldiers. In a letter to his editor, Samuel Wilkeson of the *New York Times* wrote: "The flannel shirt I have on I have worn five weeks. . . . Rails make my bed. . . . My jackknife is my spoon, knife, fork, and toothpick." De Fontaine described living conditions in reporting from the Confederate army. "Comforts of life are scarce," he wrote. "Hard bread, water, molasses and bacon, very tough and indigestible, constitute our fare; a very hard plank and a pair of blankets serves as our bed. . . . We wash our own clothes, do our own cooking, and when rations give out, 'beg, borrow, and steal'. About three times a week we have the chills."[5]

Workdays frequently could be long. During one campaign, Union correspondent George Smalley worked for 20 straight hours, including 14 hours on his horse. Some correspondents arrived back at their newspaper offices so tired that they could not hold a pen to write their stories. Shorthand reporters had to be brought in to take down the accounts.[6]

Gathering information for their news stories was challenging. A soldier correspondent with the *Atlanta Southern Confederacy* described the hard times of trying to report on General Joseph E. Johnston's army. He complained about being snubbed at the army's headquarters by everyone from the assistant adjutant general to the orderly. Then there were the officers who wanted to know why the correspondent did not mention their particular regiment or brigade. Invariably, the same officer who had snubbed the correspondent would ask him confidentially, "why do you never say anything about the general in your letters." Reporters on both sides had to constantly sift through the rumors that swirled about camps. "Each newcomer from the field of battle . . . tells a different story of the same thing to that which was told you only a few minutes since by a different person," said one newsman. Another complained about the "professional liars" in the army who "invent all manner of absurd reports, merely for the gratification of hearing them repeated to wondering listeners."[7]

The most aggressive and enterprising reporters put themselves in danger to report, standing at strategic points, going out with skirmishers, riding along the lines, crouching in trenches, and being aboard ships at battle. Correspondents on both sides were wounded during the war and several died from wounds they received.

Camp life and the rigors of being in the field also could be hazardous. Numerous reporters contracted diseases and had to be hospitalized.[8]

Specials for both sides were captured during the fighting. A *New York Tribune* reporter was seized by a group of Confederate irregulars in Virginia. They found his identification papers and were ready to hang him for being "an abolition liar for Horace Greeley." Fortunately, a cavalry patrol arrived in time to save the newsman. During the battle of the Wilderness, two *New York Herald* reporters were on the way to file stories when they were captured by Confederate troops. The rebels took everything but their shirts and pants, then marched the men for several miles before releasing them. The correspondents eventually made it to the Potomac River and rafted downstream before being picked up by a gunboat.[9]

Most captured journalists were promptly freed, but others spent weeks or months in prisons before being released. Correspondents Junius Browne and Albert D. Richardson were captured near Vicksburg in March 1863. They spent months in several different Confederate prisons while repeated efforts to have them released failed. By the end of the year, Browne and Richardson were being held at the Salisbury Prison in North Carolina. But on the night of December 17, the two men escaped. They traveled 300 miles, sometimes aided by blacks and Union sympathizers, finally making it to the Federal lines in Tennessee.[10]

Correspondents repeatedly went to great lengths to beat their competitors. After the battle of Gettysburg, reporter Frank Chapman reached Baltimore early in the morning on July 4 ahead of other correspondents. He awakened the manager of the local telegraph office at home and persuaded him to open the office. The telegraph operator sent the story, and, as he was finishing, a reporter with the *New York Tribune* dashed in with his account. Chapman was about to leave to get more information for his story but realized that the operator would have to send the *Tribune*'s account. To prevent that, Chapman pulled out a small Bible, gave it to the telegraph operator, and told him to send passages until he got back. *Philadelphia Inquirer* reporter William H. Cunnington worked to the point of exhaustion in reporting the battle of Fredericksburg. He walked from the battlefield to Fredericksburg and then rode a horse 14 miles to catch a steamer for Washington. From there he ran to the telegraph office to send his story to Philadelphia.[11]

The best specials often showed resourcefulness to get a story. A reporter for the *Boston Journal*, who was following General William T. Sherman's army in Georgia, rode 150 miles sitting on a platform atop a railroad car to get a graphic picture of the devastation from Chattanooga to Marietta. A Union correspondent in North Carolina disguised himself in a slouch hat and ragged jacket to wander behind Confederate lines for several days gathering material for a story.[12]

The position of reporter was evolving and some men clearly were not suited for it. John Linebaugh, a former Episcopalian priest, joined the staff of the *Memphis Appeal* in 1863. Assigned to the Army of Tennessee, he chose to station himself at Dalton, Georgia, about 25 miles south of where the army was camped. Linebaugh defended the decision to be so far away by telling his editors that nothing was happening in camp worth reporting. He later was in Chattanooga when the Union shelling of the city began. Instead of covering what was happening, Linebaugh promptly caught the first train south to Atlanta, later explaining that he had "a lady under my protection." The *Appeal* was scooped by the *Mobile Register and Advertiser,* which had a reporter in Chattanooga. Another problem for his editors: Linebaugh liked to use words such as "didactic" and "afflucium" in his stories. He also had a penchant for long-winded sentences. A sentence in one of his stories had 139 words.[13]

Other reporters did not let the facts get in the way of a good story. Warren P. Isham of the *Chicago Times* had a well-earned reputation as one of the most imaginative correspondents. In April 1862, he wrote about a Union general who allegedly was patronizing a bordello outside Memphis when a group of Confederate officers arrived. The general, who was "clad only in underdrawers," was forced to escape through a rear window, Isham wrote. When the general returned to headquarters, according to the story, he described a "harrowing tale of escape from spies and robbers." General Ulysses S. Grant eventually told Isham to "stop your cock-and-bull yarns," but the correspondent ignored him. Finally, when Isham created a story about a fictitious fleet of Confederate ironclads in Pensacola, Florida, he was arrested and jailed for three months.[14]

❧⊰⊱❧

Generally only the largest daily newspapers in the North and South could afford to send full-time, paid correspondents to cover the fighting. Yet many editors recognized that readers wanted news from regiments comprised of hometown men. So they made arrangements with a member of a local outfit, often an officer, to send back occasional letters to the newspaper with news of the war. Some editors took great pride in the group of correspondents they had secured. The editor of the *Atlanta Southern Confederacy* bragged in 1862 that the newspaper had "a most efficient corps of able correspondents from all points of special interest in the army." Some soldier correspondents, who went by pen names such as "Outline," "Spectator," "Vagabond," "Slingshot," and "Buttermilk," sent back only a handful of letters and were never heard from again. But others sent regular correspondence for years.[15]

As soldiers, the correspondents in no way were objective in their stories. Writing in the formal, declamatory style of the era, their letters frequently were intended as much to inspire readers back home as to inform them. As could be expected of fighting men with little or no newspaper experience, many of their stories were filled with specious, bombastic descriptions of heroic, God-fearing troops overcoming great odds to defeat the enemy. Victory on the battlefield was a sure sign of their superiority, the rightness of their cause, and the fact that God was on their side.[16]

Some soldier correspondents used their letters to do little more than glorify battles or the war in general. "Of the gallantry displayed by both officers and men, I could not, if the vocabulary of praise was searched, speak too highly," a correspondent declared in a letter. "When the history of the affair comes to be written, the brightest page will record the achievement of the Troup Artillery." And a correspondent who sent regular letters to the *Atlanta Southern Confederacy,* wrote of one attack during fighting in Tennessee: "See our brave little band as they advance with deadly impetuosity, upon the foe, and in a perfect shower of bullets meeting his numerous columns in hand to hand conflict! . . . The bristling bayonets of thousands did not deter them, but wherever their leader pointed, there they rushed with stout hearts to do his bidding."[17]

In other instances, however, the letters of soldier correspondents had real news value and provided readers with valuable insight into the impact of the war. A soldier correspondent for the *Boston Herald* described the effect of the war on Louisville, Kentucky. He described the "closed stores, the tenantless houses, the listless people in the street. No one was in a hurry . . . few seemed to have anything to do." Some soldiers for both sides could be remarkably honest in their correspondence. Their candid accounts also revealed problems within the military. A correspondent for the *Philadelphia Inquirer* described the incompetency of the quartermaster corps in providing rations and supplies. A letter from a correspondent with the *Atlanta Daily Intelligencer* described the numerous problems caused by Confederate officers who did not enforce discipline in the army. He wrote bluntly, "Some portions of the army constitute nothing more than armed mob. . . . There is such a thing as discipline and there is no excuse for not enforcing it. Lawlessness, drunkenness, and gambling are frequently not only known but even tolerated." After the battle of Chickamauga in 1863, a Southern correspondent told of walking over the battlefield where the Confederate army still was camped. Some of the troops, he wrote candidly, amused themselves by rifling through the pockets of dead Union soldiers. They also joked and made lewd comments upon reading love letters of the troops or discovering a picture of a dead man's wife or girlfriend.[18]

Newspapers in the North also received news from the Associated Press, or AP, as it was frequently known. Established in 1846 by a group of New York editors, the AP had become a national wire service by the time the war began. The AP gathered news from all over the country at its New York headquarters, and from there it was sifted, edited, and sent out via the various regional telegraphic companies. A telegraph operator in each city took down the dispatches and made carbon copies for each local subscribing AP member.[19]

The AP employed a staff of correspondents with at least one at virtually every important point in the country. The majority of newspapers in the North, particularly smaller ones, relied heavily on the AP for news of the war. They published daily columns of telegraphic news, often on the front page. Still, some member newspapers complained about the cost and quality of the AP dispatches. In late 1862, a group of Midwestern publishers met in Indianapolis to form their own wire service, the Western Associated Press. During the war, a group of former AP reporters left to start their own news and feature service based in Washington. And naval reporter B. S. Osbon launched a Navy News Service.[20]

The government supplied the AP exclusively with its war bulletins and official announcements. The Lincoln administration recognized that the wire service could be enormously helpful in reaching a national constituency simultaneously. AP reporters had wide access to the president and the War Department. The wire service also received preferential access to telegraphic facilities. The nature of the AP made it ideally suited for the administration. Unlike many reporters for newspapers, AP correspondents did not add their own commentary that would color their stories. Administration officials could count on their dispatches being sent out by the AP with just the facts. A technical aspect of the wire services news transmission also gave an advantage to an administration that wanted to control information. Because telegraphic transmissions cost less at night, many of the news dispatches from the AP in New York were sent late at night. This ensured that the news arrived just in time for compositors to get them into the next morning's papers. Editors often did not have a chance to scrutinize dispatches provided by the administration and they were published as sent from the AP.[21]

The Confederacy developed its own wire service, although it took time for obstacles to be overcome. Soon after the fighting began, the telegraphic lines to the South were cut. Confederate editors quickly recognized that some kind of wire service was needed. Banding together, they tried various things before settling on what became known as the Press Association of the Confederate States of America or P.A. Superintendent John Thrasher hired correspondents to report from Richmond and Charleston, as well as the Confederacy's largest armies. He eventually secured about 20 correspondents spread from Virginia to Mississippi. Thrasher admonished his newsmen regarding the importance of "securing early, full, and reliable" telegraphic news. Press Association correspondents were instructed to write clearly and concisely, using short sentences and avoiding ambiguous words. The superintendent ordered that all stories should be free of opinion and comment. He urged his newsmen "to sift reports" and "to not send unfounded rumors as news." He also warned correspondents to "see that you are not beaten" by reporters from other journals.[22]

In later instructions, Thrasher instructed correspondents that they represented the "whole daily press" of the Confederacy and that they should request "early intelligence of events." Correspondents were to transmit all news, which could be published without harming the military effort of the Confederate army. Thrasher warned that the "greatest caution" should be exercised in reporting troop movements and, in all cases, commanding generals should be consulted about information considered appropriate for transmission. In the event censors refused to approve a story, Thrasher told reporters to send him a copy of the story, along with the name and rank of the person prohibiting the transmission and the reason given. When news of "absorbing public interest" was occurring, correspondents were to transmit "four or five reports" during the course of a day. Finally, to maintain good relations with their sources, correspondents were expected to visit them "twice daily" and "freely exchange news" in order that the reporters might get information in return.[23]

An important aspect of the Press Association was the insistence of organizers that it be a truly cooperative news organization. Although the superintendent hired correspondents to be stationed at "points of interest," the P.A. expected its members to send "all news of interest occurring in their vicinity" at times when no correspondent was available. Terms did not prohibit "individual enterprise" if a member wanted to make arrangements with another newspaper to receive special news dispatches. However, members could not exclude other member papers from joint participation on equal terms. Unlike the AP, the Press Association did not have a relationship with the Davis administration to spread news.[24]

❦

The correspondents in Charleston reporting the secession crisis knew that fighting was imminent, but none had warning when Confederate batteries fired on Fort Sumter. The bombardment awakened *New York World* correspondent Osbon, who was aboard the Union revenue cutter "Harriet Lane." An unknown correspondent for the *Charleston Mercury* was aboard another ship in the harbor. Other specials were scattered around the city, most still asleep. All scurried to report the attack, and by the afternoon hours the Charleston telegraph office was flashing the news across the North and South. The initial accounts gave few details but provided the essential news:

> CHARLESTON, April 12—The ball has been opened at last, and war is inaugurated.
>   The batteries on Sullivan's Island, Morris Island, and other points, opened on Fort Sumter at 1 o'clock this morning.
>   Fort Sumter returned the fire, and a brisk cannonading has been kept up. . . .
>   Every available space facing the harbor is filled with anxious spectators.[25]

When a white flag was hauled up the flagstaff of Fort Sumter the next day, a *Richmond Dispatch* correspondent described the elation of Charleston residents. "You may imagine, but you cannot realize the joy, as the shouts of joy went up from thousands on the decks, wharves, houses, and steeples," he wrote. A correspondent for the *Columbus Times* reported the announcement of the surrender by

General Pierre G. Beauregard to a jubilant crowd. "Noble Carolinians! Accept my warmest congratulations on your victory," Beauregard declared. "The war has been commenced; we must continue our exertions until the enemy is driven from our harbor."[26]

In the tense days leading up to the attack, some Union reporters had been arrested or run out of the city by South Carolina authorities. But a handful had managed to stay including de Fontaine of the *New York Herald.* A native of Connecticut, de Fontaine had been working as a reporter since he was 16 years old. He traveled throughout the South before the war reporting for the *Herald,* during which time he developed a friendship with Beauregard. De Fontaine also became a Southern sympathizer during his time in the region, and when the *Herald* threw its support to the Lincoln administration after the attack, he joined the staff of the *Charleston Courier* writing under the pen name "Personne."[27]

There was little fighting for de Fontaine and other correspondents to report for the next three months. Newspapers on both sides spent the time lining up full-time and soldier correspondents. Journalists in the two capitals also reported on the war preparations taking place. Only one newsman was on hand when Colonel Elmer E. Ellsworth was killed by an Alexandria hotel proprietor as the Zouave officer tried to take down a Confederate flag flying above the premises. However, Union newspapers gave extensive coverage to the colorful Ellsworth's funeral.[28]

Correspondents on both sides got a taste for how difficult reporting would be at First Bull Run. Several days before the war's first major battle, Beauregard ordered all civilians, including Confederate reporters, to leave camp and move at least four miles away. As a result, some newsmen arrived just in time to witness the fighting, while others encountered travel problems that made them late. The battle extended over an area seven to eight miles wide, so reporters had a difficult time understanding what was taking place. To get a better view of the fighting, a correspondent for the *Cincinnati Gazette* climbed a tree, but when Confederate troops fired at him he quickly found a safer spot. Another Northern reporter narrowly escaped being captured during the Union retreat. A Southern correspondent who got too close to the Federal line was not so fortunate and was taken prisoner.[29]

The Union assault initially crushed the outnumbered rebels. Based on the early reports, Union correspondents began writing stories that said Federal forces were on the verge of victory. Some newsmen even left the battlefield to file their accounts. Then in the afternoon, the Confederate forces were reinforced with units that had just arrived on the battlefield. Beauregard ordered a counterattack and the Confederates overwhelmed the exhausted Union troops. What began as an orderly retreat by the Federals soon turned into a panicked rout. Throughout the evening, Union reporters returned to Washington with news of the defeat. However, by this point, the War Department was blocking stories from going out. Meanwhile the initial reports of a Federal victory had already been sent. The result was that residents of New York and other cities read about a Union victory on Sunday and the following day about a Union defeat.[30]

News of the Confederate triumph first appeared in most Southern newspapers on Monday and for days editors reveled in the thrilling news. The New Orleans *Daily Picayune* declared, "Such a rout of such an army—so large, so equipped, and so commanded—was never known before in the war on this continent . . . a mighty mob of disciplined men converted into a panic stricken mob." Many of the stories were full of hyperbole and purple prose. One writer claimed that First Bull Run was "the greatest battle ever fought on this continent."[31]

However, there were numerous problems in the reporting of First Bull Run. The casualty numbers reported by newspapers on both sides were far off the mark. Some early reports were based on hearsay from people who did not witness the fighting. And some Southern newspapers gave undue credit to units from their states for the victory. Editors claimed that finding out the truth of what happened from military leaders and government officials was impossible. After reading both Northern and Southern accounts, the editor of the *St. Louis Republican* complained that he could find little except "conflict and contradiction, from which it is impossible to infer anything save that there has been monstrous blundering and monstrous lying on both sides."[32]

Nonetheless, in the days that followed some newsmen revealed the human cost of the fighting. When they had time to ride over the battlefield, Confederate reporters were shocked by the scene and sought to describe it to readers. "The spectacle is too horrible for description," de Fontaine wrote. "Men and horses are scattered over the ground for several miles, lying in every possible attitude and mangled by every possible wound. Broken artillery wagons, earth torn up, corn and grain trampled down, fences laid low, houses riddle, trees and bushes cut to pieces, all bespeak to the terrible character of the opposing fires." Not surprisingly, some of the best stories of the battle came from the men who fought. Melvin Dwinell, the editor of the *Rome Courier* and an officer in the 8th Georgia Regiment, wrote an account of what it was like to be in a battle for the first time. Dwinell said the romantic visions of war he had held before were quickly shattered and replaced with the "ugly, dusty, fatiguing and laborious realization" of real fighting. The editor said he feared for his life when a cannon ball came dangerously close, but after that he was too busy to be afraid. "As the dangers really increased, and friends were seen falling thick upon either side, the apprehension, or rather the fear . . . became strangely less, and without feeling secure there was a sort of forced resignation to calmly abide whatever consequences should come," he wrote.[33]

Specials for both sides also reported on naval fighting during the fall. In the case of the Northern press, reporters for some of the largest newspapers were assigned to the navy and often traveled onboard ships. There was no such systematic reporting with the Southern press; reporters simply filed naval stories if they were in an area where fighting took place. Early in the war, most stories centered on the blockade of the Atlantic and Gulf coasts put in place by the Federal navy and the Confederate attempts to run the blockade. A *New York Times* reporter told the exciting story of the destruction of the Confederate schooner *Judah* at Pensacola, Florida, in the fall. In a nighttime raid, a small party of soldiers and marines got into the harbor. The story recounted how the soldiers soon were discovered, but under fire managed to board the schooner, spike the guns, and set it on fire before escaping.[34]

Several Northern reporters were on board ships to report the campaign against Port Royal, South Carolina. The nearly 50 ships that took part were the greatest war fleet ever assembled by the Union. Osbon, who was now reporting for the *New York Herald,* watched the battle from on board a transport ship and provided a detailed account of the fighting. "The noise was terrific," he wrote, "while the bursting of the shells was as terrific, as it was destructive." The shells exploding on the beach made "the air brown with sand." At one point, so many ships were firing that it seemed "the vessels were endeavoring to out vie each other in the rapidity with which they worked their guns."[35]

Certainly one of the biggest naval news stories was the dramatic ironclad battle between the USS *Monitor* and the CSS *Virginia* off Newport News, Virginia, in March 1862. Northern reporters had heard rumors that the Confederate navy was converting the frigate USS *Merrimack* into a formidable ironclad, renamed the *Virginia*. The *New York Herald* decided to send the enterprising Osbon to Fortress Monroe to get information about the mysterious vessel. Osbon found a small pilot boat and used it to slip past the Confederate batteries at night. He not only took notes on what he found, but made a sketch that later was published in *Harper's Weekly.*[36]

Accounts in various Northern newspapers described the *Virginia's* initial action against two Union warships at Hampton Roads. A *New York Times* reporter described the Confederate ironclad as "some devilish and superhuman monster . . . the horrid creation of a nightmare." After disabling one of the Union vessels, the *Virginia* moved in to finish off the ship. "Like a rhinoceros she skins down her head and frightful horn," he wrote, "and with a dead, soul-rendering crunch, she pierces her on the starboard bow, lifting her up as a man does a toy." Correspondents also reported the fear that quickly spread through Washington that the *Virginia* might soon be steaming up the Potomac River to start shelling the capital. Edward Fulton of the *Baltimore American* skillfully described the conclusion of the fighting the next day witnessed by hundreds of people on the shore. The *Monitor* was not an impressive looking vessel, he wrote, but "a plain structure amidship, a small pilot house forward, a diminutive smoke-pipe aft, at a mile's distance she might be taken for a raft." The *Monitor* moved around the *Virginia* repeatedly "probing her sides, seeking for weak points, until she had the right spot and the exact range" to fire effectively, he wrote.[37]

The first major action in the West, Shiloh, was one of the worst reported battles of the war by the press of both the North and South. Casualty figures for both sides were widely off the mark. Stories exaggerated the extent of the Confederate victory on the first day and the Union triumph on the second day. In part, this could be attributed to the fact that many journalists for both sides arrived late. However, numerous accounts also recounted stories that simply were not true, such as Union troops being bayoneted in their tents.[38]

Still, some reporters turned in outstanding work. Whitelaw Reid of the *Cincinnati Gazette* produced perhaps the best and most accurate Northern account of the battle. A graduate of Miami University of Ohio, Reid began writing for newspapers as a young man. He was a school principal for several years before becoming editor of the *Xenia News*. Before the war began, he joined the *Gazette,* one of the outstanding newspapers in the Midwest, writing under the pen name "Agate." Reid's story about Shiloh not only provided a comprehensive picture of the two days of fighting but also included dramatic narrative passages and interesting anecdotes of individuals. Reid described General Grant's reaction at the end of the first day when a member of his staff asked if the prospect for a Union victory was discouraging. "Not at all," he quoted Grant as saying. "They can't force our lines around these batteries to-night— it is too late. Delay counts everything with us. To-morrow we shall attack them with fresh troops and drive them, of course."[39]

Because of travel problems, the *Savannah Republican*'s Alexander did not arrive at the battlefield until noon, some six hours after the fighting had begun. Although unable to estimate the number of casualties, he reported that the fighting the first day was "hot and close and raged with great violence and fury." Alexander was at General Beauregard's headquarters later that evening when a captured Federal commander, Benjamin M. Prentiss, was brought before Beauregard, and the newsman recounted a conversation between the two men. That night Alexander slept in the tent of the quartermaster of the 53rd Ohio Regiment that had been captured in the day's fighting. With an eye for detail, he noted that the tent had been hit by 21 musket balls. The next morning resumed "another day of battle and blood," Alexander reported. The Yankees, who had been reinforced the night before, fought "with great spirit and resolution." He also felt compelled to report that the Confederate cause was hurt because many troops had spent the previous night enjoying the spoils left behind by Union soldiers, despite orders not to do so. Some soldiers resumed their search for items the next morning and were separated from their regiments when the battle resumed.[40]

Few Confederate reporters were in New Orleans to report the capture of the South's largest city later in April. New Orleans had been under a Federal blockade since the early weeks of the war, but most observers, including many in the press, seemed largely indifferent to the threat. That changed when a fleet of Union gunboats entered the Mississippi River and opened fire on the two forts guarding the city. The New Orleans newspapers reported on the shelling daily, based on official dispatches from one fort's commander. However, the dispatches were heavily censored and the reports were reassuring that the forts could hold out against the attack.

The stunning news that the Federal fleet had sailed past the forts shocked New Orleans. The Confederate government sought to suppress the information, but word got through to Mobile and from there it was telegraphed to Richmond. Two days after the Union fleet's success, the news appeared in many papers. With only about 3,000 troops to defend New Orleans, the Confederate commander abandoned the city and, on April 28, Federal forces occupied it. The Confederate government never acknowledged the fall of New Orleans to the press. And several Southern newspapers tried to minimize the loss.[41]

A handful of reporters for Northern newspapers were with the Federal fleet when it began its expedition against New Orleans. In a story for the *New York Herald,* Osbon described the six days and nights of fighting as the fleet battled the forts guarding the city. He also wrote about his own role in the fighting, including hoisting two red lanterns, the signal for the fleet to sail past the forts. Osbon published the most comprehensive story of the fighting, a three-page account that included many details. However, he was beaten by George Wisner of the *New York Times,* who put his dispatch on a steamer for Havana, Cuba. From there it was sent to New York and published ahead of his competitor.[42]

The Peninsula campaign was the first major challenge to the Northern press to provide sustained coverage of fighting deep in the enemy's country. The *New York Herald* recognized that this meant using as many reporters as possible as well as a chief correspondent to coordinate their work. It also meant using messengers to carry dispatches from the journalists and supplies to keep everyone housed, clothed, and fed.[43]

The long campaign took its toll on the newsmen and editors scrambled to replace them. The *New York Tribune* took a chance on a Washington clerk, Charles A. Page, whose only newspaper experience had been editing a weekly newspaper in Iowa. He turned out to be an outstanding reporter with a fine eye for detail. In his first account, Page noted that while both armies made noise when going into battle, "our men cheer" while the rebels "yell." Reporters covering the campaign also helped make a sensation of Belle Boyd, the young, attractive Confederate spy who had been captured. A *Philadelphia Inquirer* reporter wrote that Boyd had a "dash about her, a smart pertness, a quickness of retort, an utter abandon of manner and bearing." He noted that Boyd, who once wore a revolver in her belt, was "courted and flattered" by many of the Union officers who saw her. However, he was critical of those who had called her a prostitute, saying they "exceed the license which justice and fairness allot even to outlaws."[44]

In the meantime, the Southern press was trying to report the threat to the Confederate capital. In March Richmond was put under martial law, and two months later Confederate correspondents reported the panic that was gripping Richmond. The *Mobile Register and Advertiser*'s William G. Shepardson told about the hundreds of people who were fleeing the capital everyday. And a reporter for the *Memphis Appeal* described the "groups of excited men at every corner" and the "dense crowds before the bulletin boards of the newspaper offices" discussing the threat to the city.[45]

With few correspondents in the field, some Southern newspapers relied on soldier correspondents to provide information about the campaign. At Yorktown, Dwinell's regiment was assigned trench duty and he gave readers a vivid picture of what it was like. Soldiers spent long hours in the cold, muddy trenches silently listening for the enemy. "This duty is telling fearfully upon the men," Dwinell wrote. "Beside the great fatigue to which they are subjected, the want of sleep and exposure, the most trying of all is the continual expectation of an attack, which seems imminent all the time." After several weeks of picket duty, rebel troops in the trenches had become a "hard looking set," he noted. "Many have not had clean clothes in two weeks, have been sleeping on the mud . . . and eating fat meat, when they could get it, with their fingers, after broiling it on a stick."[46]

When the fighting returned to Manassas, Virginia, in the late summer, Northern correspondents largely were kept away. General John Pope, the new commander of the Army of the Potomac, had issued an order calling for the expulsion of all reporters from his army. Various explanations were given for the action, but the result was that many readers got only a sparse account of another Union defeat at the hands of General Robert E. Lee's army.[47]

De Fontaine observed Second Bull Run from the heights occupied by one rebel battery. In his account, he vividly described "the heavy notes of the artillery . . . mingled with the sharp treble of the small arms" that combined to sound like "some diabolical concert." He went on to write: "We do nothing but charge—charge—charge! If the enemy make a bold effort to retrieve the fortunes of the day, (and they make many) and we are repulsed, it is but for the moment, and the regiments rallying upon their support plunge back down again into the tempest of fire that before swept them down." De Fontaine also wrenchingly described the Confederate field hospitals thrown up after the battle. "For nearly half a mile along the Warrenton turnpike, the forest presented a vast spectacle of human suffering," he wrote. "Here were the various temporary division hospitals. . . . The operating tables consisted of pile of rails, covered only with a few rough boards. . . . Arms and legs were lying around the half dozen surgical altars."[48]

Southern readers did not get the account by de Fontaine and others for several days. The first news was a published dispatch from Lee to President Jefferson Davis. On September 3, correspondent George Bagby told the *Charleston Mercury* that Second Bull Run was "a battle of far greater magnitude than we supposed." When the news finally spread, Confederate newspapers rejoiced. "The skies never looked brighter than they do at this moment," the *Augusta Chronicle & Sentinel* proclaimed. "Our prospects were never more cheering than they are now."[49]

Even Alexander, usually more cautious in his praise after a battle, spoke proudly of the troops. He said that the battle had proven that the Army of Northern Virginia deserved a place among the great armies of history. "It stands before the nations of the earth, conspicuous alike for the genius of its leaders and the valor its men," the correspondent exclaimed. Still, Alexander was reminded of the sight of suffering Confederate soldiers hungry and ill-clothed. A lawyer by training, Alexander had shown since the beginning of the war that he was not afraid to point out problems with the army or the administration of the war. Early in the conflict, the correspondent reported on the problem of Confederate soldiers who carried sidearms and knives. He described how drunken soldiers often got into fights and injured or killed one another with the weapons. In blunt language Alexander wrote: "A drunken soldier, with a revolver stuck in his belt on one side and bowie knife on the other is about as fit to go at large as an infuriated maniac; and the authorities ought to see to it that no more men be suffered to enter the service unless they leave all such weapons at home, where they may be needed." But after Second Bull Run, Alexander pointed out the basic necessities that many soldier had to go without.

> The army has not had a mouthful of bread for four days, and no food of any kind except a little green corn picked up in the roadside, for thirty-six hours. Many of them also are barefooted. I have seen scores of them to-day marching over the flinty turnpike with torn and blistered feet. They bear these hardships without murmuring. . . . As for tents, they have not known what it was to sleep under one since last spring.[50]

By the time many readers were getting the news of Second Bull Run, Lee's army had crossed the Potomac River into Maryland. Several Southern correspondents, including Alexander and de Fontaine, accompanied the army into the state. Within days, the reorganized Army of the Potomac began marching north in pursuit of the rebels. When the two sides eventually met at the small village of Sharpsburg, near the banks of Antietam Creek, a host of specials were on hand to witness some of the most savage fighting of the war. As a group, they produced some of the best reporting of the war.

Several reporters went to great lengths to report the pivotal battle. Charles Coffin of the *Boston Journal* had spent the previous night at Hagerstown and was awakened by the sounds of cannons. He managed to quickly get a horse from a stable and galloped the nine miles to the battlefield. Afterward, he rode back to Hagerstown and then caught a train to Boston, writing his story en route. George Smalley of the *New York Tribune* pushed himself to the point of exhaustion to send his story about Antietam. Smalley's horse had been shot during the fighting, so he had to borrow one from another reporter. He left the battlefield and arrived in nearby Frederick at 3 A.M. The telegraph office was closed, so he had to wait until it opened at 7 A.M. Smalley sat down next to the door of the office and handed sheets of paper to the operator after he finished writing. His story was the first account of Antietam and was reprinted in hundreds of newspapers across the country.[51]

De Fontaine also wrote an exhaustive account of the battle. He set the scene of the fighting, the preliminary skirmishing the day before, the early action, and the intense fighting between the centers of both armies. He claimed that the battle was a "victory to our arms." Alexander was impressed with the performance of the Federal army and wrote that it was the army's finest moment since Shiloh. The Georgian wrote his account of the battle from near an army hospital where he graphically described the carnage with its "amputated arms and legs, feet, fingers, and hands cut off, puddles of human gore and ghastly gaping wounds." Alexander concluded succinctly, "There is a smell of death in the air." In his same report, Alexander wrote that he had favored the Confederate invasion into Maryland, but now acknowledged that it had probably been a mistake. He based this view, in part, on the poor condition of the soldiers. "A fifth of the troops are barefooted; half of them are in rags; and the whole of them insufficiently supplied with food," he wrote.[52]

❧❧

While reporters in the field were chronicling the progress of the war, another group of correspondents reported from Washington and Richmond. In the case of Washington, the reporters not only wrote about the administration and Congress, but they provided war reports as well. Washington received the first reports from the eastern war theater and transmitted them by telegraph throughout the country. An indication of Washington's importance was the fact that by the end of the war, at least 18 separate telegraph wires ran out of the capital, connecting reporters with their newspaper offices.

The Washington bureaus maintained by the press were grouped along Fourteenth Street between F Street and Pennsylvania Avenue in what was known as "Newspaper Row." Across the street was the main office of the American Telegraph Company where specials usually filed their stories. At the nearby Willard Hotel, journalists gathered with elected officials, bureaucrats, and military officers to swap news and rumors. Washington correspondents attended Congressional meeting and hearings. They regularly made the rounds of government departments hoping to pick up news. And they stopped at the White House hoping to get information from an aide or the president himself.[53]

Lincoln was generally accessible to newsmen. More than any president before him, Lincoln understood the role of the press, its tendencies, and its shortcomings. He once said, "The press has no better friend than I am—no one is more ready to acknowledge its tremendous power both for good and evil." He also once remarked that no one, not even the president, "can successfully carry on a controversy with a great newspaper, and escape destruction, unless he owns a newspaper equally great, with a circulation in the same neighborhood." Lincoln had long cultivated his relationship with journalists. During his days as a country lawyer, he contributed letters and editorials to publications in his native Illinois. William Herndon, his longtime law partner, said that like most astute politicians of his era Lincoln "never overlooked a newspaperman who had it in his power to say a good or bad thing of him."[54]

Although Lincoln granted few interviews, reporters did not hesitate to send their cards requesting information. If he was available, the president often would step out to briefly answer questions or write them on the back of the cards. Some of his advisers and cabinet members thought it was a mistake for the president to be so close to the press. Navy Secretary Gideon Welles deplored Lincoln's close relationship with newsmen. "It is an infirmity of the president that he permits the little newsmongers to come around him and be intimate," Welles wrote. "He has great inquisitiveness. Likes to hear all the political gossip." But Charles A. Dana, a journalist who served as assistant secretary of war, marveled at the president's sagacity and practicality in managing with public opinion in mind.[55]

Among the best-known Washington correspondents during the war were Lawrence A. Gobright of the AP, Ben Perley Poore of the *Boston Journal,* Noah Brooks of the *Sacramento Union,* and Reid of the *Cincinnati Gazette.* Gobright had been a mainstay of the capital since the administrations of William Henry Harrison and John Tyler. Poore, who had written for various newspapers from the capital, was a raconteur and one of the most popular journalists in the city. Brooks became close to President Lincoln and wrote many stories about the White House. He was also known for the candor of his dispatches. Reid had been a battlefield reporter until 1862 when his newspaper assigned him to Washington. He was a frank correspondent who was not afraid to criticize the military or government in his letters to the *Gazette.*[56]

Among the Washington correspondents was Walt Whitman, the writer and poet already celebrated for *Leaves of Grass.* Whitman had started working for newspapers as a young boy and by the time the war began, he had written for several publications.

Whitman was an idiosyncratic journalist who frequently clashed with his publishers, fellow editors, and the public. Whitman traveled to Washington after his brother was wounded at Fredericksburg. After finding his brother at an army hospital, he became a regular visitor at hospitals, writing about his experiences for the *Brooklyn Eagle* and the *New York Times.* Whitman was a keen observer. His first story for the *New York Times* told of his encounter with a young Massachusetts soldier who was near death and unattended in a hospital ward. "He now lay, at times out of his head but quite silent, asking nothing of anyone, for some days, with death getting a closer and surer grip upon him; he cared not, or rather he welcomed death," Whitman wrote. Whitman continued to visit the soldier, who remained sick for weeks before eventually recovering. Whitman later described what he witnessed at the hospitals. "Death is nothing here," he wrote. "As you step out in the morning from your tent to wash your face, you see before you on a stretcher a shapeless extended object, and over it is thrown a dark grey blanket—it is the corpse of some sick or wounded soldier of the reg't who died in the hospital tent during the night."[57]

A handful of correspondents reported for the Southern press from Richmond. Like their Northern counterparts, they reported on news of the Davis administration and the Confederate Congress, as well as providing war news. The best-known of the group were Salem Dutcher of the *Augusta Constitutionalist,* John R. Thompson of the *Memphis Appeal,* and George Bagby of the *Charleston Mercury* and *Mobile Register and Advertiser.* Dutcher had served in the Confederate army briefly before becoming a correspondent in the capital. Thompson had been editor of the *Southern Literary Messenger* for 13 years before the war. In addition to being a Richmond correspondent, he edited the news weekly, the *Southern Illustrated News.* Bagby had succeeded Thompson as editor of the *Southern Literary Messenger.*[58]

Southern correspondents were hampered in reporting by the fact that, much of the time, the Confederate Congress was in secret session. When sessions were open, reporters listened to little more than long-winded speeches with little news. One correspondent wrote bluntly: "The Congress of the Confederate states is doing nothing. In fact it has very little to do. Were it not for the sake of appearance, and for the purpose of keeping alive the forms of Republicanism, we might very well have our Parliament prorogued till the close of the War." Unlike Lincoln, Davis did not court the press, even though some advisers and members of his cabinet encouraged him to.[59]

The handful of female correspondents during the war mainly reported from the two capitals. Conventions of the time prevented women from going into the field for any extended period of time, so women who wanted to report had to do so from the safety of cities. The female correspondents included Jane Grey Swisshelm, who had been the first woman to get a seat in the capital press gallery. She contributed letters to the *New York Tribune* and the *St. Cloud Democrat.* Sara Jane Lippincott wrote under the pen name "Grace Greenwood" for the *New York Tribune* and the *New York Times.* She wrote both political and personal pieces, often in a satirical style. An unknown woman wrote for the *Charleston Courier* from Richmond under the pen name "Joan." She offered her services as a correspondent so that she could be near her son who was assigned to the army. In her letter to the *Courier,* she argued that "a woman proves many times a more attractive correspondent than a man. Her perceptions are keener—she picks up items of interest more intuitively, and can often times glean many from a mass where a man would detect nothing." "Joan" wrote about the work of women employed as seamstresses for the army, an appearance with Vice President Alexander Stephens, and the Yankee prisoners housed in a tobacco factory.[60]

Throughout the war, newsmen on both sides had occasionally profiled army commanders, knowing that readers wanted to read more about the men leading the armies. Following the series of Confederate victories in 1862, Alexander wrote a profile of Lee, who was being hailed throughout the South as a hero. A man of imposing appearance, Alexander wrote, Lee did not care for the trappings of rank, being content "to take the same fare his soldiers get." Although not blessed with the greatest intellect, Lee nonetheless had "those qualities which are indispensable in the great leader and champion." Alexander concluded that Lee was "the peer of any living chieftain in the New World or the Old."[61]

The portrayal of Lee as a masterful general proved to be correct at the battle of Fredericksburg in December. A reporter for the *Richmond Enquirer* skillfully described the Confederate army on the eve of the fighting. "The camp fires now gleam on every hill and hillside, and along the horizon flare up in broad sheets of pale lights," he wrote. "Our men joke and laugh around their camp fires as they prepare rations for the morrow in careless confidence, for they know we have the men and general equal to the coming trial." In another report, the correspondent described the scene as Federal troops emerged from the fog. "Whole fields are gleaming with bayonets. They continue to pour out upon the plain in a stream which seems to come from an inexhaustible fountain. The meadows are black with them, tens of thousands in solid columns." He went on to describe the murderous fire from the rebels who held the heights above Fredericksburg. "There is no breaking of ranks among the enemy, rallying and rerallying, but to no avail. They cannot stand the murderous fire."[62]

Alexander was not on hand to witness the fighting at Fredericksburg and did not reach the town until the battle was over. Still, his use of second-hand information and his own observations made for an engaging story. The Union army, he wrote, faced artillery that "poured a devouring fire into the ranks. . . . Assault upon assault was made, each time with fresh columns and increasing numbers. They never succeeded, however." The result of such savage fighting was a scene horrifying even for a war-hardened reporter. "I went over the ground this morning and the remaining dead, after two-thirds of them had been removed, lay twice as thick as upon any other battlefield I have ever seen," he wrote.[63]

The news was not any better for the North during the spring campaign of 1863. Before major fighting renewed at Chancellorsville, Union General Joseph Hooker issued General Order No. 48 requiring that all correspondents with the Army of the Potomac "publish their communications over their own signatures." The order was designed to prevent "the frequent transmission of the movements of the army to the enemy." Specials reacted variously to the requirement that they must put their names—bylines as they came to be known—on their stories. A *New York Herald* reporter said, "It is discouraging for correspondents to have their names paraded before the public as authors of carefully written letters; for sometimes the letters are written on horseback or in woods, and often with the shells screaming to us to 'hurry up'!" But another newsman remarked that using their name would make correspondents "exert extraordinary means to achieve success."[64]

Tight censorship prevented news of the Union disaster at Chancellorsville from being published in the North for several days. When the stories finally got through, most correspondents did not mince words about what happened. *New York Herald* correspondent Thomas Cook captured the retreat of one brigade after it was broken by a Confederate charge on the first day of fighting. "It was my lot to be in the centre of that field when the panic burst upon us," he wrote. "On one hand was a solid column of infantry retreating at double quick from the face of the enemy; on the other was a dense mass of beings who had lost their reasoning facilities, and were flying from a thousand fancied dangers." Another *Herald* reporter, S. M. Carpenter, skillfully captured the retreat of disheartened Union troops when it was clear that the South had won another victory. "About five o'clock in the afternoon it commenced raining," he wrote. "The water poured down in torrents; cascades leaped from the hillsides, rivers rushed through every ravine. The teams, blinded by the driving storm, staggered like drunken men. Pack mules turned their backs to the tempest and refused to move, and the soldiers crouched beneath their rubber blankets and behind the trunks of the oaks."[65]

From their offices, editors expressed outrage at the military's interference with reporting of the campaign. "There never has been during the war such an important series of events, about which the public were so imperfectly informed, as the recent operations on the other side of the Rappahannock," a *Boston Journal* editorial complained. "The government transmitted no information whatever. The newspapers' correspondents were successively obliged to pick up what intelligence they could in a hurry, and hasten off northward to secure it early publication. Hence, there has been but very little reporting from personal observation, and nothing like a connected account of the week's history."[66]

Reporting of the Confederate victory at Chancellorsville by the Southern press was poor. For various reasons, the most reliable correspondents, including Alexander and de Fontaine, were not at the battlefield. Telegraphic service between nearby Fredericksburg and Richmond also was down for a time. News from the battle was spread by the Richmond newspapers, which had taken much of their information from the Northern press. The editor of the *Augusta Constitutionalist* was so upset by the source of news that he refused to print it in his newspaper.[67]

However, the Southern press gave extensive coverage to the shattering news that General Thomas J. "Stonewall" Jackson had been mortally wounded during the fighting and died several days later. Correspondents described the immense crowd that thronged Capitol Square when the train carrying Jackson's body arrived in Richmond. In the days that followed, the Confederate press poured out one eulogy after another for Jackson. The *Augusta Constitutionalist* said of the beloved general, "His name was as terrible to the enemy as it was inspiring to his followers." And the *Atlanta Daily Intelligencer* declared, "The news of his death has cast a gloom over this community, as indeed it will over the whole land. The idol of his people and his army, his memory will ever be cherished. Truly a great man has fallen!"[68]

The reporting of the long Vicksburg campaign in 1863 was generally uneven by the Northern press and often misleading by the Southern press. Specials on both sides certainly encountered numerous difficulties in reporting the fighting. But a *Chicago Tribune* correspondent also blamed laziness by newsmen for some of the problems. "There are a few correspondents who go under fire and see with their own eyes what is doing," he wrote, "but the greater number prefer to remain on the steamer at the landing, and trust to such reports of the doings of the army as Dame Rumor may vouchsafe them. . . . To them great is the Goddess of rumor, for she saves them from the imagination, as her budget is ever full, ever varied, and ever exciting."[69]

However, after Vicksburg was captured, newspaper stories told of the spirit that troops and townspeople showed under the worst privations. Shortages of food and other basic materials were widespread. Many residents were forced to seek shelter in caves during the worst of the bombardments. A correspondent for the *Augusta Constitutionalist* described the toll the fighting had taken on Confederate troops who were forced to eat anything they could get their hands on. "[Rats] are a luxury," he wrote. "Small fishes sell at twenty dollars. Chickens at ten dollars each. Mule meat has sold readily at two dollars a pound, in market, and I eat it once a week. The soldiers have had only one meal a day for ten days, and then one man does not get what a child should have."[70]

After Vicksburg fell, Southern editors angrily denounced what they believed to be many misleading news reports, including stories that painted a hopeful picture of the ability of the rebel troops to hold out. One editor wrote bitterly, "[T]here is a heavy weight of responsibility resting on somebody's shoulders for the regular and systematic lying that has been put upon the public regarding the ability of this place to holdout. The western Press in the vicinity of the unfortunate city have been quite as badly imposed on as anybody else. We have forty times read reports, coming from Pemberton himself, that supplies were abundant, and the garrison could 'hold out indefinitely'."[71]

❧ ❧

As the showdown at Vicksburg was drawing to a close, General Lee decided to invade the North again. Nine Confederate correspondents traveled with the Army of Northern Virginia when it marched into Pennsylvania in June. The Army of the Potomac, under the command of General George G. Meade, followed after them, accompanied by more than 30 newsmen. Some Northern specials had difficulty getting to the small Pennsylvania village. Correspondents traveling from Washington took the train to Baltimore only to find that the line to nearby Frederick had been wrecked. Others got as far as Harrisburg but arrived in Gettysburg late or not at all. Confederate cavalry captured two Union newsmen.[72]

Sending stories also was challenging. The area of rural Pennsylvania had few railroad and telegraph lines, so reporters experienced numerous problems in transmitting their stories. Nonetheless, the reporting of Gettysburg by correspondents on both sides was generally excellent, as J. Cutler Andrews has noted. With the lines for both armies extending for miles, most correspondents described the fighting from their vantage point. A correspondent for the *Augusta Constitutionalist* wrote about troops attacking the Federal center on Cemetery Ridge. "As soon as we emerged from the woods and came into the open field, the enemy poured a most terrific fire into our ranks," he wrote. "When we reached the base of the range upon which the enemy were posted, they opened up on us with their infantry, and raked our whole line with grape and canister from more than twenty guns." The troops found themselves pinned in with no support, and to escape they had to fight their way out. When they regrouped, only 554 men were left of the 1,600 who had begun the attack.[73]

A *Richmond Enquirer* correspondent described the artillery barrage on July 3 that preceded the charge by General George Pickett's troops. "I have never yet heard such tremendous artillery firing," he wrote. "The very earth shook beneath our feet and the hills and rocks seemed to reel like a drunken man." It made a picture, he concluded, "terribly grand and sublime, but which my pen utterly fails to describe." The *Boston Journal*'s Coffin graphically described the hand-to-hand fighting that took place during the charge.

Men fire into each other's faces, not five feet apart. There are bayonet-thrusts, sabre-strokes, pistol shots . . . oaths, yells, curses, hurrahs, shoutings . . . men going down on their hands and knees, spinning round like tops, throwing out their arms, gulping up blood, falling; legless, armless, headless. There are ghastly heaps of dead men. Seconds are centuries, minutes, ages; but the thin line does not break![74]

Newsmen for both sides went to tremendous lengths to report the greatest battle of the war. Coffin left Gettysburg on July 4 and galloped his horse 30 miles to catch a hospital train to Baltimore. However, the train traveled so slowly that he did not arrive in the city until the following morning. Coffin spent the entire next day on another train to Boston. When he arrived at the newspaper, he locked himself in an office and wrote his account of the battle until the paper went to press. But no correspondent went to greater lengths than *New York Times* correspondent Samuel Wilkeson. He wrote his account while sitting beside the body of his 19-year-old son, an artillery officer who was killed in the fighting.[75]

The news from Gettysburg did not reach many Southerners for a week or more after the battle. In the meantime, readers could be excused for being confused. In Georgia, several of the state's dailies initially declared the battle a victory for the South. The *Savannah Morning News* carried a telegraphic dispatch on July 8, five days after the fighting had concluded, claiming that "the enemy has been completely routed." The account provided no details, however. The *Atlanta Daily Intelligencer* reported that Meade's army had "been completely demolished" and, astonishingly, that 40,000 Union troops had surrendered. A story in the *Morning News* the following day said information from the battle was incomplete, but that there had been heavy losses on both sides. An editor's note at the bottom said, "Like everything we receive of late, the above dispatch is very vague and unsatisfactory."[76]

Eventually, news of Gettysburg began to emerge in the Southern press, thanks, in part, to the reporting of Alexander. His report ran two full columns long on the front page and jumped to one-half column on page two. Newspapers across the South reprinted it. Alexander began his account succinctly as he wrote, "The bloodiest and most desperate battle of this bloody and most desperate war has just been fought here on the soil of Pennsylvania." The story apparently was written under extreme deadline pressure because he noted in the middle of it that the courier who would carry the dispatch had saddled his horse and was ready to leave. Nonetheless, Alexander was able to describe in precise detail the various smaller battles that made up Gettysburg, giving readers a vivid picture. He tried to put the best face on the loss, noting that both armies left the battlefield "worn, battle-scarred and severely punished." But Alexander recognized that some Confederate tactics were highly questionable. He also raised questions about Lee's decision to fight at the time and place he did.[77]

Five months later, Union correspondents returned to Gettysburg to report the dedication of the soldier's cemetery. Newspapers had received an advanced copy of noted orator Edward Everett's speech and, as it was the practice of the time to provide the full text of important addresses, many had already set it in type. But the president's remarks had not been written in advance and newsmen were anxious to get it. Because the reporters had to take down the speech in full, they dreaded a long speech by Lincoln. Like everyone, they were surprised that the president spoke only 10 brief, but moving, sentences. John Russell Young of the *Philadelphia Press* asked an aide if the president would continue. The president replied that he had nothing more to say.[78]

Although some major dailies did not emphasize Lincoln's "little speech," it was not as ignored as has sometimes been claimed. Many small newspapers, without the space to reprint Everett's long address, only published the president's remarks. Still, some accounts did not do justice to Lincoln's stirring words. Several reporters transcribed some of the president's words incorrectly, such as one who quoted Lincoln as saying, "The world can never forbid what they did here." But others got the president's message correct and also captured the emotion of the day. The *Ohio State Journal,* whose editor attended the ceremony, noted that when the president said, "The world will little note nor long remember what we say here, but it can never forget what they did here," an officer who had lost an arm buried his face in his hands and sobbed.[79]

By the spring of 1864, Union forces had a new commander in General Grant and a unified plan of operation for all the Union armies in the field. Correspondents had written various stories about the hero of Shiloh, Vicksburg, and Chattanooga, but they knew little about what Grant had in mind. Then on May 4, the Army of the Potomac crossed the Rapidan River and, a day later, met Lee's army at what was known as the Wilderness. The wild terrain of the area made reporting the fighting difficult and dangerous. One Union newsman was killed and another wounded. To stay abreast of what was taking place, several Northern reporters met in a little dell near the right flank of the battle line each morning and then spent the day gathering information as best they could. They returned to the spot in the afternoon to exchange material. They wrote their stories by candlelight and gave them to couriers to be taken to their newspapers. Charles A. Page's account in the *New York Tribune* provided a vivid picture of what the fighting was like. "The work was at close range," he wrote. "No room in that jungle for maneuvering; no possibility of a bayonet charge; no help from artillery; no help from cavalry; nothing but close, square, severe, face-to-face volley of fatal musketry. The wounded stream out and fresh troops pour in."[80]

Confederate correspondents encountered many of the same problems. Alexander, who by this time was reporting for the *Richmond Dispatch,* the *Mobile Register and Advertiser,* as well as the *Savannah Republican,* admitted that he had not "gone much into detail" in his account because of the difficulty of keeping track of the various rebel units. He rated the two days of fighting as "another Confederate victory," although not as decisive because the Yankees had not been driven across the Rapidan.[81]

Correspondents were in a better position to report when the fighting resumed on May 8 at nearby Spotsylvania Courthouse. Four days later, the two armies met again in what Alexander rated as "one of the fiercest battles of modern times." Grant launched his attack early in the morning, and for 18 hours some of the war's most horrific fighting raged, especially at a spot that became known as the Bloody Angle. The fighting was so close, Alexander noted, that at times opposing troops had little more than the length of their muskets between them. In the literary style that had come to characterize much of his best work, the Georgian went on to write, "The battle was fully joined and for nine hours it roared and hissed and dashed over the bloody angle and along the bristling entrenchments like an angry sea beating and chafing along a rock bound coast." *New York Times* correspondent William Swinton also captured the savage fighting at the Bloody Angle. "Nothing during the war has equaled the savage desperation of this struggle," he wrote. "In this angle of death, the dead and wounded rebels lie, this morning, literally in piles—men in the agonies of death groaning beneath the dead bodies of their comrades."[82]

✑❧

Only a handful of Northern correspondents accompanied General Sherman's campaign against Georgia during the spring of 1864. The general's hatred of the press was well known to many specials. When Sherman had heard a rumor that three reporters had been killed in fighting nears Vicksburg, he supposedly said, "Good! Now we'll have news from hell before breakfast!" The march had just begun when Sherman ordered Benjamin F. Taylor of the *Chicago Tribune* arrested as a spy and put on trial for court-martial. Taylor had written a story that said the Union lines "now extend from Knoxville to Huntsville." The order was not carried out but Taylor left the army immediately. Before the end of the month, Sherman issued a circular aimed at restricting the remaining correspondents.[83]

Few Southern newsmen covered the campaign either. The fighting was taking its toll on the Confederate press and fewer reporters were in the field. Confederate correspondents also had to deal with tightened censorship on all dispatches. Military authorities had directed that control of censorship be taken away from the provost marshal and be given to the inspector general who was far stricter in what he allowed through. Southern newspapers relied heavily on Press Association accounts, which were brief and often incomplete.[84]

The initial weeks of skirmishing and flanking during the campaign provided meager stories for reporters. That changed, albeit briefly, when Sherman changed his tactics and ordered a frontal assault on the South's heavily fortified position on Kennesaw Mountain outside of Atlanta. A reporter for the *Cincinnati Commercial* described the fighting. "From right and left, down the slopes of big Kenesaw [*sic*] and along the ridges to the west of the point of assault, the enemy poured his forces, emptying his adjacent trenches," he wrote. "The brigades charging the flanks of the mountain, subjected to a most cruel and destructive cross-fire, after repeated and heroic efforts, failed to reach the crest and retired in comparative disorder to the best cover they could find near the base of the hill."[85]

By mid-June, the *Atlanta Daily Intelligencer* declared, "Our city is in a state of siege." The editor complained that residents needed passes to get through the military guards posted around the city. "[W]e are certain they do no good, and only annoy those who have other business to attend to." Its competitor, the *Southern Confederacy,* called attention to the conduct of some Confederate troops in the city. An editor noted sarcastically that a brigade armed with shotguns was needed to patrol the streets at night and gather up all the drunken soldiers. Also needed was a load of lumber to build a guardhouse for all the men arrested in just one day. Later in the month, the editors of both newspapers packed their presses and fled south to the safety of Macon, leaving even fewer Confederate reporters to cover the fighting.[86]

By the end of July, Sherman had decided to lay siege to Atlanta. Union reporters described the battery duels and cavalry raids that took place. The handful of Confederate reporters still in Atlanta, both full-time and soldier correspondents, sought to report on life in a city that had changed dramatically. A correspondent for the *Columbus Times* reported that the shelling had made Atlanta all but deserted. The only people seen on the street were an occasional resident searching for vegetables and a few boys selling grapes from under the cover of bombproof trenches. General John Bell Hood maintained his headquarters in a cottage, formerly occupied by the head of the Confederate Press Association. The newsman reported that Hood could frequently be seen on the balcony smoking his long-stemmed pipe.[87]

"Rover," an occasional correspondent for the *Augusta Chronicle & Sentinel* and probably a soldier, was the only correspondent for the Southern press to report the dramatic climax of the campaign when Atlanta fell. In a straightforward account, he wrote that with the exception of some individuals, including soldiers who participated in looting, the evacuation was accomplished in good order. The army spent most of September 1 removing what ammunition and supplies it could carry. Many of the soldiers had expressions of sorrow on their weather-beaten faces, he reported. By nightfall the great majority of the army had left Atlanta. The troops remaining burned the ammunition and other property left in the city. The conflagration and explosions could be seen and heard from miles away, "Rover" wrote.[88]

Only a few Northern reporters accompanied Sherman's army on its march from Atlanta to the sea. Although the general did not try to keep correspondents away, most recognized that it would be difficult, if not impossible, to send stories from a march where there was no way to send stories. Correspondents did not know

Sherman's plans, but on November 18, the *Atlanta Daily Intelligencer* reported on what was believed to be the army's first target: Georgia's capital, Milledgeville. "It is now evident that Sherman has inaugurated a winter campaign," the newspaper declared, "and that Georgia is the field which he designs to desolate." A *New York Herald* reporter described the foraging that took place on the march:

> To draw the line between capturing and stealing, when permission is given troops to take everything which will sustain life or assist military operations, would puzzle the keenest observer. . . . An army passes along a road. A planter's house stands by the wayside; without a halt the whole premises are overrun as if by ants. . . . A column ten miles long generally furnished enough men to pick the premises clean.[89]

News of what had happened to Milledgeville emerged on December 1 when the *Macon Telegraph and Confederate* printed a letter from R. M. Orme, publisher of the *Southern Recorder*. In a detailed account, Orme reported how the Federal cavalry had appeared outside the capital on November 20, cut the telegraph lines, and ridden through the town causing alarm. Two days later, Union troops arrived. While the Federal army was in Milledgeville the city was "one vast camp," he reported. Fences were used for fuel, and garden and private yards were mere paths for horses and men. The arsenal, magazine, and railroad depot were burned, although the state house, governor's mansion, and asylum were left standing, the editor wrote.[90]

When Sherman's army left Savannah in February on its march through the Carolinas, a handful of Northern reporters accompanied the troops. They reported the widespread destruction that Union troops inflicted on the Palmetto state. When the two wings of Sherman's army reached the outskirts of Columbia two weeks later, David Conyngham of the *New York Herald* was with the general and his commanders on a bluff overlooking the capital.

> There was General Sherman, now pacing up and down in the midst of the group, all the time with an unlit cigar in his mouth, and now and then abruptly halting to speak to some of the generals around him. Again, he would sit down, whittle a stick, and soon nervously start up to resume his walk. Above all the men I have ever met, that strange face of his is the hardest to be read. It is a sealed book even to his nearest friends.[91]

With great satisfaction, the Northern correspondents reported the fall of Charleston where the war had begun. "The city is a ruin," wrote the *Boston Journal*'s Coffin. "The tall rank weeds of last year's growth, dry and withered now, rattle in every passing breeze in the very heart of that city which, five years ago, was so proud and lofty in spirit." Coffin and another reporter visited the office of the *Charleston Mercury*. The newspaper's staff had fled before the Union army arrived, taking the printing press and other equipment. The newsmen took obvious joy in reporting that three lines of newspaper type were left behind. The type claimed that Charleston authorities had no plans to abandon the city.[92]

Confederate newspapers reported the final months of the war mainly through the efforts of the Press Association and scattered reporters, many of them soldier correspondents. By this point, the South's two most reliable newsmen, Alexander and de Fontaine, were no longer reporting from the field. Alexander left the army after Savannah was captured and de Fontaine moved to Columbia, where he edited a newspaper in the city. Most of stories by Confederate correspondents were short and incomplete. That mattered little, however, because less than half the South's newspapers still were publishing.

In the meantime, the siege of Petersburg was seemingly making little progress, correspondents reported. James B. Sener of the *Richmond Dispatch* reported on the burial party needed to recover the Union dead killed by the disastrous attempt to blow up Confederate lines using a tunnel. "At the hour named . . . three gaily-dressed, flashy looking officers raised an elegant white flag, mounted on a handsome staff, and advanced from their line of works," he wrote. "Simultaneously, two shabbily dressed but brave Confederates, mounting a dirty pocket handkerchief on a ramrod, proceeded to meet them. A brief parley ensued, civilities were exchanged, and then the details came to do the work of the truce—the burial of the dead." The impact of the siege on the Virginia countryside was clearly visible, Union newsmen reported. "Those who saw these lands when they first became the theatre of active operations, would have difficulty in recognizing a single field," a *Philadelphia Inquirer* correspondent wrote. "The houses are nearly all still remaining, but every other trace of the old inhabitants has disappeared."[93]

❧ ❧

At the end of March, correspondents reported that the Army of the Potomac was on the move again. Then on April 7, the Confederate capital fell. Newspapers described the joyful celebrations across the North when people heard the news. In New York, the news "spread by a thousand mouths" and "almost by magic the streets were crowded with hosts of people, talking, laughing, hurrahing, and shouting in the fullness of their joy." Many newspapers rushed out special editions that were snapped up by eager readers. "The demand seemed inexhaustible and almost beyond the power of our lightning-press to supply," said one journal.[94]

Several newsmen accompanied Federal troops into Richmond. Among them was Thomas Morris Chester, a reporter for the *Philadelphia Press* and the only black newsman for a major newspaper. Chester's mother had been a slave in Virginia, and his father owned a restaurant in Harrisburg. Chester was educated at a private academy and as a teenager he briefly spent time in Liberia as part of the controversial colonization program. Chester wrote his dispatch while seated in the chair of the speaker of the House of Delegates. He described the Federal army entering Richmond. "The citizens stood gaping in wonder at the splendidly equipped army marching along under graceful folds of the old flag," he wrote. "Some waved their hats and women their hands in token of gratitude."[95]

Unlike the opening of the war, only a few specials from the North and none from the South were on hand when Lee surrendered to Grant at Appomattox Courthouse. *New York Herald* reporter Sylvanus Cadwallander said General Lee "looked very much jaded and worn, but, nevertheless, presented the same magnificent *physique* for which he has always been noted. . . . His demeanor was that of a thoroughly possessed gentleman who had a very disagreeable duty to perform, but was determined to get through it as well and as soon as he could." General Grant wore "a hat somewhat the worse for wear, without a sword of any kind," Cadwallander wrote. "His appearance, never imposing, contrasted strongly with that of Gen. Lee," he continued. "But his quiet, unassuming deportment rarely failed to impress everyone with his force of character, no matter what his surroundings might be."[96]

Newsmen were forced to wait outside Wilber McLean's home, so no correspondent witnessed the surrender. But a resourceful Henry E. Wing of the *New York Tribune* had made arrangements to get the news first. A member of Grant's staff agreed to provide a signal to Wing: If Lee surrendered, the staff member would come out of the house, take off his hat, and wipe his forehead three times with his handkerchief. When the officer gave Wing the signal, the correspondent jumped on his horse and galloped off to the telegraph office to file his story. The war was over and Wing got his scoop.[97]

TWO

ILLUSTRATIONS
AND PHOTOGRAPHS

People wanted to see the news of the Civil War that they read about. A cast of artists and photographers provided the images. Never before had a significant event in the United States been captured pictorially so widely and provided to such a vast audience. Thousands of illustrations appeared in magazines and newspapers during the war and more than a million photographs were made.

The great majority of illustrations and photographs appeared in the North. Three illustrated weeklies published the sketches of full-time artists in the field. Cameramen made photographs that could not be published but were turned into illustrations and shown in galleries. The South had fewer magazines and most closed because of insufficient staff, materials, and advertising. The South also had fewer photographers and most of them did not have the equipment, supplies, or financial wherewithal to record the war. Newspapers on both sides could not print the kind of elaborate illustrations that the magazines published. But recognizing their appeal with readers, some of the largest newspapers published woodcuts of maps, portraits, and other subjects.

Artists and photographers considered themselves reporters who worked with pictures instead of words. The best illustrations and photographs had a realism that captured the war in all its many faces. Certainly, the illustrators and cameramen had different professional goals and ethical standards, but most of them wanted to faithfully record the conflict for a public that craved news and information.

Americans primarily saw the war on the pages of weekly illustrated magazines. On the eve of the conflict, the most popular magazines were *Frank Leslie's Illustrated Newspaper, Harper's Weekly,* and the *New York Illustrated News.* At the time, all three were classified as newspapers because they reported current events. *Leslie's* even called itself a newspaper in its title. However, all three emphasized material more common to magazines, chiefly features and illustrations. The magazines were patterned after the illustrated weeklies of England, particularly the *Illustrated London News.* Their distinctive appearance and size made the publications immediately recognizable. The magazines regularly devoted as many as half of their 16 pages in each issue to illustrations, many of them full page in size. As a small folio, they could be easily folded in half for carrying or fitting into a bag. The size also allowed them to be shipped easily.

Henry Carter, an English immigrant and engraver who published under the *nom de guerre* of "Frank Leslie," founded *Frank Leslie's Illustrated Newspaper* in 1855. The magazine carried articles on music, drama, arts, fashion, book reviews, serialized fiction, and current events. But most striking were its large illustrations of news events. The magazine, which sold for 10 cents, was a big hit and by its fifth year had a circulation of more than 150,000. Fletcher Harper, the youngest of the brothers who started the Harper Brothers publishing firm, founded *Harper's Weekly* in 1857 and patterned it after *Leslie's.* Subtitled *A Journal of Civilization,* it was advertised as a "family newspaper" that emphasized news. Each issue contained domestic and foreign news, light essays, serial fiction, miscellany, and editorials. And like its competitor, *Harper's* emphasized illustrations, usually publishing a full-page picture on the front page and numerous pictures inside. On the eve of the war, *Harper's* had a circulation of almost 100,000. John King founded the *New York Illustrated News* in 1859, fashioning it after *Harper's* and *Leslie's.* The *Illustrated News* had an outstanding staff of artists, but the news and fiction were inferior to its competitors. The magazine never enjoyed the large circulation of *Harper's* and *Leslie's,* and it had a succession of editors before merging with a fashion publication late in the war.[1]

Making illustrations was a complicated process requiring large staffs of artists and engravers. Working with a sketch provided by an artist in the field, studio artists reproduced the sketch in reverse on blocks of wood. Engravers then cut away the bare white surface, leaving only the drawn lines in relief to be printed like type. Once completed, the blocks were bolted together to form a picture. Anywhere from 10 to 15 engravers would be used to complete a single picture. A two-page illustration could require as many as 40 blocks. An electrotyped metal impression then was made from the blocks for printing on the high-speed rotary presses used by the magazines. Depending on how long it took for the sketch to arrive at the magazine, it could take anywhere from one to three weeks for pictures from the war to go from an artist's sketch pad to the pages of a magazine.[2]

An estimated 30 full-time sketch artists—called "special artists" by the magazines—covered the war, the vast majority working for publications in the North. Some had formal training and their ranks included graduates of the Royal Academy of London and the National Academy of Design. Artists had varied experiences before the war. Several worked as book illustrators, others as designers and lithographers. A few were portrait and landscaper painters and at least one was a magazine cartoonist. Most were in their early twenties, a few in their thirties. All were white men.[3]

The most prolific Union artists were Alfred Waud, Theodore R. Davis, Edwin Forbes, Henry Lovie, and Francis H. Schell. Some, such as Waud, spent most or all of their time with one army. Others traveled widely. Schell made pictures in Florida, Kentucky, Louisiana, Maryland, North Carolina, Texas, and Virginia. William T. Crane sketched drawings in Florida, Georgia, and North Carolina. And Lovie made pictures in Illinois, Kentucky, Mississippi, Missouri, Tennessee, Virginia, and West Virginia.

With a haversack hanging on their hip and a sketchpad and pencils in hand, the artists were immediately recognizable in the field. They usually made pencil drawings for battle scenes but preferred crayon and charcoal for camp illustrations. Being a successful sketch artist not only required artistic talent but also sharp observation skills and a good memory. Davis described the qualities an artist should have: "Total disregard for personal safety and comfort; an owl-like propensity to sit up all night and a hawky stile of vigilance during the day; capacity for going on short food; willingness to ride any number of miles on horseback for just one sketch, which might have to be finished at night by no better light than that of a fire."[4]

Because they had to make their sketches quickly, artists developed their own shorthand for recording war scenes. A pencil smudge showed a clustering of trees and underbrush. Wavering circles indicated shells exploding in the air. A row of short lines suggested battalions and regiments in formation. Artists usually only sketched a few soldiers and officers in detail to remind them of what they were doing or looked like. Sometimes they had the time to make a more polished sketch, but often they had to send just an initial sketch with notes in the margins for the engravers. The notes included comments such as "more tents" or "trees here." Some sketch artists included explicit instructions for the engravers. In one drawing, an artist wrote: "Make scene as wild as possible, I am entirely disabled by diphtheria . . . or heaven knows what. Contrast the black smoke well with the powder smoke. Finish gunboats from former sketches, no changes except pilot houses who have this shape."[5]

Sketch artists had various ways of working in the field. Lovie, who ran a lithograph business in Cincinnati and supplemented his income as an artist, knew that he should make battle illustrations with a full view of a scene and then supplement it with details. He would take a vantage point on a hillside to draw a panoramic view of the fighting and the terrain. Then when the fighting was over, he went down on the battlefield to draw the aftermath, often talking to officers to get information about what took place.[6]

✑❧ ❧✑

Civil War photography had its roots in the daguerreotype era. A Frenchman, Louis Daguerre, invented the process that took his name. Daguerreotypes were first used widely for portrait photography. Individual and family portraits, previously only possible for the wealthy as paintings, were for the first time affordable to virtually everyone. In 1840, the first daguerreotype studios opened in New York, Boston, Philadelphia, and Charleston. Within a few years, studios opened throughout the country. By the mid-1850s, it is estimated that three million daguerreotypes were taken annually. Just as daguerreotypes were becoming popular, the wet collodion glass plate process was invented. It was cheaper and easier, reducing the exposure times and permitting the duplication of prints on photographic paper. Another big advantage was that the wet plate process could be done in the field to capture news event. Delivery wagons were turned into photographic wagons carrying all the camera equipment and developing chemicals needed to make pictures.[7]

On the eve of the war, a mass audience for photography was developing due in large part to the low cost of prints and marketing by various photographic supply companies. The paper process of making prints made it possible to duplicate photographs almost endlessly. The pictures could be sent through the mail and stored in albums. Firms such as the Edward A. Anthony Company in New York provided camera, plates, chemicals, paper, and studio equipment to photographers across the country. They also mass produced and sold the most popular pictures made by various photographers.[8]

Less is known about the photographers who recorded the war. Many worked in obscurity: their names never attached to their pictures. Even with the dozen or so who have been identified, only a few left behind any significant personal information. Many photographers had experience before the war either as portrait photographers or assistants. When the fighting began, they took advantage of the demand for portraits, making pictures of the new recruits for both armies. However, for many photographers their war experience ended there. Making pictures in the field was too difficult and expensive for most of them.

Taking photographs usually was a two-man operation and took 7 to 10 minutes for each picture. The photographer set the large camera upon a tripod to keep it steady. He pointed the camera at the scene to be shot and then put his head under a black cloth to focus the lens. At the same time, an assistant prepared the negative plates. Each plate was coated with collodion, a mixture of sulfuric ether and alcohol. The plate then was sensitized in a bath of silver nitrate. The sensitized plate was removed from the bath, the excess silver blotted off, and then secured in a light-tight wooden holder behind a hinged door. The process was done in the dark with the only light coming from a small, safelight window. The prepared plate was rushed to the photographer who moved the focusing frame out of the way and replaced it with the plate holder. He then slid the front panel out to expose the plate to the interior of the camera. Finally, the photographer removed the lens cap to expose the plate and record the image. Exposures in good light typically took 10 to 15 seconds. The lens cap then was put back on, the plate cover replaced, and the plate taken back to the developing wagon. There the assistant removed the plate from the holder and poured a developer over it. After about two minutes, water was poured over the plate to stop the developing. The plate then was dried and stored. Prints were made at the studio.[9]

In the field, photographers traveled in small wagons with canvas sides. Dubbed "what-is-it" wagons by curious soldiers, they carried a photographer's cameras, equipment, chemicals, and, often, personal belongings. Making and developing pictures was difficult work. On hot days, the heat under the tarps could be debilitating and the wagon reeked of the ether used in the collodion. Breathing the fumes made photographers woozy and the silver nitrate turned their hands black. J. Pitcher Spencer recalled later the "immense difficulties" of making pictures in the field. "[I]t took unceasing care to keep every bit of the apparatus, as well as each and every chemical, free from contamination which might affect the picture," he wrote. "Often a breath of wind, no matter how gentle, spoiled the whole affair."[10]

Because of the long exposure time it took to make pictures, the majority of war photographs were posed. Individuals or groups were set up by the photographer and instructed to simply look at the camera and not move while their picture was made. The more skilled and creative photographers did more, capturing subjects when they were at ease. Cameramen were unable to photograph the fighting, so they made pictures of the aftermath: dead soldiers, wrecked equipment, devastated cities, and countryside. Viewers saw the pictures in galleries, where they could purchase copies. They also saw them in the illustrated magazines, which regularly turned the best photographs from major battles and campaigns into intricate drawings.

Artists and photographers worked under the same military restrictions as reporters. But because most of their pictures were made after fighting had taken place, they had far fewer problems with military commanders. Probably the most serious incident took place during the Peninsula campaign when *Harper's* published two "bird's eye" pictorial maps. One of the maps showed the position and identity of infantry units, the location and sizes of the artillery, and even the position of General George B. McClellan's headquarters. Secretary of War Edwin M. Stanton said the magazine was "guilty of giving aid and comfort to the enemy" and he ordered it suspended. Fletcher Harper promptly met with Stanton and argued that the journal had not revealed any useful information to the Confederacy. He also reminded the secretary of *Harper's* strong support for the administration. Before Fletcher left, Stanton revoked the suspension.[11]

In the field, artists and photographers also dealt with the same dangers and dif- ficulties as correspondents. After riding some 1,000 miles on horseback over three months, Lovie complained to his editor at *Leslie's* that he was exhausted. "Riding from ten to fifteen miles daily through mud and underbrush and then working until midnight by the dim light of a tallow dip, I am nearly 'played out'," he wrote. "I must beg for a furlough for rest and repairs. I am deranged about the stomach, ragged, un- kempt, and unshorn, and need the co-joined skill and services of the apothecary, the tailor and the barber and above all the attentions of home." Waud described what the conditions could be like in a story for *Harper's* in 1863. The artist wrote about being soaked by rain for two days. When he left the protection of cover, he was fired upon by Confederate sharpshooters and had to do "some tall riding to get out of the way."[12]

Several artists and photographers were debilitated by exhaustion or disease and had to leave the field for a time. At least one sketch artist was killed in the fighting and at least two were wounded. The conditions took their toll on many men, especially the sketch artists, who often stayed in the field for weeks without a break. Waud and Davis were among a small group of artists who worked through the end of the war.[13]

❧⚬❧

Before the fighting began, artists had been in Charleston for weeks illustrating the secession crisis. *Leslie's* sent William Waud to the city and instructed him to use dis- cretion in making his sketches. Waud, a convivial Englishman and the brother of Alfred Waud, made the rounds of meetings, rallies, and regimental reviews, sketching as residents celebrated secession and prepared for the fighting. *Leslie's* also encouraged soldiers with artistic talent on both sides to send pictures of "important events and striking incidents." The magazine promised to "pay liberally." *Harper's* was unable to send an artist to Charleston, but the magazine made arrangements for several officers with the Union garrison to send sketches. As soldiers, their pictures were limited to the forts in the harbor, but the magazine could boast that it had illustrations from the most strategic points.[14]

When Confederate batteries began firing on Fort Sumter, Waud seemingly was ev- erywhere. He sketched gun crews on Morris Island firing shots across the harbor. He drew soldiers on the floating battery stripped to their waists as they fired the big guns. He also drew the badly damaged fort. *Leslie's* bragged that it had "the only reliable war illustrations." With no other artists except for the Union officers, *Harper's* largely relied on the imagination of the artists back in New York to record the event. They produced the dramatic—and highly unlikely—front-page illustration of Charleston residents weeping as they watched the attack from rooftops. The *Illustrated News* also did not have an artist in Charleston, but it managed to publish the sketches of re- porter B. S. Osbon of the *New York World*. He drew three sketches that the magazine published, including the torn American flag flying from a makeshift pole at the fort during the attack.[15]

No photographers recorded the start of the war. During the winter and spring of 1861, Charleston photographer George Cook had corresponded with friends in the North who were concerned about his safety. A fellow photographer in Philadelphia wrote to Cook suggesting that Major Robert Anderson, the commander of the Union garrison, would be a newsworthy subject for a portrait. Anderson turned down Cook's initial request, but the photographer asked the wife of South Carolina Governor Francis W. Pickens to persuade the major to agree to have his picture taken. In February Cook hired a boat to ferry him and his equipment to the fort where he made a group portrait of Anderson and his officers. Cook promptly made negatives and sent copies of the photograph to two friends in the North. It quickly became a best seller in Charleston and New York. Six weeks later, *Harper's* published a front-page illustration of Anderson and his officers based on the photograph.[16]

During the attack and even afterward, Cook apparently was content to stay in his studio tending to business. However, other Charleston photographers recorded the aftermath of the bombardment. Alma A. Pelot took a boat to the fort on April 15 and spent the day making pictures. Afterward, the studio bought an advertisement in the *Charleston Mercury* touting its "sixteen views of the most important and interesting points of Forts Sumter, Moultrie, and the Floating Battery." J. M. Osborn, a photographer with the Osborn & Durbec's Southern Stereoscopic and Photographic Depot, took more than 40 pictures of Fort Sumter, Fort Moultrie, Morris Island, and other scenes of the fighting. The pictures showed Confederates posing next to the big guns, men cleaning up the damage, and dignitaries inspecting the captured fort.[17]

During the months when the Union and Confederacy prepared for war, photographers on both sides stayed busy. The thousands of new recruits for the Union and Confederate armies wanted pictures of themselves in uniform for loved ones. They marched into studios across the North and South to pose for portraits. To meet the demand, some enterprising photographers traveled to army camps to make individual and group portraits of soldiers. They set up temporary studios in tents, hung up a sign, and soon soldiers were standing in line to have their picture made. The demand for portraits remained high throughout the war as new recruits enlisted. During one round of enlistment, an observer wrote, "The streets are filled with bright uniforms, and the photographic galleries are crowded with soldiers and their friends. What a blessing it is that they who go to the war can not only leave behind their images, but take with them the semblance of those they leave at home!"[18]

Unquestionably, the best-known photographer when the war began was Mathew Brady. Brady had opened a daguerreotype studio in New York in 1844 and quickly established himself as one of the city's leading portrait photographers. His lavishly appointed studio on Broadway was near the city's finest hotels. He lured many of the best-known figures of the era, including Henry Clay, Daniel Webster, and James Fenimore Cooper, from their hotels to his studio to have their portrait made. Business boomed and within 10 years, Brady employed more than 25 workers, including camera operators, technicians, and finishers. Brady later opened a studio in Washington, D.C., and announced that his goal was to create "a gallery which shall eventually contain life-like portraits of every distinguished American now living."[19]

The ambitious Brady wanted to make a complete photographic record of the war. He and his staff not only took portraits of individual soldiers, but they also made pictures of the thousands of Union troops training outside Washington. The pictures showed the rows of white tents formed in squares around the drill field and the raw recruits learning to march in formation. They captured the men digging trenches for the protection of Washington and stringing telegraph wires out of the city. They also showed men relaxing in camp, washing their clothes, and worshipping at outdoor chapels. Brady sold the popular pictures mounted on cards with the inscription "Illustrations of Camp Life."[20]

Brady had an outstanding group of assistants led by Alexander Gardner. Born in Scotland, Gardner briefly owned the *Glasgow Sentinel* but he became interested in the new art of photography. With his wife and several family members, Gardner immigrated to the United States in 1856. Gardner had seen Brady's photographic work at an exhibit in Scotland and contacted him after arriving in the country. Brady hired Gardner as an assistant and the talented photographer soon because indispensible.[21]

A few cameramen in the South also sought to capture images of camp life. New Orleans photographer J. D. Edwards traveled to Pensacola, Florida, to record troops training there. Among the photographs he made was a picture of members of the "Quitman Rifles" from Company B of the 9th Mississippi standing around a camp fire while one man was cooking. Ben Oppenheimer, a photographer in Mobile, Alabama, also made pictures of the troops in camp. One photograph showed a group of Confederate soldiers in their homespun uniforms standing in line with their weapons.[22]

❧ ❀ ❧

The illustrated magazines in the North captured the patriotic celebrations set off by President Lincoln's call for troops to put down the rebellion. Sentimental pictures captured young men going off to join the military as their families bid them farewell. A front-page picture in *Harper's* showed volunteers in Washington, D.C., being sworn in. An illustration from New York captured a large crowd watching the parade of new recruits marching down Broadway. Another picture showed temporary barracks erected in Central Park. *Harper's* also reprinted the group portrait of Anderson and his officers made before the attack, dubbing them "The Heroes of Fort Sumter."[23]

The Zouaves were popular subjects for magazine artists. Numerous illustrations showed the colorful soldiers in their baggy pants and distinctive fezzes. They captured the Zouaves as they drilled in New York and later paraded through the streets of the capital. When Zouave Colonel Elmer Ellsworth was killed trying to cut down a Confederate flag from an Alexandria hotel, artists recreated the scene of his death. The illustrated magazines also published pictures showing bare-chested Zouave troops making gallant bayonet charges.[24]

During the first months of the war, the illustrated magazines scrambled to keep up with the demand for pictures. All three made regular appeals for Union soldiers with any artistic talent to send sketches from the army. The *Illustrated News* offered to pay for any sketches that were published, no matter how crudely drawn. And *Leslie's* offered a year's free subscription for any soldier who submitted a sketch as a sample of his artistic ability.[25]

Both full-time and part-time artists sketched the action of Federal troops during initial skirmishing in the summer. They made pictures of the fighting at Great Bethel, Philippi, and Laurel Hill. In July when the Army of the Potomac began its advance against Richmond, several photographers, including Brady and his assistants, joined the artists. They took two wagons full of equipment and supplies.

Among the sketch artists was Alfred Waud. Known to his friends as "Alf," Waud was born in London and studied art in England before moving to the United States in 1850. He worked as an engraver for various publications and also illustrated several books. Waud wanted to be a maritime painter and he made numerous illustrations of the ships in Boston and New York. But when the war began, he signed on to be a sketch artist for the *Illustrated News*.[26]

Like the reporters covering a battle for the first time, Waud and his colleagues had no idea what to expect at First Bull Run. The artists sketched frenziedly during the battle trying to capture scenes none had ever witnessed before. Waud drew the Union batteries and the men fighting from behind whatever cover they could find. An illustration of one charge was published on the front page of the *Illustrated News*. The same issue carried a picture of Union batteries firing on Confederate troops. Waud even included a picture of himself in the illustration sketching the scene. *Harper's* published several illustrations of the battle, including a two-page picture of a Union charge and a large picture of the Union retreat. Several of the pictures showed Federal troops performing heroically. In the first of what would be many illustrations of alleged Confederate atrocities, another picture showed Confederate troops bayoneting wounded Union soldiers. *Leslie's* also captured the Union troops fighting heroically, but the magazine did not ignore the embarrassing retreat. Two illustrations showed the hysteria as officers fled with the troops. One showed a white-suited civilian caught up in the melee.[27]

No photographs were made at Bull Run, at least none that survived. Brady claimed that he made pictures at the battle, and he had a photograph taken of himself with the caption "just returned from Bull Run." A flattering story in the *New York Times* said that Brady was seen "at every point, before and after the fight, neglecting no opportunity and sparing no labor in the pursuit of his professional object." However, no pictures by Brady or anyone else ever appeared. Brady told a journalist later that he made pictures at the battle but that his "apparatus" was damaged on the trip back to Washington.[28]

Down in Charleston, Cook recorded the aftermath of the battle weeks later. He made photographs of Union prisoners who were captured at Bull Run and sent to Castle Pinckney in the Charleston harbor. One picture showed 19 men with the 69th New York, an Irish regiment, standing in front of their cell. One of the prisoners had formerly worked with the popular group, Christy's Minstrels, prompting the men to dub their cell the Musical Hall. Cook's revealing pictures were the first photographs of prisoners from the war.[29]

In the weeks after Bull Run, when no fighting took place, artists and photographers looked for other subjects, so they made numerous pictures of camp life. One illustration showed troops relaxing in camp after an evening parade. Another captured three soldiers on picket guard. An illustration in *Leslie's* showed troops huddling in camp on a stormy night. Another captured Lincoln and some of his cabinet members reviewing the Army of the Potomac. Artists also illustrated the Army of the Potomac's new commander, General McClellan.[30]

Alfred Waud lived in the camp with the army and made numerous pictures of the troops. He shared a tent with an officer, sleeping on a hospital stretcher, and using a valise for a pillow. However, the artist was increasingly unhappy with the demands of the *Illustrated News*. The magazine expected him to cover a large area, from Fortress Monroe to the Shenandoah Valley, in addition to various events in Washington. An exhausted Waud also did not like the way the magazine's engravers reproduced many of his sketches. Early in 1862, Fletcher Harper asked Waud if he would like to join the *Harper's* staff. Waud jumped at the opportunity and spent the rest of the war with the magazine.[31]

With little fighting to illustrate, *Harper's* regularly sought to explain the war to readers with large, elaborate pictures. Made by the studio artists in New York, the illustrations showed the various uniforms of the Union and Confederate armies, ships that had been converted into gunboats, and "The Songs of the War," among other subjects. Half- and full-page portraits, usually made from photographs, showed key military and civilian leaders. *Harper's* also published numerous maps. A page in one issue featured small maps of seven Southern harbors. And an impressive four-page, foldout map of the South in a November issue showed cities, town, roads, rivers, and other features in detail.[32]

❧❦❧

Southerners did not get to see the war in the same way as Northerners did. When the fighting began, the illustrated weeklies stopped circulating in the Confederacy, although occasionally copies would get through the lines. In the absence of the magazines, the *Southern Illustrated News* tried to fill the void. Founded in 1862 by the

Richmond publishing firm of Ayers and Wade, the magazine declared its intent to provide pictures of the war "honestly and faithfully drawn and engraved by competent and experienced artists." In its first issue the *Southern Illustrated News* promised to never publish "pictures of victories that were never won, nor to sketch the taking of capitals that never surrendered, as have the illustrated weeklies of Yankeedom." *Leslie's* fired back, dismissing the magazine for printing on "whitey brown wrapping picture" and publishing "wonderfully bad woodcuts." Indeed, the *Southern Illustrated News* had problems from the start. The first issue contained only one illustration, a small engraving of General Jackson on the first page. The magazine suffered from a constant shortage of supplies and a lack of sketch artists and engravers to make pictures. Most of the illustrations published were of simple subjects and generally crude by the standards of the North's magazines. The *Southern Illustrated News* limped along for two years until it finally closed in 1864.[33]

Newspapers also recognized the appeal of illustrations. Although they did not have the staff or facilities to print the kind of elaborate pictures that the magazines published, the largest newspapers, most notably the *New York Herald, New York Times, New York Tribune,* and *Philadelphia Inquirer,* published numerous woodcuts of maps, and, to a lesser extent, other subjects. The *Herald,* in particular, regularly published illustrations, sometimes two or more in a single issue. In its extensive coverage of the battle of the ironsides in 1862, the *Herald* published a map of Hampton Roads. The next day the newspaper also published woodcuts of the two vessels and sketches of the *Monitor's* skipper and chief engineer.[34]

At least two artists were with the Union squadron during the Mississippi River campaign in early 1862. Lovie and Alexander Simplot traveled with General Grant and his staff on board the steamer, *New Uncle Sam.* Some men became sketch artists during the war by accident, and the 24-year-old Simplot was one of them. A graduate of Union College, Simplot was a schoolteacher in Iowa when the fighting began. He was on the wharfs in Dubuque with a large group to see a group of men off to the war. Awed by the cheers of the crowd and the roar of artillery, he made a sketch of the scene and sent it to *Harper's.* Editors liked his picture and a few weeks later, Simplot was assigned to cover the fighting in the West. He was paid from $5 to $25 per sketch.[35]

Simplot and Lovie captured the fighting at forts Henry and Donelson, where Federal forces won important victories. In one illustration published by *Leslie's,* Lovie drew a graphic picture of a mounted battery being directly hit by a gunboat. Some of the crew was shown killed, one with a lost arm and another with his head and arms blown off. The two men also made other pictures, including Grant's headquarters, a field hospital, and Confederate prisoners.[36]

Lovie continued traveling with Grant and, as a result, got outstanding pictures of the battle of Shiloh. He was with Grant's command when it arrived at Pittsburgh Landing on the first day of the fighting. Lovie, who increasingly showed his willingness to show the horrors of war, witnessed the chaos as frightened Federal troops tried to flee the initial Confederate attack. He focused on specific incidents such as the ambulance corps lifting wounded soldiers into wagons. One of his pictures also showed an aspect of the war the press rarely discussed: a group of frightened soldiers huddling under a bluff. For its part, *Harper's* devoted the front page of its May 3 issue to the "Heroes of the Battle of Pittsburgh Landing." The magazine featured individual portraits of 11 commanders, including Grant, Sherman, and Don Carlos Buell. *Harper's* also published several illustrations of the fighting.[37]

William Waud joined Admiral David Farragut's naval expedition against New Orleans to sketch for *Leslie's*. One of his pictures showed Union sailors trying to camouflage their ships by tying tree boughs to the masts. He drew Farragut's men trying to douse burning rafts that the rebels had sent downstream in a desperate attempt to set the fleet afire. The adventuresome Waud also climbed up the mainmast of the USS *Mississippi* to draw a series of sketches of the fleet sailing past the forts guarding the city. When the fleet anchored in New Orleans, he made another drawing of Federal sailors rowing to shore to demand the surrender of the city. *Leslie's* published Waud's pictures in several supplements to the regular editions. *Harper's* also had an artist with the fleet at New Orleans and he provided numerous pictures. However, the illustrations lacked the detail and action of the best naval illustrations.[38]

The Peninsula campaign proved to be one of the most significant events of the war for photographers. Brady remained convinced that he could record a photographic history of the war. He needed the approval of the War Department and Secretary of War Stanton agreed, provided that Brady assumed the cost. Brady purchased more cameras and equipment, enough to supply a fleet of photographic wagons. He also set up supply bases in various locations and lined up cameramen. The venture was costly but Brady believed he could sell enough copies of the photographs to more than cover his expenses.[39]

At least four photographers accompanied the Union army on the Peninsula campaign, including James F. Gibson. Working with Alexander Gardner, the young Gibson made some of the best-known pictures of the war at Antietam and Gettysburg. But he received his initial experience on the Virginia peninsula. Gibson and the other photographers produced pictures of camp life, artillery batteries, and the curious new observation balloon Intrepid, as well as group portraits of officers and soldiers.[40]

Because of bad weather, photographers were unable to photograph the aftermath of many battles during the campaign. However, they managed to get pictures of casualties at army field hospitals. The revealing photographs included a group of wounded soldiers strewn about a farmyard at Savage Station, Virginia. As historian Bob Zeller has noted, for the first time photography revealed the human toll of war. And *Harper's New Monthly Magazine* said the image "brings the war to those who have not been to it. . . . It is a picture which is more eloquent than the sternest speech."[41]

The photographs of the Peninsula campaign and those sold to the public garnered plenty of attention for Brady and his studio, if not for the men who actually made the pictures. The *New York Times* wrote, "Brady was the first to make photography the Clio of war. . . . His artists have accompanied the army on nearly all its marches. . . . The result is a series of pictures christened 'Incidents of War', and nearly as interesting as the war itself: For they constitute the history of it, and appeal directly to the great throbbing hearts of the north." And the *New York World* gushed: "Mr. Brady's 'Scenes and Incidents' . . . are inestimable chroniclers of this tempestuous epoch, exquisite in beauty, truthful as the records of heaven. . . . They [photographers] have threaded the weary stadia of every march; have hung on the skirts of every battle scene; have caught the compassion of the hospital, the romance of the bivouac, the pomp and panoply of the field review—aye, even the cloud of conflict."[42]

❧❧❧

Although war photography had made major strides over the past year, no one had captured the real horror of the battlefield. That changed with the battle of Antietam. It is not known when Gardner and Gibson arrived at the Maryland battlefield. But on September 19, Brady's two assistants began working and, over the next five days, the men made some 70 photographs of the battle's aftermath, including some of the best-known pictures of the war. The photographs included Confederate dead along the Hagerstown Pike, near the Dunker Church, and in the so-called Bloody Lane, as well as a Union burial party. The photos of the dead soldiers were exceptionally graphic, some showing bloody faces, contorted bodies, and bloated features. The burial party photograph was a haunting image of a shallow grave and headstone under a large tree, with three soldiers underneath the broad branches, two with rifles on their shoulders.[43]

The Antietam photos were exhibited at Brady's gallery in October. The *New York Times* enthusiastically praised the work, once again giving credit to Brady even though he took none of the pictures. "Mr. Brady has does something to bring home to us the terrible reality and earnestness of war. If he has not brought bodies and laid them in our dooryards and along the streets, he has done something very like it." The writer noted that there was a "terrible fascination" with the images "that draws one near these pictures, and makes him loath to leave. You will see hushed, reverend groups standing around these weird copies of carnage, bending down to look in the pale faces of the dead, chained by the strange spell that dwells in dead men's eyes." And Oliver Wendell Holmes, whose son was wounded at Antietam and rushed to the battlefield to search for him, later wrote of the pictures:

Let him who wishes to know what war is look at this series of illustrations. It was so nearly like visiting the battlefield to look over these views, that all the emotions excited by the actual sight of the stained and sordid scene, strewed with rags and wrecks, came back to us and we buried them in the recesses of our cabinet as we would have buried the mutilated remains of the dead they too vividly represented.[44]

The photographs from Antietam were the last Gardner photos to be published in association with Brady. The burly Scotsman had decided to start his own studio and gallery in Washington at 511 Seventh Street that featured a large sign advertising "Views of the War." Gardner took several of Brady's most talented associates, including Gibson and Timothy O'Sullivan. He also took more than 400 negatives the men had shot from First and Second Bull Run, the Peninsula campaign, Antietam, and other battles. By all accounts, the split between Gardner and Brady was amicable. The two men remained friends.[45]

Sketch artists also illustrated the fighting at Antietam. Forbes of *Leslie's* witnessed the fighting from a hill near the Pry House. He later wrote that it was "probably the most picturesque battle of the war." Forbes went on: "The engagement was a spectacle which was not surpassed during the whole war. Thousands of people took advantage of the occasion, as the hills were black with spectators. Soldiers of the reserve, officers and men of the commissary and quartermasters' department, camp-followers, and hundreds of farmers and their families, watched the desperate struggle." Alfred Waud made numerous sketches from the battle. They included a picture of a Union field hospital where amputations were being done. As it often did, *Harper's* published some of his remarks about the pictures and how he made them. The artist noted the tremendous casualties from the fighting. Schell also made pictures at Antietam. Perhaps his most provocative illustration showed nearby residents, who, the day after the battle, brought their families to gawk at the dead troops still lying on the battlefield.[46]

Some magazine illustrations sought to recreate war scenes, usually for propaganda purposes. A picture in a summer 1862 issue of *Harper's* captured the "Sacking of a City in the West by the Guerillas." It showed a highly stylized street scene with Confederate guerillas wrecking a town. In the foreground, a woman on her knees pleaded with a rebel guerilla, while an old man was about to be beaten over the head by another soldier. The accompanying text said: "Guerilla warfare involves, as a matter of necessity, the four highest crimes in the calendar—murder, rape, robbery, and arson. The bond which unites members of a guerilla band together is love of plunder, list, and violence. War, as carried out by civilized armies, has no attraction for them. It would not pay them." Another illustration showed Union prisoners being marched through a Southern town. Angry townspeople, including women and children, expressed their hatred for the troops.[47]

In the weeks leading up to the battle of Fredericksburg, *Harper's* published various pictures of the city. After the Federal defeat, it published a front-page illustration of

Union soldiers bravely scaling the high ground held by the Confederates. A revealing two-page picture also showed in detail the confusion in the Union rear as soldiers were tending to the wounded and more troops were being sent into battle. As the magazine noted in the accompanying text: "As a general rule, battle pictures represent the shock of the actual conflict; the scenes in the back-ground are often quite as striking as worthy of being preserved." *Harper's* also quoted the artist who wrote of the scene: "All this and more is seen by the reserve, patiently waiting until their turn shall come to take part in the struggle of the day. The wounded are brought past them, carried so that their injuries are terribly apparent to those who are forced to stand still, not knowing how soon the same fate may be theirs."[48]

Although illustrations from battles such as Antietam and Fredericksburg were undeniably popular with readers, the news magazines recognized that the war was more than just fighting. Artists increasingly drew the everyday aspects of army life when soldiers were at ease. Many of the pictures showed the more enjoyable aspects of camp life: recreation, sports, parties, religious services, and holiday celebrations. Artists also occasionally drew the darker sides, including military executions and the punishments meted out for small crimes.[49]

Although several of the artists in the field provided sketches of army life, none did it better than Winslow Homer. The Massachusetts native had been a freelance artist for *Harper's* before the war. His work was notable for its detail and sense of realism, and editors soon began giving him important assignments. One was to cover Lincoln's inauguration, and he produced a two-page drawing of the president giving his address in front of the capitol. During the war, Homer made several trips to the front and some of his drawings, notably one of a cavalry charge, took readers into the thick of the fighting. But most of his drawings examined everyday life: a bivouac fire, surgeons at work, Thanksgiving in camp, news from the war, winter quarters, a football game, and payday.[50]

Many of Homer's pictures were single images, but others featured multiple scenes tied together by decorative motifs. His illustration, "News from the War," showed the various means of communication used during the war—letter, telegraph, rider, train, and bugle. One image captured a woman reacting to tragic news, slumped over a table, her face hidden. Another showed an artist, probably his colleague Alfred Waud, sketching two soldiers. In the scene, onlookers delighted in watching the artist work. During the war, Homer became a serious painter. He turned some of his wartime subjects, including "A Sharpshooter on Picket Duty" and "Prisoners from the Front," into paintings that were praised by critics.[51]

As Fletcher Thompson has noted, over the course of the war the best sketch artists increasingly "abandoned the futile attempt to portray everything they saw, and instead sketched episodes and incidents that were representative of the larger scene." This episodic technique was especially useful in capturing troops on the march, life in camp, and other daily events of the Union army. A two-page illustration by Alfred

Waud showed troops struggling to cross the Potomac River in a driving rain. Another captured a lone soldier doing picket duty on a snowy morning, while another pictured soldiers cooking a meal during the halt of a wagon train, and another captured the interior of a hospital railroad car.[52]

⸙ ⸙

Blacks in the South had been the subjects of artists and photographers since the beginning of the war. Most pictures had focused on the men, women, and children freed as a result of the Union occupation of the coastal areas of the South. The illustrations of blacks ranged from the positive and heroic, to the demeaning and stereotypical. *Harper's* devoted its front page in late 1861 to scenes of contrabands at Beaufort, South Carolina. It showed proud men and women doing a variety of tasks. However, an illustration on the cover of an 1862 issue resorted to common stereotypes. It portrayed a "Scene in the Parlor of Mr. Barnwell's House at Beaufort, South Carolina" and showed shiftless blacks languishing around, dancing, and playing music.[53]

After President Lincoln issued the Emancipation Proclamation, artists and photographers increasingly made pictures of the thousands of newly freed blacks. One illustration captured several families gathered around a wagon that was on its way to an army camp. Another showed a long line of freed men, women, and children walking to the Union lines at Newbern, North Carolina. Photographers captured many similar images.[54]

When blacks were permitted to enlist in the military, artists and photographers began making pictures of proud men in uniform. In the case of the magazines, they also showed the new troops fighting. A two-page illustration in *Leslie's* of the assault on Confederate works at Fort Hudson in 1863 showed members of the Second Louisiana Regiment bravely engaged in hand-to-hand fighting. The magazine quoted a report in which General Nathaniel P. Banks called the regiment "heroic," and added, "No troops could be more determined or daring." *Leslie's* also published a two-page illustration entitled "The Negro in the War" that comprised 12 separate pictures of black troops fighting, on guard and relaxing in camp.[55]

Portraits continued to be popular during the war. In their studios, photographers turned their cameras on politicians, officers, and other well-known figures. The news magazines frequently made the pictures into illustrations, publishing them when a figure was in the news or during periods when there was little fighting happening. Although numerous politicians were photographed, none more so than President Lincoln. In fact, Lincoln was the most photographed president of the 19th century. In all, he sat for photographs on 61 occasions and 119 pictures were made, about half during the war. Gardner took 30 pictures of Lincoln, more than any other photographer.[56]

Soon after Lincoln arrived in Washington, *Harper's* commissioned Brady to photograph the president. Gardner actually made the portrait, photographing the bearded Lincoln seated next to a table. The picture was made into an illustration for the magazine. Two years later, Gardner photographed the president again, this time in his own studio. One picture showed Lincoln with his head leaning against his hand, a photograph that Lincoln called "the best that I have seen yet." Later in 1863, Lincoln returned to Gardner's studio. He was photographed with his secretaries, John Hay and John Nicolay. In another portrait, Lincoln was captured staring straight into the camera, a portrait many believe to be the best ever taken of the president.[57]

One of the most commercially popular photographs ever taken of Lincoln was made in February 1864 with the president's son, Tad. Lincoln was seated with his arm resting on a book lying a table. Tad was standing on the other side of the table leaning over with his arm also resting on the table. The picture was reproduced in *Harper's* and other publications. One of the last pictures made of Lincoln was taken in Gardner's studio in February 1865. The president had a half-smile, but the toll the war had taken on him was clearly seen on his face.[58]

Although not covered as extensively as the fighting in the East, the war in the West also was the subject of pictures made by artists and cameramen. Chicago photographer John Carbutt traveled to Columbus, Kentucky, to photograph Illinois troops stationed there. He made pictures of the 4th U.S. Heavy Artillery changing guards with Columbus in the background. He also photographed the 134th Illinois drilling. Two Cincinnati photographers followed Ohio regiments to Vicksburg in 1863. In addition to making camp portraits, they photographed scenes around the strategic city. One picture showed a large American flag flying from the top of the Vicksburg Courthouse after the city was captured.[59]

Illustrators extensively covered the Vicksburg campaign in the West. Davis and Schell captured the final weeks of fighting for the strategic riverfront city. The two men sent back numerous sketches but some of the most revealing showed how the Union troops lived and fought in the trenches outside Vicksburg. The pictures captured the men eating meals and washing their clothes. They also showed the shelters built with any material that was available. Davis, who spent several nights in the trenches, illustrated how the troops fought the Confederate sharpshooters. His pictures showed marksmen putting their caps on top of the trenches to draw the fire of Confederate sharpshooters who exposed themselves to Federal riflemen. When the Confederacy surrendered after the long siege, Davis and Schell captured the event. Davis illustrated Confederate General John Pemberton meeting with Grant to discuss the surrender terms. Pictures showed the rebels stacking their weapons while Union soldiers sat atop the trenches watching the scene. Another illustration captured Federal troops marching into Vicksburg.[60]

At the same time the Vicksburg campaign was coming to a close, artists were doing their best to follow the Union army into Pennsylvania where all expected a major battle would be fought. Alfred Waud is believed to have arrived at Gettysburg with the main body of General George G. Meade's army on the night of July 1–2. Just a week earlier, the artist had buried his friend L. W. Buckingham, a correspondent with the *New York Herald* who had been killed trying to escape an ambush by Confederate guerillas. Waud still had the reporter's personal belongings when he finally arrived in Gettysburg. Other artists never made it. George Law of *Leslie's* was captured by Confederate troops at Chambersburg. Thomas Nast of *Harper's* got as far as Harrisburg, but he was detained for several days after one of his in-laws was arrested for flying a Confederate flag.[61]

The indefatigable Waud was in the midst of the fighting for the next two days and produced several excellent illustrations, including the fighting around the Devil's Den. His sketch of Pickett's charge appeared as a two-page spread in *Harper's*. Forbes arrived on the second day and tried to make some sketches but soon found that the fighting was "too hot" for him to risk getting close. The fighting on the third day was so intense that he stayed behind the Union lines where he drew the reserve troops marching by him toward the front. When he walked over the battlefield on July 4, Forbes was shocked by the ghastly scene. He visited many of the places where the fighting had taken place and sent several sketches to *Leslie's* but they lacked much detail. The *Illustrated News* did not have an artist at Gettysburg and it showed in the magazine.[62]

But more than the artists, it was the photographers who captured the frightening losses at Gettysburg, even though they arrived after the battle ended. Gardner learned about the battle on July 3 and, accompanied by O'Sullivan and Gibson, left Washington immediately. Gardner's son was attending school in Emmitsburg, Maryland. Worried about his safety, the photographer and his assistants stopped on July 5 to check on the boy. While there, they were briefly detained and questioned by General J.E.B. Stuart's fleeing cavalry. When the photographers arrived in Gettysburg, many of the dead had not been buried. The men initially photographed the scenes at the Rose Farm, Devil's Den, and Big Round Top where Confederate casualties remained unburied on the battlefield. They later made pictures of fighting locations, breastworks, as well as the town and cemetery.[63]

Gardner had learned from his experience at Antietam that photographs of the aftermath were in demand by a curious public. So he and his assistants focused on the shocking scenes at Gettysburg. Of the approximately 60 pictures the men made, three-quarters were of corpses, dead horses, and other battle carnage. The graphic photos showed dead rebels, some where they had been killed at Big Round Top, the Slaughter Pen, and other places. Other pictures showed the deceased lined up for burial in an open field. In an era before journalism ethics were defined, the photographers set up some of the casualty pictures. The best known of these was the picture of the dead Confederate sharpshooter at Devil's Den. Gardner found the young soldier beside a large boulder on the southern slope of the rocky outcrop. He took several photographs of the body and then spotted a stone wall a short distance away. With the help of others, Gardner dragged the body to the wall and positioned the soldier with his knapsack under his head and his rifle leaning against the rocks.[64]

Brady was not about to miss an event already being hailed across the North. He arrived in Gettysburg a week after Gardner and his assistant left. The casualties had already been buried by that time. However, the landmarks of the battlefield were becoming well known, so Brady and his staff photographed many of them, including Little Round Top, McPherson's Woods, Lee's headquarters, the Lutheran Seminary, and Evergreen Cemetery. Brady did not personally take any of the photographs at Gettysburg, but his artistry and vision were evident. He selected many of the scenes and camera angles for the pictures. That was probably most evident in the photograph of three Confederate prisoners on Seminary Ridge. The captured men were posed in the same proud manner of many portraits that Brady made during the war. Recognizing the popularity of the pictures from Gettysburg, *Harper's* published numerous illustrations based on Brady's photographs. Even though Gardner and his staff arrived first and made the only pictures of the casualties, *Harper's* did not use any of their photographs.[65]

In the weeks after Gettysburg, other cameramen made pictures of the battlefield that was becoming increasingly famous, thanks in large part to the extensive press coverage. The photographers included Charles and Isaac Tyson, who owned Gettysburg's Excelsior Gallery. The small shop, which focused on portraits, remained opened in the initial hours of the fighting as Union soldiers came in to have their pictures made. Before Confederate troops captured the town, the brothers fled and did not return until several days after the battle was over. The studio was not damaged in the fighting, and soon the Tysons were taking photographs of the battlefield and town, no doubt with the plan to sell pictures to tourists who already were starting to visit Gettysburg.[66]

✧◦✧

The great majority of Civil War photographers were civilians. The best-known exception was Andrew J. Russell, a Union military railroad photographer. Russell produced hundreds of photographs, mainly of the railroads of northern Virginia, which the army constantly tried to keep operating despite all the fighting that wrecked them. In his position, Russell had remarkable access to the scene of fighting. He made pictures of soldiers, including the widely seen photograph of a large group of Union troops in abandoned Confederate works near the Rappahannock River. He also photographed dead Confederate soldiers behind the stone wall at Marye's Heights at Fredericksburg.[67]

Russell also made pictures of the enemy when he photographed a group of Confederate soldiers who watched him work one day. Russell or an assistant had taken a camera to Stafford Heights across from Fredericksburg to photograph a destroyed bridge. In a series of five pictures, Russell not only shot the bridge but also a group of rebels who had come out to see what he was doing. The soldiers moved closer and closer as they became more comfortable in the presence of the camera. In fact, one photograph showed the Confederate troops at the end of the bridge essentially posing for the camera. Unfortunately, few outside the military saw Russell's photographs during the war. They were not shown in a gallery and not reproduced in magazines.[68]

One of the most widely photographed areas was the coastal area of South Carolina that Union forces captured early in the war. Some 17 photographers worked in the area taking hundreds of photos. One of the cameramen was Samuel E. Cooley, who advertised himself as the official photographer of the army's Department of the South. In actuality, Cooley only worked for the government by contract, but the sign he placed on his photography wagon probably helped his business.[69]

During the fighting at Charleston harbor in 1863, photographers managed to capture actual naval action. Cameramen Philip Haas and Washington Peale took a panoramic picture of one battle with plumes of smoke coming from a gunboat. A picture made on the beach near the Union camp showed dozens of soldiers and bystanders watching the battle. In the distance were several ships; most are dim but one was clearly visible. Cook captured another photograph of a battle while under fire himself. On September 8, the Charleston studio owner climbed onto the parapet of Fort Sumter and rested his camera on a broken gun carriage. There he made two pictures of Union gunboats firing less than 1,000 yards away. The three ironclads in the pictures were barely visible. Nonetheless, Cook's feat was praised by the *Charleston Courier,* which called it "one of the most remarkable acts . . . ever recorded in the history of war." The photographs were never published during the war, but Cook sold many copies at his studio.[70]

After Gettysburg, Alexander Gardner spent most of his time in Washington overseeing his gallery. He issued a 28-page catalogue listing 568 images, including many taken at Gettysburg. Prints and album cards were sold from 25 cents to $1.50. The pictures were available by mail from Anthony and Gardner's studio. Unlike Brady, Gardner gave credit to his photographers who made the pictures.[71]

Gardner named Timothy O'Sullivan his "superintendent" of field photography and the young man took advantage of the opportunity. Little is known about O'Sullivan. His family immigrated to the United States when he was a child. O'Sullivan joined Brady's staff as a young man. He photographed the Union-occupied areas of the Southern coast in 1862 and later various battles in Virginia. Gardner persuaded O'Sullivan to join him when he started his gallery. O'Sullivan and Gardner's brother, James, traveled with the Army of the Potomac during the spring campaign in 1864, along with several photographers from Brady's gallery. O'Sullivan made a revealing picture of wounded soldiers outside the Sanitary Commission depot in Fredericksburg and other scenes of the battle-ravaged town. O'Sullivan also got pictures of Confederate dead near Spotsylvania, several of which were likely arranged.[72]

The busy O'Sullivan later spotted a meeting of Grant with his officers on the grounds outside Massaponax Church. Looking for a good vantage point to capture the scene, he climbed up to the second story of the church and from a window made three revealing pictures, no doubt with the permission of Grant. In one photograph, Meade was examining a topographic map and in another Grant was writing a dispatch. Also in the picture was Charles A. Dana, the assistant secretary of war.[73]

During the campaign, artists followed the Union army to the Wilderness, Spotsylvania Courthouse, and Cold Harbor. Alfred Waud managed to sketch his pictures deep in the woods of the Wilderness. One picture showed a division advancing in rough formation through the trees, the men firing all the time. Forbes drew the charge of Union brigades at Spotsylvania. At Cold Harbor, Waud illustrated a Union charge and troops turning captured Confederate artillery on the enemy. Illustrations also showed the many casualties from the intense fighting. Waud drew a wounded soldier being lifted onto a blanket by his comrades.[74]

No photographs similar to Antietam or Gettysburg were made of the aftermath of the major battles in Virginia in the summer of 1864. Cold Harbor was not recorded for more than a week after the carnage. However, Brady's staff kept busy taking portraits of officers, including Grant who was quickly becoming famous across the North. A portrait of Grant captured the general outside a tent with his arm resting on a tree. It became one of the best-known pictures made of the general. In another picture, Brady sat with General Ambrose Burnside and other officers in camp as Burnside read a newspaper. John Reekie also made pictures in the Richmond area. His photograph of a burial party at Cold Harbor was one of the most disturbing and memorable of the war. It showed a young black man posing next to a stretcher full of human remains, including several bleached skulls. In the background other men were digging graves.[75]

The Federal army's failure to capture Petersburg by direct assault gave photographers the opportunity to make pictures of the troops as they laid siege to the city. Cameramen photographed the "Dictator," the heavy mortar on a specially prepared railroad platform. O'Sullivan also photographed black troops at captured Confederate trenches. They also made numerous pictures at a plantation, which had suffered little damage from the war.[76]

In the meantime, George Barnard was photographing Sherman's spring campaign against Atlanta. Barnard, who photographed some of the early fighting in Virginia, had been hired as the photographer of the topographical branch of the Army of the Cumberland's Department of Engineers. His main job was to reproduce maps but he also photographed the army as often as possible. In late 1863, Barnard made pictures in Chattanooga and Knoxville after the two cities were captured by the Union.[77]

Barnard stayed behind when Sherman launched his campaign. But soon after the Union army arrived outside Atlanta, he was summoned to the city. It is not clear why Sherman, who had repeatedly shown his dislike for journalists, allowed Barnard to photograph the army, but likely it was because of his position with the topographi-cal branch. The photographer shot the spot where General James B. McPherson was killed, enhancing the scene by adding artillery shells, a hat, a leather satchel, and the bleached bones of a dead horse. Barnard photographed a lone Sherman on horseback. He also photographed the captured rebel fortifications outside Atlanta; one revealing picture showed a group of soldiers being photographed. The picture showed Barnard or his assistant, a camera, and the portable darkroom.[78]

John F. E. Hillen also illustrated the Atlanta campaign. Perhaps no Civil War artist had as varied experiences as Hillen. Born in Belgium, he immigrated to the United States and worked as an engraver and illustrator. When the war began, he enlisted in the 34th Ohio Volunteer Infantry and served in West Virginia where he made sketches that *Harper's* published. Hillen was captured at Chickamauga in 1863 and spent time at a prison in Stevenson, Alabama. His drawing, "Arrival of Rebel Pris-oners to the Stockade Prison," no doubt reflected his own experience. After being released, Hillen joined Sherman's army in its march to Atlanta. He sketched the fighting outside Atlanta and produced more drawings for *Leslie's* for the remainder of the war.[79]

Davis also accompanied Sherman's army on the Georgia campaign. His front-page illustration in a May issue showed Union troops marching through a mountain pass in northwest Georgia. He also made a dramatic picture of a Union commander riding through the lines exhorting his troops at the battle of Dallas that was pub-lished as a two-page illustration. He drew a close-up view of Federal troops fighting at Ezra Church. He also illustrated a council of war held by Sherman. Because it took so long for the sketches to reach New York, *Harper's* did not publish illustra-tions of the fall of Atlanta for more than three months. Then, in a flurry, it published numerous pictures of Sherman's march through Georgia, including the capture of Savannah.[80]

After Savannah fell, William Waud traveled to the city and provided pictures of the strategic port. Davis and Waud then joined Sherman's campaign through the Carolinas, and by March *Harper's* was publishing their illustrations. Some of the most revealing pictures captured the travel difficulties that Union troops encoun-tered. A sketch by Davis showed troops crossing a swamp in South Carolina. Later in the month, the magazine ran a large picture of black troops marching into a captured Charleston. Most of the many illustrations from the campaign only hinted at the widespread destruction and foraging that took place throughout the Carolinas. However, a picture by Waud showed Columbia burning while Federal soldiers celebrated.[81]

⚮⚮

In the final months of the war, photographs and illustrations showed the horrifying condition of Federal prisoners who had endured months or years in Confederate prison camps. The South began releasing sick and dying prisoners in late 1864. When the soldiers returned home, their angry families asked photographers to record the emaciated conditions that many were in. The pictures showed some men who were little more than skin and bones barely able to sit for the camera. Illustrations were made from the pictures and published by *Harper's* and *Leslie's*. Illustrations and photographs of captured Confederate prison camps also horrified viewers. They showed the squalid conditions in which thousands of captured Federal troops lived.[82]

Artists and photographers illustrated the fall of Richmond. Artists sketched the triumphant entry of Union troops and the crowds of cheering blacks who greeted them. One illustration showed Lincoln touring Richmond, including a visit to President Davis's home. Others showed the destruction of the city by the fleeing rebels, including pictures of homeowners searching for their possessions among the rubble.[83]

Alexander Gardner returned to the field after the fall of Richmond. He left for the Confederate capital immediately after learning it had been captured. Gardner and Reekie documented the destruction of the city, making more than 100 pictures. Many of the photographs showed the shells of burned buildings. Others captured Richmond's historic landmarks and distinguished buildings, including the Capitol, city hall, First African Baptist Church, and Washington monument. A two-plate panorama of the city taken by Gardner, rich with detail, not only showed the burned areas of the city, but also those that survived largely intact.[84]

Photographers arrived too late to shoot Lee's surrender to Grant at the McLean home. By the time O'Sullivan arrived, the generals and their staff were gone. However, he photographed soldiers still at the courthouse with their rifles stacked. He also made a picture of the McLean family on the steps of their home. No sketch artists were present at the surrender. Waud returned later and recreated the scene of Lee leaving the surrender on horseback. He also depicted Federal troops sharing their rations with the hungry Confederate soldiers. The pictures appeared in books on the war.[85]

Brady, who had been away from the scene of fighting for months, wanted to capture the end of the war by photographing the Confederate capital. Soon after he and his assistant got to Richmond, word spread that Lee had arrived home. The ambitious Brady had to get a picture of the Confederacy's most famous commander. He had known Lee since the Mexican War, and, with the help of the general's wife, persuaded him to pose for pictures, some with his son and a lieutenant on the back porch of his house in Alexandria. The photographs showed a tired, but proud, Lee, still in full uniform.[86]

CHARLESTON

MERCURY

EXTRA:

Passed unanimously at 1.15 o'clock, P. M. December 20th, 1860.

AN ORDINANCE

To dissolve the Union between the State of South Carolina and other States united with her under the compact entitled " The Constitution of the United States of America."

We, the People of the State of South Carolina, in Convention assembled, do declare and ordain, and it is hereby declared and ordained,

That the Ordinance adopted by us in Convention, on the twenty-third day of May, in the year of our Lord one thousand seven hundred and eighty-eight, whereby the Constitution of the United States of America was ratified, and also, all Acts and parts of Acts of the General Assembly of this State, ratifying amendments of the said Constitution, are hereby repealed; and that the union now subsisting between South Carolina and other States, under the name of "The United States of America," is hereby dissolved.

THE

UNION

IS

DISSOLVED!

Charleston Mercury extra edition, December 1860. The *Charleston Mercury* rushed out a small one-page extra the day that South Carolina became the first state to secede from the Union. (Library of Congress)

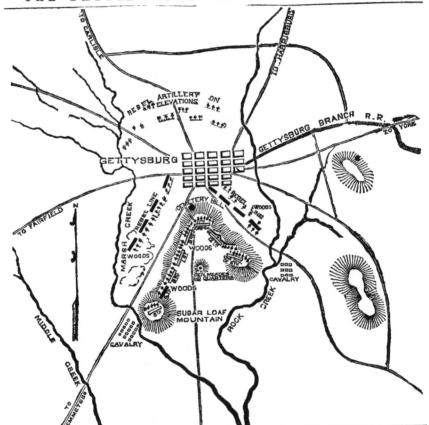

Gettysburg battlefield map, July 1863. The battlefield at Gettysburg was shown in a map that appeared on the front page of the *New York Tribune*. (Penn State University Libraries)

Flag of Truce, date unknown. Union and Confederate troops exchanging wounded soldiers were pictured in a sketch made by artist Alfred Waud. (Library of Congress)

Gallant Charge, Fredericksburg, Virginia, December 1862. The Union assault at Fredericksburg was pictured in an illustration published in *Harper's Weekly*. (Library of Congress)

Photographer's wagon and tent, date unknown. A cameraman and his assistant were photographed outside their wagon and tent. (Library of Congress)

Contrabands, Cumberland Landing, Virginia, May 1862. A group of fugitive slaves, including children, was photographed. (Library of Congress)

Abraham Lincoln, Antietam, Maryland, October 1862. Alan Pinkerton, President Abraham Lincoln, and Major General John McClernand posed in camp for a photograph. (Library of Congress)

Reading newspaper, Cold Harbor, Virginia, June 1864. General Ambrose E. Burnside was pictured reading a newspaper in camp with photographer Mathew Brady (closest to tree). (Library of Congress)

Confederate dead along Hagerstown Road, Antietam, Maryland, September 1862. Confederate troops killed in fighting at the Hagerstown Road were photographed after the battle of Antietam. (Library of Congress)

Alfred Waud, Gettysburg, Pennsylvania, July 1863. Waud, a sketch artist for *Harper's Weekly,* posed for a picture after the battle of Gettysburg. (Library of Congress)

General Robert E. Lee, Arlington, Virginia, April 1865. After the surrender at Appomattox Courthouse, Lee posed for a picture on the porch of his home. (National Archives)

Long ABRAHAM LINCOLN a Little Longer.

Long Abraham Lincoln a Little Longer, *Harper's Weekly*, November 1863. Following his reelection as president in 1864, a tall Lincoln stood even taller, as portrayed in this cartoon from *Harper's Weekly*. (Penn State University Libraries)

General Ulysses S. Grant and staff, Massaponox, Virginia, May 1864. Grant and his staff officers were photographed on the grounds of Massaponox Church. (National Archives)

THE COPPERHEAD PARTY.—IN FAVOR OF *A VIGOROUS PROSECUTION OF PEACE!*

The Copperhead Party, *Harper's Weekly,* February 1863. The Copperheads, or Peace Democrats, threatened the Union, as depicted in this cartoon from *Harper's Weekly.* (Library of Congress)

The Press, the Field, *Harper's Weekly,* April 1864. Reporters and illustrations were depicted working in the field in an illustration made by artist Thomas Nast. (Penn State University Libraries)

Newspapers in camp, date unknown. The popularity of newspapers among soldiers was depicted in a sketch made by artist John Forbes. (Library of Congress)

THREE

EDITORIAL SUPPORT
AND CRITICISM

The American press had always taken great pride in its editorial role, and the newspapers of the North and South were not about to be silent even with a devastating war raging. Editorial cartoons were a more recent form of popular commentary, but editors of the illustrated magazines believed they too had an important part to play in the debate about many aspects of the conflict. The desire of the press to editorialize perhaps was expressed by the *New York Times,* which declared in 1863: "While we emphatically disclaim and deny any right as inhering in journalists or others to incite, advocate, abet, uphold or justify treason or rebellion; we respectfully but firmly affirm and maintain the right of the press to criticize freely and fearlessly the acts of those charged with the administration of the Government; also those of their civil and military subordinates."[1]

The topics of editorials and cartoons during the war varied. Issues relating to the fighting and its administration were far and away the most popular subjects, but editors and artists addressed economic, social, and diplomatic matters as well. Writers and artists had no shortage of advice for the political and military leaders directing the war efforts. They endorsed candidates at various levels of government. Issues of national interest received the most attention from editors. But they also turned their pens on state and local subjects.

Political leaders on both sides recognized the impact that the press could have on public opinion. The Lincoln administration sought to influence and counter editorial opinion through various means. Officials rewarded friends in the press with patronage. They published anonymous editorials in friendly publications and encouraged supporters to start publications that supported their views. Union and Confederate soldiers also started camp newspapers to express their views and preserve morale.

Certainly, the press took its opinion role seriously. Since the country's founding, American newspapers had been intensively partisan and aggressive. Steeped in the tradition of political partisanship, editors did not hesitate to criticize or support political and military leaders. Nineteenth-century editors believed passionately in the power of the printed word. They were convinced that the press had a significant impact on public opinion. It was one of the reasons that so many publications were started. It was also why editors spoke so passionately about the importance of a free press. All newspapers, from the smallest to the largest, published editorials. The editor usually wrote the commentary, although at large dailies an assistant editor sometimes handled the task. Magazines did not put as big an emphasis on editorials, but many still spoke out on issues.[2]

Editorial cartoons had been published since the revolutionary era, but they took on an increased significance with the advent of the illustrated weeklies. In the North, *Frank Leslie's Illustrated News, Harper's Weekly,* and the *New York Illustrated News* featured cartoons prominently, as did *Vanity Fair,* a magazine of humor and satire. In the South, the *Southern Illustrated News* published editorial cartoons, albeit less frequently and of generally lower quality than its Northern counterparts. Depending on space, the magazines usually published one, two, and sometimes three cartoons in each issue. Many editorial cartoonists did not sign their work; others only used their last name. As a result, many cartoons published during the war cannot be credited to anyone.[3]

❧ ❧

During the secession winter of 1860–1861, the press of the North and South editorialized on many issues: whether or not states could legally leave the Union, the decision of South Carolina and other states to secede, the various attempts at compromise, and whether a war should be fought to save the Union. Not surprisingly there was no editorial unanimity on any of the issues, either in the North or South. The organization of the Confederate government and the election of Davis as president sparked even more commentary, as did President Lincoln's inaugural address and his decision to resupply the Union garrison at Fort Sumter. As it became increasingly clear that the crisis was going to come to a head in Charleston, it often seemed that editorial writers could not keep up with the flurry of events.

The Confederate attack on Fort Sumter produced a range of editorial reaction. The press of the North largely blamed the South for starting the war, and the press of the South blamed the North. "The confederate States are determined to have war; and now war exists by their act," the *Boston Advertiser* declared. "It is now a question of life and death for the nation." But the *Montgomery Advertiser* maintained that Confederate leaders had done "all that men could honorably do to bring about a peaceable solution." It was due to "the madness and perversity" of Northern leaders that "all efforts to that end have failed." As they had done in the debate over secession, many newspapers in the South drew parallels to the American struggle for independence during the Revolutionary War. "Charleston has become to the South, in eighteen hundred and sixty-one, what Lexington was to our once common country in seventeen hundred and seventy five," announced the *Memphis Appeal.* "It is the scene of the first triumph which inaugurates the war of Southern independence."[4]

However, there was no unanimity on the subject, especially in the North, portending the editorial division that would be seen throughout the war. The *Daily Times* in Hartford, Connecticut, blamed the Republican Party for the attack, arguing that "this horrible drama" could have been avoided. The *Knoxville Whig* argued that both sides were responsible and said there was "no reason" for the fighting to have started. "The Administration in Washington was unwise, stubborn, sectional, and ignorant of the state of public sentiment in the South," the newspaper said, "the administration at Montgomery has been wicked, reckless, and awfully guilty."[5]

President Lincoln's call for 75,000 troops to put down the rebellion sparked a wave of patriotic editorials from both sides. The *New York Times* said the attack on Fort Sumter "awoke strange echoes, and touched forgotten chords in the American heart. American Loyalty leapt into instant life, and stood radiant and ready for the fierce encounter." Confederate newspapers became even more defiant. The *Augusta Chronicle & Sentinel* said the Confederacy had to be ready to defend the South. "This is no ordinary time," the newspaper proclaimed. "None of us have ever seen the like of it before—let all then get ready. Arm and drill, arm and drill, should be the word now, all over the land."[6]

In the days following the attack, the press debated the reasons to fight a war. Editorials claimed the North was fighting to preserve the heritage of republican liberty established by the founding fathers. The *Philadelphia Ledger* said the Union had to fight to preserve constitutional authority and the principle of majority rule. "We are fighting for everything for which this Government was established," the newspaper declared. "We are fighting to preserve our republican institutions in their purity." Antislavery editors recognized that the war would be fought to restore the Union, and that few people in the North believed that emancipation should be a goal of the fighting. But they also predicted that slavery would be crippled, if not eliminated entirely, as a result of the war. "This outburst of spirit and enthusiasm at the North may spring chiefly from indignation at the wrongs of the white man," said the National *Anti-Slavery Standard*, "but it will none the less finally right those of the black man."[7]

Most of the press in the South contended the war was about more than just the issue of slavery. "The matter is now plain," the *Charleston Mercury* said. "State after State in the South sees the deadly development, and are moving to take their part in the grand effort to redeem their liberties." Others continued comparing the fight with that of the American patriots. "The resistance of the South has been based on the same eternal principles which justified and glorified the patriots of 1776," declared the *New Orleans Daily Picayune*. "The people of the South are in arms to defend them against the aggressions and invasions of the degenerate sons of the illustrious patriots."[8]

Newspapers on both sides also editorialized about their foes. The *Daily Palladium* in New Haven, Connecticut, claimed the Confederacy's armed forces were overestimated. "Their assault upon the National Government was as cowardly as their conspiracy was wicked," it said. "The whole proceedings of these traitors . . . has been characterized by the most contemptible cowardice." The *Albany Patriot* said the Union army was no match for Confederate forces, boasting that the county's women and children could "whip" the Federals. However, the *New Orleans Bee* warned not to take the fighting ability of the North lightly. "They belong to the revolutionary stock, and have displayed their valor in many a battle field," it said. "They are as brave as the men of the South, and were their cause a just one, were they as we are, defending their houses and firesides, their freedom and independence against ruthless invaders, they would be as we trust we shall be, invincible."[9]

The South's Unionist journals, accused of disloyalty and, in some cases, treason, found it increasingly hard to oppose secession. The *North Carolina Standard*, one of the most steadfast Unionist newspapers in the Confederacy, declared after Lincoln's call for troops: "The proclamation of Mr. Lincoln has left to the people of the border states no alternative but resistance or unconditional submission. . . . It is a war which could not have been avoided. It has been forced upon us. We must fight!" One newspaper that refused to change its views paid the price. The *Alamo Express* repeatedly criticized Confederate leaders and accused them of starting a war on the question of supplying Fort Sumter "with pork and beans for a few days." When the newspaper published an extra edition that satirized that capture of a small detachment of Federal troops, it went too far for some in San Antonio. A mob broke into the *Alamo Express* office, destroyed its press, and set fire to the building.[10]

The North had a far more sizable opposition press. More than 100 Democratic newspapers sympathized with the South and opposed the war, among them the *New York World, Chicago Times, Cleveland Plain Dealer, Indianapolis State Sentinel, Detroit Free Press, Dayton Empire, Dubuque Herald, Cincinnati Enquirer,* and *Crisis.* They believed the South had a right to leave the Union. Many Democratic editors also supported slavery. They viewed slavery as a state issue and argued that only individual states had a right to eliminate it. When the governor of Ohio prepared to answer Lincoln's call for troops in April, the *Dayton Empire* declared: "Governor Dennison has pledged the blood and treasure of Ohio to back up a Republican administration in its contemplated attack upon the people of the South. . . . Does he promise to head the troops which he intends to send down South to butcher men, women and children of that section?"[11]

While leaders of the North and South spent the months following the attack preparing for war, they battled public attitude about what fighting would be like. Many Americans had a romantic view of war. Many also believed the war would end quickly. By the summer, some editors were leading the chorus demanding that Union forces invade the South and crush the rebellion. The *New York Tribune* coined the battle cry "Forward to Richmond!" and declared that the Confederate Congress should not be permitted to convene as scheduled on July 20. "Forward to Richmond!" appeared at the top of the *Tribune's* editorial page for more than a week and other militant newspapers picked up the call for action. On the other side, President Davis believed the South's best strategy was to be defensive, arguing that the Confederacy could win the war by attrition. Others in the South ridiculed the idea, including some editors who claimed the South could easily defeat the North. The *Charleston Mercury* urged the Confederacy to adopt an aggressive military strategy. "We have avoided battle," the newspaper complained in June. "We have let our enemies take their own time to assail us."[12]

❧❦

After the Union defeat at First Bull Run, most Northern newspapers did not downplay the seriousness of the loss. Many said the Union could learn valuable lessons. "Let us take comfort in that we now know the worst," said the *Philadelphia Inquirer.* "It is better that this rebellion should have the first victories than the last." Some editorial writers sought scapegoats for the loss. The *New York Evening Post* argued that the defeat was the "best thing that could have happened." The rout would take the "conceit out of us" and ensure that "when we do settle it we shall insist on so crippling the slave interests that it will never lift its head again." The *Baltimore American* blamed editors such as the *New York Tribune's* Horace Greeley who it claimed had prodded the military to action. It said the defeat "will doubtless now satisfy . . . those newspaper generals in New York, and elsewhere in that latitude, who have long been vociferating for an 'advance'." A distraught Greeley said he would gladly serve as a scapegoat for the loss and declared that in the future the *Tribune* would support the Union's military leaders. "Henceforth, it shall be the Tribune's sole vocation to rouse and animate the American People for the terrible ordeal which has befallen them," Greeley wrote.[13]

Southern editors cheered the victory at First Bull Run, often with great hyperbole. The *Memphis Appeal* compared the rout with other historic battles, including Napoleon's defeat at Waterloo. "It would not, perhaps, being going too far to surmise that it will be the battle of the present war, and will virtually break the back of the Washington government," the newspaper said. Some editors called on Confederate officials to follow up on the victory and take the fight to the North. "We have whipped them in open field, and proved ourselves their masters in war; but it must never be said that the North invaded the South, and that the South could not retaliate the humiliation," the *Richmond Examiner* proclaimed.[14]

The issue of slavery did not disappear once the war began. Outspoken abolitionists and radical Republicans took every opportunity to urge the Lincoln administration to free the slaves. Although Lincoln hated slavery, he also recognized that it was a politically sensitive subject, especially in the border states, where many people sympathized with the South. The abolitionist press initially put aside any criticism of the president in order to show unanimity against the South. However, antislavery editors did not check their criticism for long. One of the most outspoken publications arguing that ending slavery should be a Union war aim was *Douglass' Monthly,* published by former slave Frederick Douglass. "To fight against slaveholders, without fighting against slavery, is but a half hearted business, and paralyzes the hands engaged in it," Douglass wrote. "[H]enceforth let the war cry be, down with treason, and down with slavery, the cause of treason."[15]

In August, Union General John C. Frémont declared martial law in Missouri and issued an order freeing the slaves of all rebels in the state. However, a cautious Lincoln was concerned that Frémont's order would alarm the crucial border state of Kentucky, which had considerable Southern sympathies. He asked the general to make the order consistent with the Federal confiscation policy. When Frémont refused, the president modified it to confiscate only those slaves who had aided Confederate forces. Abolitionist editors were outraged. William Lloyd Garrison published the president's order with thick black rules around it, the traditional sign of mourning. The *Liberator's* editor declared the president guilty of "a serious dereliction of duty. Either the government must abolish slavery, or the independence of the Southern Confederacy must be recognized." And Douglass asked, "What is the friendship of these so-called loyal slaveholders worth? . . . From the beginning, these border Slave States have been the mill-stone about the neck of the government."[16]

When Lincoln did not move fast enough on the issue, an exasperated Greeley decided to put the weight of public opinion against the president by publishing an open letter to him in the *New York Tribune.* Titled "Prayer of Twenty Millions," the letter began: "Dear Sir: I do not intrude to tell you—for you must already know—that a great proportion of those who triumphed in your election, and all who desire an unqualified suppression of the rebellion now desolating our country, are sorely disappointed and deeply pained by the policy you seem to be pursuing with regard to the slaves of the rebels." Greeley went on to demand ungrudging execution of the confiscation laws granting freedom to the slaves of those resisting the Union. The president knew he must publicly respond to the popular Greeley. Significantly, Lincoln chose another newspaper to publish his reply, the *National Intelligencer*. In one of his most memorable public statements, Lincoln wrote: "My paramount object in this struggle *is* to save the Union, and is *not* either to save or to destroy slavery. If I could save the Union without freeing *any* slave I would do it, and if I could save it by freeing *all* the slaves, I would do it; and if I could save it by freeing some and leaving others alone, I would also do that."[17]

The president's savvy response in summarizing the contentious issue defused Greeley's criticism. A month later after the Union victory at Antietam, Lincoln issued the preliminary Emancipation Proclamation. It not only decreed freedom for slaves in the Confederate states on January 1, 1863, but cited sections of the Confiscation Act dealing with slavery and ordered military service to enforce the provisions. Greeley was thrilled with the announcement and the next day the *New York Tribune* proclaimed: "It is the beginning of the end of the rebellion; the beginning of the new life of the nation. GOD BLESS ABRAHAM LINCOLN!" The *Chicago Tribune* said that the president had "set his hand and affixed the great seal of the nation to the grandest proclamation ever issued by man. . . . From the date of this proclamation begins the history of the republic as our fathers designed to have it—the home of freedom, the asylum of the oppressed, the seat of justice, the land of equal rights under the law, where each man, however humble, shall be entitled to life, liberty, and the pursuit of happiness." And an ecstatic Douglass proclaimed, "We shout with joy that we live to record this righteous decree."[18]

Furious Democratic newspapers argued that Lincoln had exceeded his constitutional authority with the proclamation and predicted that it would strengthen Confederate efforts to defeat the Union. "The abolition of slavery is a State question, and cannot be exercised by the General Government without a total revolution in our whole governmental theory," declared the *Crisis*. The *Chicago Times* said that Lincoln was guilty of "a monstrous usurpation, a criminal wrong, and an act of national suicide." And the *New York World* said that Lincoln was now "adrift on a current of radical fanaticism."[19]

Newspapers in the South ridiculed the Emancipation Proclamation. The *Augusta Chronicle & Sentinel* boasted, "If you want our slaves, come and take them if you can." It declared that "no scheme more atrociously wicked ever entered the mind of man." Lincoln had been "forced to throw off the mask," the newspaper said, and "the world now beholds the rottenness of his heart." Other editors claimed the freed slaves would suffer a worse fate in the North. "The slaves are only to change masters; they are to be stolen instead of freed; in place of being set at liberty, those that can . . . are to be put to work for the Yankee Armies," argued the *Mobile Register and Advertiser*.[20]

The Davis administration dealt with its own editorial critics in the press, most notably the *Richmond Examiner* and *Charleston Mercury*. Under the leadership of the Rhett family, the *Mercury* had been one of the leading supporters of Southern independence. However, the *Mercury* was the first and one of the most vocal critics of Davis. Robert Barnwell Rhett, Jr. had never trusted Davis and he was furious about the Confederacy's failure to aggressively follow up its victory at First Bull Run. For the rest of the war, the *Mercury* skewered the Davis administration for its incompetence and autocracy. *Examiner* editor John M. Daniel pilloried the administration every chance it had. Although the *Examiner* championed the Confederate cause and urged a vigorous prosecution of the war, the newspaper had no use for Davis and his cabinet. By the fall of 1861, Daniel argued that several Confederate leaders would have made a better president. When R.M.T. Hunter left the cabinet, and Davis named the unpopular Judah P. Benjamin secretary of state, Daniel claimed that Davis kept lesser men in his cabinet because he was "jealous of intellect." In early 1862, Daniel declared that the Confederate government was failing its citizens. "In the midst of a revolution no greater calamity can befall a people than for their affairs to pass into the control of men who could not understand it in the beginning, and are incapable of appreciating the demands of the crisis as they arrive," he wrote.[21]

As the summer of 1862 drew to a close, the North was in despair over the course of the war. The Confederate army had defeated Union forces at the Seven Days' battles and General McClellan's campaign against Richmond had become bogged down. The administration replaced the cautious McClellan with General John Pope. Lee then crushed Pope's troops at Second Bull Run. The *Augusta Chronicle & Sentinel* proclaimed after the victory that the "skies never look brighter" and "prospects were never more cheering." The Confederate army had routed Federal troops and "even now they may be thundering at the gates of the Capital, making Lincoln, Seward, and others . . . tremble in their very shoes," the newspaper said. After the stinging defeat, the Lincoln administration was deluged by editorial criticism. The *New York World* called the administration "weak and inefficient" and said it had "forfeited all right to complain of its loss of public confidence." The *New York Tribune* said it had given up hope "for any display of genius or decided military capacity."[22]

Despite the criticism, both the Lincoln and Davis administrations had editorial supporters that they could count on. Among the most loyal Republican publications were the *Chicago Tribune, New York Times, Sunday Morning Chronicle, National Intelligencer, Philadelphia Press, Albany Journal,* and *Springfield Republican*. The newspapers supported the administration's policies on virtually every issue. They beat the drums for war, exaggerating Union victories and minimizing Union defeats. And they repeated the message in editorial after editorial that the South could never be victorious. As was the custom for presidents, Lincoln rewarded his friends in the press with patronage and political appointments.[23]

The president's supporters published pieces written by administration officials and even the president himself. Perhaps the best-known newspaper piece written by Lincoln was titled "The President's Last, Shortest, and Best Speech," and it told the story of two Tennessee women who visited Lincoln to ask for the release of their husbands who were being held as Confederate prisoners of war. One of the women said her husband should be set free because he was, in her words, "a religious man." The president ordered the men released and, according to the story, told the woman:

> You say your husband is a religious man; tell him when you meet him that I say I am not much of a judge of religion, but that, in my opinion, the religion that sets men to rebel and fight against their government, because, as they think, that government does not sufficiently help some men to eat their bread on the sweat of other men's faces, is not the sort of religion upon which people can get to heaven.

For unknown reasons, the president's name was not signed to the story. However, it was widely reprinted in newspapers across the North, as Lincoln no doubt hoped it would be.[24]

One of Lincoln's most stalwart supporters was the *Sunday Morning Chronicle,* published in the capital by John Forney. A veteran editor, Forney launched the weekly in the midst of the secession crisis to support the administration. "Our only politics will be unfaltering devotion to the union of these States," Forney wrote. "[W]e shall do whatever an independent journal may do to strengthen the hands of the President and his Cabinet." When others attacked the administration for incompetency in its administration of the war, Forney's rushed to the defense. "It is quite certain that the labor and difficulties which have beset Mr. Lincoln and his advisers from the very start have no parallel in our history," the *Morning Chronicle* declared, "and, therefore, there is no precedent criterion by which to judge the administration as in the case of its predecessors." And when critics complained that Forney's publications were too pro-administration, he defended his support for the White House. "[W]hen our country is agonized by war, and assailed by assassins and robbers, indifference or neutrality would be more than treason." In late 1862, Forney converted the *Sunday Morning Chronicle* into a daily publication, likely at the suggestion of Lincoln who feared the effect on the Army of the Potomac of criticism by the *New York Tribune,* which had become increasingly critical of the administration. With the administration's support, thousands of copies of the *Morning Chronicle* soon were going to the army.[25]

President Davis also had numerous supporters in the Southern press, notably the *Richmond Enquirer, Charleston Courier, Augusta Constitutionalist,* and *Mobile Register and Advertiser.* The newspapers faithfully supported the administration and repeatedly defended the president from critics. They praised the heroic efforts of soldiers and civilians, decried apathy and disloyalty, emphasized Union problems, and explained the consequences of defeat.

Unlike Lincoln, Davis did not court the press. He did not regularly make himself available to reporters. And while the president had newspaper supporters, the administration did not have any publications that could be their editorial mouthpiece. Secretary of War Stephen Mallory suggested securing a sympathetic newspaper to explain the wisdom of administration measures that were unpopular, but the president ignored the advice. A Davis supporter even contacted an editor about starting a pro-administration publication in Richmond. The idea did not go anywhere and Davis neither knew of nor approved of the idea. Attorney General Thomas Bragg expressed his frustration that the president generally ignored the press, noting that the *Richmond Examiner* assailed the administration almost daily.[26]

In the meantime, the South was dealing with its own problems, including shortages and rising prices that left many of the poor hungry and destitute. Editorials condemned speculators who drove up prices, making food, clothing, and other materials unaffordable to many. The *Richmond Examiner* declared that "Southern merchants have outdone Yankees and Jews. . . . The whole South stinks with the lust of extortion." When the Confederate Congress passed a law to regulate impressments, the *Carolina Sparta* expressed hope that the measure would force "all those who have locked up their corn cribs and smoke houses against their friends and neighbors" to share their food supplies. Reports that speculators were growing rich at the expense of poor Southerners outraged the *North Carolina Standard.* "The worst enemies of the Confederacy are those who speculate upon salt, flour, bacon, corn, leather, cotton and woolen goods," it declared, "and they have no concern except to keep the war raging that they may make money."[27]

As important fighting was taking place, Democrats and Republicans battled in the midterm elections of 1862. Benefitting from Northern frustration with the course of the war and controversial administration measures, Democrats scored major victories. The party gained 35 seats in the House of Representatives, won gubernatorial races in New York and New Jersey, and took control over the state legislatures in Illinois, Indiana, and New Jersey. The election produced a barrage of editorial commentary. Democratic newspapers criticized the administration's prosecution of the war, the arrest of political opponents, and the Emancipation Proclamation. They called on Democrats to save the Union from Republicans, who they claimed were usurping people's rights. "This war, which we are told by Abolitionists is being conducted to put down the rebellion, is, in reality, to further their mad schemes of negro emancipation and negro equality," wrote the *Dubuque Herald.* "We who oppose those unconstitutional measures are denounced as traitors, and not only denied the meanest privileges, but our Constitutional rights are swept away." And the *Jonesboro Gazette* called on Democrats to, "recollect that you want to send men to the legislature, who will take the means to prevent the State from being overrun by free niggers, and the labor of white men being reduced to free nigger prices."[28]

For their part, Republican editors said the election was not a referendum on the administration but said voters wanted the president to find better generals. "[N]othing but a series of vigorous and comprehensive measures instantly inaugurated and firmly pursued by the President, can save the country from disunion, and the North from the despotism which would surely follow that event," the *Chicago Tribune* said. The *New York Times,* generally a supporter of Lincoln, said the election results showed a lack of confidence in the president's administration of the war. "We must have a fixed, steadfast, immovable determination that henceforth all men and all things shall bend to the one sole object of making the speediest conquest of this rebellion," it editorialized.[29]

Southern newspapers claimed that the Democratic victories showed that the North was tired of the war. The *Richmond Examiner* argued that the Republican Party had brought the United States to the brink of ruin by waging an unjust war. It said Republicans had "deceived, misled [and] seduced the people of the North and voters had shown their disgust with the party. The elections of the North, if they show nothing else, at least prove that the Northern people are growing sick of Black Republican rule," the newspaper said. The *Charleston Mercury* did not believe the election result would mean an end to the war, but it argued the growing strength of the Democrats would be a distraction for Republicans and that would help the South. "The Black Republican Party of the North drove the Southern States into secession, and made the war from which that section now suffers," it editorialized. "Failure to overpower the Confederate States and restore the Union must be fatal to its popularity and power for all time."[30]

Movements for peace on both sides had begun soon after the war started. In the North, the so-called Peace Democrats, also known as Copperheads, led the charge. In the South, Unionists, who had always been opposed to leaving the Federal government, headed the calls for peace. With support for the war so widespread in the South, Unionists were relatively few in number and generally worked underground. The Copperheads were far more numerous, visible, and outspoken. Peace supporters on both sides had editorial support as well as plenty of opposition.

In January of 1863, Democrats led by Clement L. Vallandigham, a Democratic congressman, launched a peace movement in Ohio. Vallandigham argued that the Confederacy could never be conquered and that the North had waged a war on personal freedoms "which have made this country one of the worst despotisms on earth for the past twenty months." Fearing unrest from the peace movement, General Ambrose E. Burnside, commander of the Department of the Ohio, issued General Order No. 38 declaring that anyone committing "expressed or implied" treason would be subject to trial and punishment by expulsion or death. Vallandigham, who was trying to drum up support for the Democratic gubernatorial nomination in Ohio, defied the order in a speech in which he called the war "wicked, cruel and unnecessary." Soldiers arrested him at his home and he was convicted of "expressing treasonable sympathy." He was sentenced to a Federal prison for the rest of the war, but President Lincoln commuted his sentence and banished him to the Confederacy.[31]

Democratic newspapers howled in protest over Vallandigham's arrest and exile. They said it violated constitutional protections of free speech and accused the government of exercising arbitrary power against citizens. "Each successive attack upon the liberties of the people, borne as these latter attacks are borne, shake our confidence in their patriotic integrity," the *Dubuque Herald* wrote. "They only deserve liberty who prize its blessings, and they tyranny, who crouch before its blows." The *Chicago Times* called Vallandigham's expulsion the "funeral of civil liberty." It said Vallandigham was being punished by "those who daily pollute their souls with perjury in breaking their solemn oaths to 'preserve, protect and defend the constitution of the United States'." But Republican newspapers such as the *Chicago Tribune* said Vallandigham deserved the harsh punishment. Moreover, it argued the government should arrest other enemies of the country. "[I]t is time for a more thorough handing of the home enemies of the Government," the paper declared. "Let Vallandigham head the list, and all the people will say amen." The *New York Times* said the exile would help the Union cause because it would show the determination of the North "to suppress this rebellion and to grind to powder all those who would sustain it."[32]

Confederate newspapers viewed Vallandigham's arrest as a desperate sign of the Lincoln administration's despotism. "This performance in Cincinnati is evidently the first practical opening of Mr. Seward's new campaign for consolidating all power in the hands of his Dictator, and ferociously stamping down the last murmurs and struggles of those liege subjects, who used to be citizens," the *Richmond Enquirer* declared, referring to Secretary of State William H. Seward. And the *Richmond Examiner* said, "[I]f sympathy for any individual and an enemy were permitted, sorrow for the fate of V. would be felt by most men of heart in the South."[33]

In the South, opposition to the draft and general weariness with the war fueled the moves toward peace. Governors Joseph E. Brown of Georgia and Zebulon B. Vance of North Carolina fought conscription at every turn, even taking their battles to the courts. The Northern peace movement precipitated efforts toward peace in North Carolina where more than 100 rallies were held across the state. Supporters urged the Confederate government to begin peace negotiations and suggested reunion on the basis of proposals offered by Democrats in the North. Peace factions also developed in other Southern states, most notably in Georgia. Governor Brown introduced resolutions in the state legislature urging Davis to initiate peace negotiations after every Confederate victory.

One of the most outspoken advocates of peace in the South was William W. Holden, editor of the *North Carolina Standard* in Raleigh. Encouraged by the peace movement in the North, Holden began advocating peace negotiations in mid-1863. "The people of both sections are tired of war, and desire peace," he wrote. "We desire it on terms honorable to our own section; and we cannot expect it on terms dishonorable to the other section." Insisting that he advocated "no peace which will not preserve the rights of the sovereign States and the institutions of the South," he argued, "what the great mass of our people desire is a cessation of hostilities." Another editor who supported peace was Nathan B. Morse, editor of the *Augusta Chronicle & Sentinel.* Morse, who moved to Georgia from Connecticut just before the war began, argued that the South "should employ all the arts of policy for the attainment of peace." "It becomes us as a wise and Christian people, engaged in a struggle for all that is dear to man and only seeking our rights, to bear the sword in one hand and the olive branch in the other," Morse wrote.[34]

But other Confederate editors argued strongly against any moves toward peace. "We are in the fight and must carry it on to the bitter end; until we can close it with honor," said the *Southern Recorder* in Milledgeville, Georgia. "The sword can be sheathed after victory." They also criticized Holden and Morse for weakening the Confederate war effort. The editor of the *Mobile Register and Advertiser* called Morse "a viper in our bosom who should be driven forth." He even signaled his willingness to fight a duel with his fellow editor if there was no Georgian to protect the state's honor.[35]

❧◈❧

To spread opinion and preserve morale, some Union army regiments launched their own newspapers during the war. Going by such names as *American Patriot, First Kansas, Camp Kettle, Pennsylvania Fifth, Stars and Stripes, Eleventh Ohio, Federal Knapsack, Banner of Freedom,* and the *War Eagle,* more than 100 camp publications were started using small hand presses carried on equipment trains or the printing presses of abandoned Southern newspapers. The newspapers were small, usually a single sheet, and published "as often as circumstances will permit," in the words of one. Not surprisingly the soldier newspapers reflected a strong sense of unit pride. *Our Regiment,* published in Mississippi by the 13th Illinois, boasted: "We have in our regiment, not only men of all the principal nationalities in the [old] world as well as the new, but we have men of every profession, trade, and occupation." The *Black Warrior,* published by a black unit from Rhode Island, said its goal was "to raise the status of colored troops . . . to sustain our government under whose banner we have enlisted by moral as well as physical force; and to war against copperheads and traitors."[36]

The camp newspapers celebrated Union victories, printing pictures of U.S. flags and proclaiming the good news effusively. After the twin victories at Vicksburg and Gettysburg, the *Union Volunteer* recounted "the glorious events . . . [which] have sent a thrill of joy to every patriotic heart." As a rule, the camp newspapers avoided political affiliations. "We belong to no party," said the *Athens Post* in 1863. "We are strictly for the Union. Our motto is '*our country, may she ever be right, but our country right or wrong*'." But camp publications were staunch supporters of President Lincoln and their military leaders. The *Union Daily* praised the "unswerving firmness, and honesty of Mr. Lincoln." "When we find a ship that has withstood the test of wind and waves, and has rod so far unswervingly through the breakers of revolution, let us stand by her," it said. And *Grant's Petersburg Progress* declared, "We believe in the United States, one and indivisible, in Abraham Lincoln, our adopted Father, in U.S. Grant . . . and the freedom of the contraband, the speedy extinction of the Rebellion, and the perdition of Jeff Davis here and hereafter."[37]

Union soldiers also used their newspapers to ridicule Southern leaders, especially President Davis. The *Soldier's Letter,* published by the 2nd Colorado Cavalry, proposed an epitaph for the Confederate president:

> Pause for an instant, loyal reader,
> Here lies Jeff, the great seceder,
> Above, he always lied you know,
> And now the traitor lies below.

A story in the *Shield* titled "Jeff Davis's Dream" described the president encountering Satan in hell and being told by the devil that he had been waiting for someone more wicked than him to arrive. They also regularly ridiculed Southern women, especially for showing disrespect for Union soldiers. The *Soldier's Budget* published a letter allegedly from a woman to her cousin who was a Confederate soldier. "John, as you are a prisoner . . . I believe I will take your place and . . . I will kill live Yankees. . . . I wish I was a man. . . . I would tar [sic] their hearts out and cook them and make them eat them."[38]

There were far fewer Confederate camp newspapers, but they took the same approach as their Union counterparts: to preserve morale and urge soldiers to keep fighting. "Hold up your heads—brave the storm—stand by your country—achieve your independence," the *Missouri Army Argus* implored. "Almighty God will fight with you and for you." The *Vidette,* published by members of General John H. Morgan's command, printed the words to "Morgan's War Song," which began: "Ye, sons of the South, take your weapons in hand, For the foot of the foe has insulted your land, Sound, sound the alarm, Arise, arise and arm." Many of the publications took great delight in denouncing the enemy. The *War Bulletin* pledged to defend the South against "the mercenary minions of the child-murdering, woman-insulting, negro-stealing, Bull Run-ing infidel Yankee nation."[39]

❧⊙❧

During the first two years of the war, Union forces had given Northern newspapers little to cheer about editorially. The Union victory at Gettysburg changed that, and Northern editors exalted in the news from Pennsylvania. The *New York Times* declared that the Army of the Potomac had redeemed itself with the crucial triumph.

> The Army of the Potomac has not only won a great battle, and delivered the nation from the gravest peril of the war, but it has triumphantly vindicated its claim to be classed with the veteran and heroic armies that history delights to honor . . . After such a history of misfortune, disappointments and defeats, is it not amazing that any soul or spirit was left in the hearts of the men of the Army of the Potomac? . . . It has leaped at once from the depths of its disappointment and gloom to the height of glory and success.[40]

In the face of the demoralizing defeat, the *Charleston Courier* said it was time for the Confederacy "to show the kind of stuff we are made of." "Is this a time to yield to despondency and gloom?" the paper editorialized. "We have beaten the enemy. . . . We shall smite him again and defeat him utterly." The *Augusta Chronicle & Sentinel* said the South should not lose heart and it compared the defeat to losses the American patriots faced. "People struggling as we are, must expect disaster," it declared. "What nation every achieved its independence without it? . . . There has been no point in our experience yet reached, at all comparable in gloom to that which was suffered by the patriots of '76."[41]

Initially, the North and South depended on men volunteering to meet the manpower needs of the two armies. However, it became clear after the first years that new measures were needed to keep the military adequately manned. For the first time in American history, the Union and Confederate governments were forced to use drafts. The Confederate Congress approved the first of three conscription acts on April 16, 1862. They required all white males between the ages of 18 and 35 to serve in the military for three years or until the end of the war. Men in certain occupations deemed essential to the Confederacy were exempted from service. The following year President Lincoln signed the Enrollment Act requiring men in various age groups, beginning with those aged 20 to 45 to serve in the military. The act provided exemptions for some and drafted men could either pay an exemption fee or hire a substitute.

The drafts prompted a great deal of editorial debate on both sides. One of the most vocal opponents of the draft in the South was the *North Carolina Standard*, which argued that conscription would lead to a military despotism. "This is the people's war, and not a war to be waged by forced levies," the paper editorialized. "If the people will not volunteer in sufficient numbers to carry it on, and to repel the invader, then let them bear the consequences." The *Atlanta Daily Intelligencer* argued that a conscription law would take away power from the states and put it in the hands of the Confederate government. "The way to whip the Yankee is not by a surrender of your personal rights, nor the sovereignty of your State to the Central power at Richmond," it declared. "Whenever this is done we shall virtually surrender what we have demanded from the old Union." But the *Rome Courier* said it was useless to "talk about State Rights, when there are no rights, civil or religious, of person or property, left to anyone, unless we succeed in this context."[42]

In the North, newspapers that supported the Lincoln administration generally backed the draft, while opposition papers were highly critical of it. The *Chicago Tribune* maintained that conscription was a military necessity and that patriotic men should be proud to serve their country. "There is only one way of dealing with the great question of raising men for the army—and that is, we repeat it, by enforcing the Conscription law," the newspaper editorialized. But the *Cleveland Plain Dealer* argued that the Federal government was exceeding its authority in holding a draft. It argued that the citizens "have given sons, husbands, fathers for the way; they have given unexampled supplies of money; they have given more still—their moral support. They ask in return to give them assurances of an end to legislation hostile to the spirit of American freedom."[43]

Groups protested the draft and sometimes the demonstrations turned violent. By far the worst bloodshed took place in New York during five days in June of 1863. Some working class New Yorkers believed that Protestants were forcing the war on them for the freedom of blacks. Soon after the draft began, hundreds of angry men attacked the draft office. Mobs looted the homes of prominent citizens, burned Protestant churches, and lynched blacks. They also attacked Republican publications in the city, including the *New York Tribune*. Police, later joined by soldiers, battled the rioters for two days, inflicting severe casualties. In all, an estimated 1,000 people died in the violence.[44]

The *New York World*, the chief Democratic publication in the city, blamed the president and Republicans for the riots. "Does any man wonder that poor men refuse to be forced into a war mismanaged almost into hopelessness, perverted into partisanship?" it asked. "Did the President and his cabinet imagine that their lawlessness could conquer, or their folly seduce, a free people?" But the *New York Tribune* claimed that Confederate sympathizers organized the violence against blacks and other targets. "Resistance to the Draft was merely the occasion of the outbreak; absolute disloyalty and hatred to the Negro were the moving cause," the newspaper declared. "It was not simply a riot but the commencement of a revolution organized by the

sympathizers in the North with the Southern Rebellion." Not surprisingly, the South-
ern press reveled in the news of the riot. Editors argued that the violence showed the
North was tired of the war. "This affair is a revolution," the *Richmond Examiner* said.
"We get a glimpse of what is slumbering under the shoddy."[45]

However, the Confederacy was dealing with its own problems. By the fall of 1863,
the scarcity of goods, high prices, and speculation were weakening morale. Criticism
of the government was increasing and Confederate leaders recognized that civilian
unrest was threatening to split the South. At the same time, there were increasing calls
for the South to negotiate peace with the North. Seeking to suppress disloyalty and
enforce the draft, the Confederate Congress, at the request of Davis, voted to suspend
the writ of habeas corpus. Many Southern editors were outraged by the move. They
argued that the president was assuming power not granted to him by the Confederate
constitution. The *Augusta Chronicle & Sentinel* accused Davis of creating a "military
despotism" and complained that "in the midst of a revolution undertaken for the
vindication of our rights . . . every vestige of popular liberty is destroyed."[46]

The issue of enrolling black troops in the Federal army produced another out-
pouring of editorial commentary. Black leaders had repeatedly called on the president
to enlist black soldiers, arguing that it would strike another blow at slavery. But the
cautious Lincoln feared that any Federal program would arouse prejudices in the
North and alienate the border states. Douglass was one of the most outspoken supporters of enlisting black men. The editor urged his fellow blacks to "fly to arms, and
smite with death the power that would bury the government and your liberty in the
same hopeless grave." Douglass said it was far better for black men to die free than
to live as slaves. But Democratic newspapers opposed the measures and claimed that
white soldiers would refuse to fight alongside black troops. "If Negro regiments and
brigades are put into the army of the Potomac, we would not be surprised to see those
same soldiers who fought so desperately . . . throw down their arms and refuse to
fight at all, or turn their cannons and bayonets against the enemies of the Union who
are now holding sway in Washington," said the *Democratic Watchman* in Bellefonte,
Pennsylvania.[47]

In 1863, the War Department established the Bureau of Colored Troops to over-
see recruitment of black troops and screen applications for officers in black companies. By the end of the year, approximately 50,000 black troops had enlisted in the
Union army. Editorial supporters cheered when the 54th Massachusetts Infantry became the first black regiment to serve in the war. The regiment performed heroically
in a nighttime assault on Fort Wagner, one of the principal defenses of Charleston.
But the 54th lost nearly half its men in spearheading the assault, including Colonel
Robert Gould Shaw who died leading the charge. The National *Anti-Slavery Standard*
declared that Fort Wagner was a "holy sepulcher" to the black race. And the *New York*

Tribune said the battle made Fort Wagner "such a name to the colored race as Bunker Hill has been for ninety years to the white Yankees."[48]

As 1864 began, President Lincoln faced the real danger that he would not be reelected or even renominated. Radical Republicans had long been critical of Lincoln's administration of the war. They also believed the president had not moved fast enough in ending slavery. The radicals wanted a new nominee and they had precedent on their side. No president since Andrew Jackson had won a second term. Several Republicans were interested in the nomination, including Secretary of Treasury Salmon P. Chase and 1856 party nominee John S. Frémont. The Democratic Party also was divided between members who wanted a strong prosecution of the war and those who favored increased efforts to secure peace. They eventually nominated former Union commander George McClellan to appease war Democrats, and as his running mate, Congressman George Pendleton, a supporter of the peace movement.[49]

The election produced one of the greatest outpourings of editorial debate during the war. In the months between party conventions and the elections, newspapers published hundreds of editorials to bolster their candidates and disparage their opponents. Republican newspapers such as the *Philadelphia Inquirer* praised the president and claimed he had "a powerful hold on the popular heart." Democratic newspapers such as the *Cleveland Plain Dealer* hailed "Little Mac" who they said had been an outstanding leader but was treated unfairly by the administration.[50]

Supporters of Lincoln and McClellan savagely criticized their opponents. On July 4, the *Crisis* celebrated the nation's birthday by proclaiming how far the nation had fallen under Lincoln, "From constitutional liberty under Washington to unlimited submission to Lincoln is a fall second only to that of Satan's," the newspaper said. The *New York Daily News,* which often regularly printed anti-administration verse, published "A Federal Nursery Rhyme," a stanza of which went:

> Abe in the White House
> Proclamation writing;
> Meade on the Rapidian
> Afraid to do the fighting;
> Seward in the Cabinet
> Surrounded by his spies;
> Halleck with the telegraph
> Busy forging lies.

For its part, the *Morning Chronicle* said McClellan had done little more than be "a querulous partisan" since he resigned from the army "allowing himself to be used by a body of men who almost openly profane the name of their country, and exult in her defeats and mourn over her victories."[51]

Southern newspapers said Lincoln's reelection would mean the war would continue, but if McClellan was voted into office the South could expect peace negotiations to begin. "The great object to be obtained is the defeat of Lincoln," the Augusta *Chronicle & Sentinel* editorialized. "His re-election means war: relentless, exterminating war. The emancipation of the slave; the subjugation of the people of the South; the confiscation of property; the obliteration of all political rights." Editors also took great joy in the split that the election was causing in the North. "In the confusion and discord at home, the North has managed by its bigotry, its ferocity and its insolence, to raise up hosts of enemies abroad," the *Mobile Register and Advertiser* declared. "Verily, the way of the transgressor is hard, and the robber nation is destined to reap the harvest of a terrible retribution."[52]

Republican newspapers exalted over Lincoln's overwhelming reelection. The *Springfield Republican* said the fact that the United States held an election during a devastating civil war was a triumph for democracy. The "quiet and order" of the election, the paper editorialized, "give to the republican institutions new strength and added luster." In the South, the *Richmond Examiner* said Lincoln's reelection ensured that the war would continue. "This is what we have now to deal with; and on the way in which we meet it depends the whole future of our race and nation," it declared. "If we shrink from the conflict, better were it for us and ours that had never been born."[53]

Throughout the war, newspapers on both sides tried to put a positive face on defeats in an effort to preserve morale. After the Union loss at Fredericksburg, the *Morning Chronicle* insisted that, "We are wrong at looking at the affair at Fredericksburg as an overwhelming disaster. It is simply a temporary defeat." During the Atlanta campaign in 1864, Georgia newspapers certainly tried to put on the best face on what was taking place. In a June editorial, the *Albany Patriot* asked for patience from readers, despite the steady backward march of Johnston's army. The newspaper said the general simply was "maneuvering for position" and "saving his men." A month later, with Sherman's army just across the Chattahoochee River from Atlanta, the *Patriot* still was boasting of Johnston's achievement. "Gen. Johnston has immortalized himself in his retreat from Dalton," the newspaper declared. "No living man could have retreated an army the size of Johnston's, a distance of seventy-five miles, and kept the confidence . . . of his men as he has done." The *Atlanta Daily Intelligencer* responded to readers who accused the newspaper of downplaying the Confederate army's retreat and the threat to the city. "Yes! General Johnston is falling back. Yes! The enemy; the Yankees; the terrible, great big, bugaboo Yankees . . . are thundering at our gates. . . . Mr. Despair, and all the rest of your lowering brood, does this picture please you?"[54]

With the capture of Atlanta, the Union had a new hero in General Sherman. The *Baltimore American* said the general would go down in history, not only for his capture of the city, but his pithy telegraph message describing it. " 'Atlanta is ours, and fairly won', says General Sherman, in his modest dispatch," the newspaper declared. "He has unconsciously uttered words of pith and conciseness, that have already become historic, and that have taken their place among the immortal brevities of famous commanders." But the *Columbus Times* would have nothing to do with any despondency, and it downplayed the loss of the young, but strategic city. "Who ever heard of such a fuss being made over the fall of a twenty year old town, three hundred miles in the interior of a State, as we and the Yankees are making over the *evacuation* of Atlanta," the Georgia newspaper sneered.[55]

Throughout the war, newspapers on both sides had published editorials accusing the other side of battlefield atrocities. In an editorial bearing the headline, "A Nation of Barbarians," the *Southern Federal Union* said of Union troops, "They rob, they kill, they bear false witness, they covet their neighbor's ox, his wife, his man and maid servants, they commit adultery, they are idolaters, indeed they have violated every article of the decalogue. Thanks be to the God that made us; we are no longer of them." During the Union army's march through Georgia, a new round of atrocity editorials appeared in the Southern press. The *Confederate Union* expressed outrage at the destruction that Union troops inflicted. "A full detail of all the enormities practiced upon the inhabitants of this place and the vicinity would fill a volume, and some of them would be too bad to publish," the newspaper declared. "In short if any army of Devils, just let loose from the bottomless pit, were to invade the country they could not be much worse than Sherman's army."[56]

The *New York Tribune* reveled in the capture of Savannah and mocked Southern newspapers that had claimed Sherman's march was a "retreat" or "escape" through Georgia. "Savannah is fallen like a ripe apple into Sherman's lap," the newspaper exalted. "The 'retreat' through Georgia is consummated, and the 'escape' of Sherman seems to be at this moment tolerably well secured." The *Richmond Examiner* said Sherman's successful campaign in Georgia must serve as a wake-up call for the Davis administration.

> Sherman now believes he can live on the country anywhere . . . So he can, if he marches through a country in which there are neither armies, nor extensive fortifications. . . . No doubt but that he can come on through the Carolinas to Richmond, if Confederate forces are not in the way; but perhaps Mr. Davis is now convinced of the necessity of employing armies against the progress of an enemy in the interiour of the country.[57]

For the first time since the war had begun, real pessimism started to creep into Southern editorials. The *Daily Sun* in Columbus, Georgia, said it would be insulting people's intelligence to proclaim that "all is well." "The prospect is rather gloomy," an editor wrote, "but it is not desperate." The *Montgomery Mail* said that without "Providential interference," which seemed unlikely, the Confederacy could not prevail. "It would be wicked to deceive others" and "unwise to deny the truth to ourselves," the newspaper editorialized. And the *Augusta Constitutionalist* said, "In taking a sweep of the field, unless we fortify ourselves by reason and thought, despondency most likely would take possession of us."[58]

The South required desperate measures and President Davis signaled his willingness to do whatever was necessary, including enlisting slaves in the Confederate military. The idea of using slaves had been quietly discussed in Confederate circles for some time, but it did not spark serious debate until several newspapers published editorials in support of the move. "We must either employ the negroes ourselves, or the enemy will employ them against us," the *Jackson Mississippian* announced. During the fall of 1864, various Southern leaders began calling for greater use of blacks in the military. The *Richmond Enquirer* floated a trial balloon that received widespread attention. The newspaper argued that "neither negroes nor slavery will be permitted to stand in the way" of the South's success. "This war is for national independence on our side, and for the subjugation of the whites and the emancipation of the negroes," the newspaper editorialized. "If we failed the negroes are nominally free and their masters really slaves. We must, therefore, succeed." However, the idea of enlisting blacks was too much for other Southern newspapers. "[T]he existence of a negro soldier is totally inconsistent with our political aim and with our social as well as political system," the *Richmond Examiner* wrote. "The Employment of negroes in our armies, either with or without prospective emancipation, would be the first step . . . to universal emancipation."[59]

The strong feelings on the subject were evident on the pages of the *Atlanta Daily Intelligencer*. An editorial in September supported enrollment of former slaves, noting the Federal army had proven that blacks could fight as soldiers. The South was embroiled in a "fearful life and death struggle," the editorial argued, and all able-bodied men, black or white, were needed. However, the next day the newspaper did an about face. In a front-page note, the *Daily Intelligencer*'s editor said an associate had written the editorial, and he claimed that the newspaper could not support enlisting slaves. "If we cannot win our independence without imitating the Yankee nation in the use he makes of the negro, we are in a worse condition than we believe we are," he wrote.[60]

The Northern press exulted in the controversy roiling the Confederacy over the issue. The *Philadelphia Inquirer* said it was poetic justice for leaders that had fomented revolution. "[T]he leaders of the Rebellion are now beginning to experience for the first time the dire troubles of wide and violent political divisions with their little household," the newspaper wrote. "They are now to experience the bitter fruits, within their own lines, of that agitation for "abolition" on the one side and fire-eating resistance on the other with which, for a quarter of a century, they made the politics of the United States one unceasing round of horrible discord." The *New York Tribune* also noted the absurdity of the Confederacy talking about rewarding blacks for their service with the promise of freedom. "That Slavery is the best possible condition for the Negro, is the first article in the Rebel creed," the paper editorialized. "That the Negro loves his master above all men, takes pride in his service, and would by no means accept freedom if it were offered to him, used to be the second. The stress of circumstances has somewhat modified this canon."[61]

When Richmond fell, Northern newspapers hailed the news. Among the first troops to enter the Confederate capital were units from the all-black 25th Corps. The *Boston Advertiser* noted the significance of the event for black Americans. "[I]t is . . . historical justice," the newspaper noted, "that the troops who were first to enter Richmond were, at least in part, of that despised race whose wrongs have entered so largely into the merits of this struggle." Union editors also reveled in the news that Confederate leaders had been forced to flee from the capital. The *New York Herald* called them "fugitives from justice" and said "they only hope to escape from the consequences of their own acts."[62]

A few days later, Northern newspapers celebrated the surrender news from Appomattox Courthouse. The *New York Times* eulogized the thousands of men who died to restore the Union and bring freedom to all Americans.

> The thrilling word PEACE—the glorious fact of PEACE—are now once again to be realized by the American people. . . . We have achieved the great triumph, and we get with it the glorious Union. We get with it our country—a country now and forever rejoicing in Universal Freedom. The national courage and endurance have their full reward.[63]

With the fighting over, editorial writers turned to the subject of what to do next. Newspapers such as the *National Intelligencer* called for Americans to remember all that they had in common, including many national traditions. "Our instant work is *to create an American sentiment*," the newspaper wrote. "We should call back pleasant memories and proud traditions. . . . Let us henceforth be humble; let us be wise; let us be brothers." Some Southern newspapers remained defiant. The *Albany Patriot* refused to attribute defeat to Northern superiority on the battlefield and blamed the Southern people for their apathy. "We are yet unconquered and until the sword of the enemy is at our throats, we upbraid our fellow citizens for their recent nefarious conduct," it proclaimed. "God help our country."[64]

However, many other newspapers in the South encouraged citizens to accept defeat graciously. "The revolution has failed," the *North Carolina Standard* proclaimed. "Mr. Lincoln has made good his declaration that he would 'hold, occupy, and possess the forts and other property of the United States, and that he would enforce the laws of the nation'." The *Augusta Chronicle & Sentinel* said readers should learn from the way Lee surrendered graciously. "The example set us by Gen. Lee ought to be promptly followed," the newspaper said. "He saw that the hour had come for yielding up the struggle, and he had the magnanimity to acknowledge it."[65]

⤷ ⤶

Before the war many magazines had been nonpartisan in order to reach the largest number of readers in the North and South. That changed when the fighting began. *Harper's Weekly* announced its new pro-Union stance in a May editorial. "Southerners have rebelled and dragged our flag in the dirt," the magazine declared. "The rebels have appealed to the sword, and by the sword they must be punished." The illustrated weeklies voiced their opinions about the war in editorials. However, they made their greatest impact with editorial cartoons.[66]

As a rule, 19th-century editorial cartoons were not subtle. During the war, many artists sought to demonize the enemy. Editorial cartoonist also used crude caricatures and stereotypes. Racism was widespread, not just toward blacks, but Jews and other ethnic groups. Some cartoonists used humor to make their points, but the majority were more serious. Not surprisingly, the favorite targets of cartoonists were the North and South's political and military leaders. Other popular objects included the enemy, foreign powers, military contractors, draft dodgers, and citizens considered disloyal.[67]

A cartoon published in *Harper's Weekly*, just weeks after the attack on Fort Sumter, showed a stern-looking Columbia grabbing the throat of a startled rebel, who held a piece of the Constitution he had torn away from her. The rebel's legs were labeled "treason" and "secession." Another drawing early in the war depicted a "Daughter of Columbia" using a broom to push away her husband who was returning home from three months in the army. The woman said, "Get away! No husband of mine would be here while the country needs his help."[68]

As the Confederacy was trying to get diplomatic recognition from England and France, cartoonists skewered America's longtime allies. A drawing entitled "Recognition or No" portrayed Napoleon III looking through a spyglass at a ridiculous little figure waving a Confederate flag. Standing in his way was a proud-looking Uncle Sam holding an American flag. The figure of John Bull asked Napoleon, "Can you recognize this thing they call the C.S.A." Napoleon replied, "Well, I think I could, if 'twere not for the Big Fellow who stands in front." After a series of Union victories in 1862, another cartoon showed a petulant John Bull angry after receiving news of the war. He was contrasted with a proud Uncle Sam pictured as a blacksmith forging a metal band bearing the slogan "Union."[69]

Shortages and high food prices were a popular subject for Southern cartoonists. A drawing with the caption "Great Rise in Beef," showed a steer with long legs.

A citizen, towered over by the steer, remarked, "Oh, Lord, I wish you were not quite so high." Another drawing provided a "Recipe to get Rid of Extortioners." It showed frightened extortionists tied to a stake with undervalued Southern currency burning beneath them. Editorial artists also poked fun at the South's situation late in the war when food and provisions for Confederate troops became increasingly scarce. A drawing, titled "An Expedition in Pursuit of Live Stock," pictured two soldiers trying to catch a frog to eat. The first panel showed the soldiers hovering over the frog discussing how to grab it. The second panel showed the soldiers diving for the frog while it jumped away.[70]

Union cartoons regularly demonized the enemy. A *Harper's* cartoon titled "Jeff Davis Reaping the Harvest" showed a monstrous-looking Davis, scythe in hand, walking through a swamp at night harvesting skulls. A rattlesnake was coiled at his feet and a buzzard was perched in a tree above him. Another drawing portrayed the inauguration at Richmond in 1862. Davis was portrayed as a skeleton wearing a crown seated on bales of cotton on top of a cask of whiskey. He was holding a torch labeled "desolation" and a flag with a skull and crossbones. Surrounding him were scenes of destruction, while citizens celebrated, drinking and holding signs, with slogans such as "hurrah for our new president." A morbid cartoon in *Harper's* titled "Some Specimens of 'Seceesh' Industry" showed a series of pictures, including a "goblet made from a Yankee skull," "furs formed of scalps and beards," and a "necklace of Yankee teeth."[71]

A popular subject throughout the war was ridiculing young men who did not enlist in the Union army or who paid substitutes. One *Harper's* cartoon suggested the uniform for the "Stay-at-Home Light Guard." It showed a man in a dress wearing a cooking pot on his head. He was holding a broom as if it was a rifle and wearing on his side a duster as if it was a pistol. Another cartoon, titled "Scene, Fifth Avenue," depicted a wealthy, well-dressed couple talking. The man said, "Ah! Dearest Addie! I've succeeded. I've got a Substitute!" To which the woman replied, "Have you? What a curious coincidence! And I have found one for YOU!" Cartoonists also skewered military contractors who were criticized for making enormous amounts of money at the expense of the army and its soldiers. One drawing showed a fat, well-dressed contractor talking to a gaunt-looking soldier. The contractor said to the soldier, "Want beefsteak? Good Gracious, what is the World coming to? Why, my Good Fellow, if you get beefsteak, how are Contractors to live. Tell me that."[72]

In addition to its cartoons, *Harper's* occasionally published large, elaborate editorial illustrations intended to celebrate the Union cause or demonize the Confederacy. On the first anniversary of the war, the magazine published a two-page illustration entitled "Uprising of the North." It showed an image of Fort Sumter burning, surrounded by Union troops going into battle. The soldiers were carrying flags bearing the names of various states. In the background was a picture of the U.S. capitol with the words "liberty" and "Union."[73]

Thomas Nast drew many of *Harper's* editorial illustrations. Nast was born in Germany and immigrated to the United States with his family when he was a young boy. Nast studied art and when he was 15 years old he joined the staff of *Leslie's Illustrated*. In 1862, he moved to *Harper's Weekly* where he initially worked as a sketch artist in the field. But Nast had a strong moral viewpoint about the war and, increasingly, the magazine used him to make patriotic editorial illustrations.[74]

In an illustration entitled "Southern Chivalry," Nast mocked the Confederate claims of valor by drawing alleged war atrocities, including a rebel soldier beheading a Union soldier, and Confederate soldiers bayoneting defenseless Union soldiers. Another illustration entitled "Thanksgiving Day" showed Columbia kneeling in thankful prayer at the "Union altar." In smaller scenes surrounding the main image, soldiers, sailors, and other groups were also giving thanks. The illustration "New Year's Day" contrasted how the holiday was observed in the North and South. The central images showed prosperous Northern civilians celebrating at a lavish party, while poor Southern civilians mourned over a grave. Nast commemorated the Emancipation Proclamation with another large illustration. The central image showed a black family comfortably enjoying time at home. On one side of the central image were smaller scenes of blacks living in slavery, enduring beatings, and being sold. On the other side were blacks living in freedom, earning money, and attending school.[75]

Perhaps Nast's most powerful illustration was entitled "Compromise with the South." It was published during the summer of 1864 when prospects for Lincoln's reelection looked bleak. The title of the picture referred to the Democratic Party platform, which had pronounced the war a failure and advocated peace negotiations with the South. The illustration showed Columbia weeping as a proud Confederate soldier, with his foot on a Federal grave, shook hands with a disabled Union veteran. In the background, a black Union soldier was once again enslaved, along with his family. The illustration was widely reproduced by the Republican Party for the rest of the presidential campaign.[76]

During the first year of the war, cartoons repeatedly skewered Union military and political leaders. Artists joined others in criticizing General McClellan for refusing to aggressively move against Richmond in the summer of 1862. A drawing in *Leslie's*, titled "'Masterly Activity', or Six Months on the Potomac," showed McClellan and Confederate General Pierre G. Beauregard seated on large chairs and watching each other through periscopes. Beneath each general, soldiers for the two sides engaged in assorted camp activities but did no fighting. Another drawing depicted Federal soldiers being carried aloft by the U.S. Balloon Corps. The caption said, "Flying Artillery—A Hint to General McClellan how to 'advance to Richmond'" and suggested that balloons could be used to get Federal troops moving. After the defeat at Second Bull Run, a cartoon in the *New York Illustrated News* portrayed Union commanders looking around bewilderedly for Stonewall Jackson, making remarks like "Oh! There he is" and "No. There he is." Meanwhile, Confederate troops were sneaking up from behind ready to attack. A *Leslie's* cartoon showed Union generals climbing a greased pole and unsuccessfully trying to reach the prize of Richmond.[77]

When the Confederacy was winning on the battlefield, Southern cartoonists mocked the enemy. A drawing in the *Southern Illustrated News,* titled "Schoolmaster Lincoln and His Boys," showed the president shaking a ruler at four bandaged students, McClellan, Pope, Nathaniel Banks, and Ambrose Burnside, all generals who were defeated by the South. Another showed a childlike Lincoln playing "war" with his puppets. He was manipulating Joseph Hooker, while other Union generals lay discarded on a shelf. The Union army's inability to capture the Confederate capital was mocked in a drawing that showed a ridiculous looking Lincoln playing a banjo and singing "I Wish I Was in Dixie." A map of Richmond was in the background and tools of Lincoln's rail splitting days were scattered around him.[78]

The disastrous Union defeat at Fredericksburg was too much for some editorial artists. A scathing cartoon showed an angry Columbia pointing her finger at Lincoln and Stanton. Columbia declared, "Where are my 15,000 sons—murdered at Fredericksburg!" Lincoln replied with his familiar line, "This reminds me of a little Joke—" to which Columbia said, "Go tell your joke at Springfield!" Another drawing early in 1863 reflected the frustration with the performance of the Federal army. Two men were shown greeting in the street. One said, "So the Army of the Potomac has crossed the Rappahannock again." The other man replied, "Ah! Indeed! Which way!"[79]

❧∼❧

Slavery was a regular subject for artists. A cartoon in the *New York Illustrated News* early in the war showed the Southern economy, which was based on cotton production, carried on the back of a slave. The Confederacy was represented as a bomb with a lighted fuse. The Emancipation Proclamation also prompted numerous editorial cartoons. A *Leslie's* drawing showed an angry Southern overseer with a whip yelling at a slave who had just awoken. The overseer said, "Darn you, Casear, are you going to get up, or d'ye want me to wake ye." The slave said, "Lor' sakes, Mr. Hogan, I dreamed it was Fust of January and I was going to sleep as long as I liked." A *Leslie's* cartoon near the end of the war ridiculed the Southern debate about enlisting slaves in the army. It showed a Southern planter and General Lee fighting over who would get a slave.[80]

As the war turned for the North, cartoonists increasingly poked fun at the Confederacy and its leaders. In an effort to aid the war effort, President Davis regularly declared days for fasting and prayer that often were ridiculed by the press. By the fall of 1862, food was becoming scarce in Richmond and a *Leslie's* cartoon published at the time was titled "A Lucky Coincidence—Fast Day in Richmond." It showed a slave woman telling her master that she had just been to the market where there was no food. Just then she learned of the proclamation. "Oh, massa, so berry lucky," said the woman in the black dialect regularly used by cartoonists. One of the more unusual drawings published after Gettysburg showed the startled face of Davis peering between the mountains of South Mountain Gap. The caption read, "Jeff Davis' Face, as Seen through South Mountain Gap, Fourth of July, 1863." Another cartoon later in the summer, entitled "Jeff Davis's Last Appeal to Arms," showed the president speaking to soldiers on the street. The soldiers have lost arms in the fighting and waved hooks. At the end of the year, *Leslie's* published a cartoon titled "Wreck of the Ship 'Confederacy'." It showed Davis and Secretary of the Treasury Christopher Memminger frantically hanging onto a ship's mast as it sank into the ocean.[81]

Not surprisingly, Lincoln was a popular subject of Southern cartoonists. Editorial artists joined others in attacking Lincoln for issuing the hated Emancipation Proclamation. A cartoon, titled "King Abraham before and after Issuing the Emancipation Proclamation," showed Lincoln taking off his mask to reveal his true persona: Satan. The proclamation lies on the ground in front of him. Another drawing in the *Southern Illustrated News,* titled "One Good Turn Deserves Another," pictured Lincoln dressed as Uncle Sam with arms stretched out to a black man. The message was clear: In exchange for freeing the slaves Lincoln expected blacks to enlist in the Union army. In another drawing, Lincoln was again depicted as Satan, showing his disdain for the Constitution as he carried Lady Liberty away to "his infernal regions."[82]

The Copperheads were favorite targets of cartoonists. In one powerful drawing, three coiled copperhead snakes with human heads looked angrily at a determined-looking Columbia who carried a sword and shield. The caption read, "The Copperhead Party—In Favor of a Vigorous Prosecution of Peace!" In a cartoon about Vallandigham being exiled, the Southern sympathizer was portrayed as a shuttlecock who was being hit back and forth by Lincoln and Davis. Cartoonists condemned the mob that attacked black residents during the New York City draft riots. One showed rioters beating an old black man protecting a little girl. The caption said simply, "How to Escape the Draft." Another drawing portrayed New York as the "Naughty Boy Gotham, Who would not Take the Draft" from his mother, President Lincoln, who was dressed in a robe.[83]

During the election of 1864, the illustrated magazines generally supported Lincoln while mocking his Democratic opponent. One of the most devastating cartoons showed the president seated and holding up in his open hand the tiny figure of McClellan holding a shovel. Looking at the general and smiling, Lincoln uttered one of his favorite lines, "This reminds me of a little joke." A drawing in *Leslie's* showed the tricky position that McClellan was in as the Democratic nominee. It portrayed the general as part of a circus act trying to balance on a short stilt labeled "peace" and a longer stilt labeled "war." On the eve of the election, *Harper's* published a two-page illustration by Nast showing a proud Columbia voting for the Lincoln ticket. Slogans said, "No Compromise," "Down with Slavery," and "Down with the Rebels." After the president's victory, *Harper's* published a clever cartoon that pictured the tall, lanky Lincoln even taller. The caption said, "Long Abraham Lincoln a Little Longer."[84]

As the Union increasingly seemed poised for victory, cartoons reveled in the good news. A cartoon in *Leslie's* celebrated the capture of Savannah and General Sherman's message about the capture: "I beg to present to you, as a Christmas gift, the city of Savannah, with 150 heavy guns and . . . about 25,000 bales of cotton." The general was shown putting Savannah into a Christmas stocking while Uncle Sam slept peacefully. During the peace conference, another drawing showed a smiling Lincoln with his arms open wide. Distraught Confederates leaders, lead by Vice President Alexander Stephens, stood by unsure of what to do. The caption read, "The Peace Commission Flying to Abraham's Bosom." Another cartoon showed Union General Phil Sheridan catching Confederate troops in a net while others fled. The caption was a play on words and read, "Sheridan's Last Haul—Lee Gets His Phil'."[85]

The rumor that Davis was captured wearing women's clothes was too good for some artists to pass up. (It proved to not be true.) One showed Davis dressed in a skirt and hat and carrying a hatbox labeled "C.S." for Confederate States. The cowering president was surrounded by Union troops staring and laughing at him. And a *Leslie's* cartoon, titled "Jeff Arming for the Final Struggle," showed a woman helping Davis put on a hoop skirt.[86]

But other editorial artists encouraged the North to reach out sympathetically to its defeated foe. A poignant drawing in *Harper's,* with the caption "A Man Knows a Man," showed a black Union soldier and a white Confederate soldier warmly shaking hands. Each man had lost a leg and was using a crutch.[87]

FOUR

CENSORSHIP AND
SUPPRESSION

An aggressive and outspoken press presented issues for the governments of the Union and Confederacy during the Civil War. Newspaper correspondents for both sides were determined to report stories from the battlefield, but military and civilian leaders were just as determined to ensure that they did not reveal critical information. At the same time, editors wanted to voice their opinions on issues, but political leaders wanted to make sure they did not hurt morale and the war effort. The results were censorship and newspaper closings on a scale never seen before during wartime, particularly in the North.

The attempts to restrict and control the press presented new constitutional issues. The United States had never experienced broad censorship and courts had not ruled on issues of freedom of the press during wartime. Violence against the press was not unusual in 19th-century America, but it rose to an unprecedented level during the war as citizens and soldiers repeatedly sought to forcefully silence newspapers considered disloyal. *Harper's Weekly* summarized the issue in an editorial early in the war. The magazine argued that the press represented the people and, as such, should be given the maximum freedom. The question was "whether newspapers, working for private ends or in the interest of the unpatriotic malcontents, should be suffered to weaken the hands of Government, during war-time, by malevolent opposition."[1]

Few disputed the necessity of some censorship during wartime, particularly a war that was fought entirely on American soil. But in many cases the restrictions imposed by both sides were arbitrary, hasty, and heavy-handed. At the same time, numerous journalists for the North and South were guilty of revealing important military information in their stories. And some editors showed a lack of responsibility in voicing slanderous opinions about political leaders. Journalists protested the censorship rules considered unreasonable, and they raged in editorials against the mob violence. However, with no real protection for freedom of expression in the mid-19th century there was little they could do.

The governments of the North and South had few precedents to guide them in censoring journalists because the American press did not actively report conflicts until the Mexican War, and even then only on a limited basis. During the Mexican War, military authorities had suppressed at least five newspapers and those not shut down were sometimes subjected to government censorship or the threat of violence. But authorities only censored one correspondent's story. The telegraphic network in the southwest was limited, and reporters sent their stories back using various combinations of the mail, pony express, railroads, and the telegraph.[2]

During the first year of the war, administration of censorship in the North was passed from one department to another. It was initially under the Treasury Department, then transferred to the War Department, then to the State Department, and, finally, back to the War Department. Reporters and editors were understandably confused about the rules they had to work under. The provisional Confederate Congress approved a bill giving the president the power to censor the telegraph, but it took months for censors to be put in place.

The confusion was evident in the days after the surrender of Fort Sumter when a mob of Southern sympathizers fired on Union soldiers passing through Baltimore. To prevent news of the attack from spreading, police immediately cut the telegraph lines running out of the city. Secretary of State William H. Seward also seized the telegraph office in Washington and prohibited correspondents from sending stories about the violence in which several people were killed and wounded. The office reopened the next day and the telegraph company distributed instructions to guide operators in sending dispatches. The instructions said that only messages from the president or heads of government departments could be sent. Messages about military operations and anything "injurious to the interests of the Government" were prohibited. Seward dismissed complaints from journalists about the instructions, saying that stories "would only influence public sentiment, and be an obstacle in the path of reconciliation."[3]

As prospects grew for the first major battle, General Winfield Scott became alarmed by newspaper stories detailing the Federal army's preparations. Scott, who had dealt with the press during the Mexican War, issued a one-sentence order prohibiting the transmission of any telegraphic dispatches concerning military operations unless he approved them. Correspondents protested the order and in a new agreement, Scott permitted them to telegraph the progress and results of battles without submitting their stories to a censor. Under the pact, reporters were bound not to report the arrival or departure of troops, disagreements or mutinies in troops, and predictions of any troop movements.[4]

At the same time, Southern leaders also were taking steps to establish telegraphic censorship. A month after the attack on Fort Sumter, the Confederate Congress approved a bill giving the president the authority to put government agents in telegraph offices to supervise the transmission of dispatches, require telegraph employees to take an oath of allegiance to the Confederate government, and impose penalties of fines and imprisonment for anyone convicted of sending damaging news by telegraph. A few weeks later, the government later gave the Confederate postal service authority to censor the mail.[5]

The Confederate government also issued its first instructions for journalists. In a letter to newspapers published in the *Richmond Enquirer,* Secretary of War Leroy P. Walker appealed to correspondents not to publish any information that might hurt the Confederate cause. He wrote:

> It must be obvious that statements of strength, or of weakness, at any of the points in the vicinity of the enemy, when reproduced in the North, as they would be in spite of all the vigilance in our power, would warn them of danger to themselves or invite an attack upon us; and in like manner, any statements of the magnitude of batteries, of the quantity and quality of arms, or of ammunition, of movements in progress or in supposed contemplation . . . might be fraught with essential injury to the service.[6]

A correspondent for the *Mobile Register and Advertiser* said that damaging stories published in newspapers had forced Walker to issue his appeal. Writing from Richmond, he said, "No regiment has passed Lynchburg that Lincoln has not had the fullest notice of. There is not a battery in the country that has not been as full described by correspondents as [a] Frank Leslie's or Harper's artist could have done. They keep old Scott as well posted about the strength of our forces at every point . . . as if he were present at every dress parade and heard the morning orders read." However, the *Charleston Mercury* disputed the idea that Union leaders received information about the Confederate army from the press. The paper said the Union had spies throughout Virginia and it argued that readers had a right to be informed.[7]

Confederate commanders took their own steps to suppress the publication of stories. An order published from Yorktown, Virginia, over the signature of a colonel forbid "newspapers scribblers" from giving information about the size of forces, the movement of units, and the results of fighting. The colonel went on to say that since the order had been violated, he was directing commanders to use every means to frustrate "this foolish and pernicious itching for newspaper notoriety." But Southern correspondents showed they were not going to accept restrictions without protest. Two reporters claimed that in his "itching" for notoriety after the fighting at Big Bethel, the colonel immediately sent a newspaper story that emphasized the gallant conduct of him and his own troops. The colonel also had not given credit to another commander who led troops in the fighting.[8]

꧁◌꧂

There was widespread confusion at the battle of First Bull Run. Initial telegraphic accounts of the fighting suggested an imminent Union victory. But when the fighting ended in a Federal rout, Northern correspondents returned to Washington to find the telegraph offices closed. Most newspapers could not print the news of what actually happened for more than a day. The affair cast doubts on the credibility of the government and the press. *New York Times* editor Henry Raymond said that citizens had the right to know the truth. "[W]e cannot conceive of any state of things which can justify the Government in deliberately suppressing what it knows to be true; and thus promulgating what it knows to be false," he wrote.[9]

It was clear that new measures were needed. Soon after taking over command of the Army of the Potomac, General George McClellan invited reporters to his headquarters for a meeting. McClellan opened it by speaking in flattering terms of the importance of journalism and its influence on the public. He also said that he would like to give correspondents wide latitude and come up with an agreement among themselves of what should and should not be published. But within a few weeks, the War Department decided that formal rules were needed. It issued an order that no information about army movements could be sent until "after actual hostilities." Violators could be given the death penalty or any other punishment as might be prescribed by court-martial.[10]

Throughout the fall, Union correspondents and censors clashed over what could be transmitted. At the battle of Ball's Bluff, Federal forces suffered major casualties, including the death of Colonel Edward D. Baker, a senator from Oregon. McClellan was at the telegraph office when the news was received, and the general ordered no news about the battle to be sent, except the official report. Although newspapers across the North denounced the prohibitions, censors continued the wide latitude they had been given. A news story about the visit of a Russian military observer included comments about the organizational differences between U.S. and European armies. The censor cut a large part of the story.[11]

Before the end of the year, editors convinced members of the House of Representatives Judiciary Committee to investigate to what extent and under whose authority telegraphic censorship was taking place. During committee hearings in January and February, newsmen testified about the difficulty of working under the new censorship rules. They claimed that the government censors were not qualified and were given unnecessarily wide discretion to block information from being sent. The chief censor acknowledged that his definition of what was public information was limited. He said that the public had a right to known anything said by the president or a cabinet member in public, but he argued that the press had no right to publish "the private affairs of the Gov't."[12]

The committee's 14-page report was critical of the government's censorship policy. Although the original purpose of the rules was to prevent the publication of damaging military information, the report said, "almost numberless" dispatches of "a political, personal, and general character have been suppressed." The report listed examples of inoffensive dispatches that were blocked for no apparent reasons. It concluded that because of the importance of the telegraph "it should be left as free from government interference as may be consistent with the necessities of the government in time of war."[13]

As it turned out, the committee report had little impact because in January Congress passed a law giving the president the authority to take control of telegraph and railroad facilities. All telegraph lines and offices were placed under military control, and new Secretary of War Stanton was given authority over the government's censorship efforts. Stanton promptly sent a message to the press saying that "public safety requires all newspapers to abstain for the present from publishing intelligence in respect to military operations by the U.S. forces." He sent another message to the chiefs of police of major cities that published military information received by telegraph or other means. Stanton also made sure the War Department sent its own dispatches about the war to the press.[14]

Confederate correspondents also were finding that getting information from military and government sources to be increasingly difficult. A reporter with the New Orleans *Delta* complained that the military was so secretive that he felt "considerably embarrassed" about what he could and could not publish. Newsmen also told how in the course of doing their work, they risked being arrested as spies. A reporter for the *Petersburg Express,* who aroused the suspicion of the local militia, was jailed in Winchester, Virginia, and remained there until the secretary of war secured his release. A native of Ireland, the correspondent said he had been raised in Richmond and been a loyal citizen for 15 years.[15]

The war departments of both the Union and Confederacy gave officers in the field wide latitude in dealing with correspondents as they saw fit. Commanders took matters into their own hands by barring reporters from their camps and taking various forms of disciplinary action against journalists. Officers believed the action was necessary to deter reporters from publishing information valuable to the other side. But reporters complained that commanders acted arbitrarily and that too often newsmen did not know the rules they were expected to operate under. The *New York Times* said the right to know news from the war should not be left to "the caprice, the resentments, or the fancied self-interests of individual officers." It went on: "It is very rarely that a military man can be found who is capable of understanding what public opinion is, or who can be made to comprehend that the Press has any other rights than those which he may be pleased to confer upon it."[16]

One Confederate general who definitely took matters into his own hands was General Joseph E. Johnston. Soon after the new year began, Johnston issued Order No. 98 calling for all correspondents to be expelled from his army. The order followed the publication of a story in the *Richmond Dispatch* by William G. Shepardson that identified the location of the winter quarters of various brigades of the army. Before issuing his order, a furious Johnston had asked new Secretary of War Judah P. Benjamin to punish Shepardson for the breach of secrecy. Benjamin replied that the law provided no penalty for the "outrageous breach" and said that he would ask Congress for legislation to deal with such cases. However, the secretary also told Johnston: "I think some of the mischief . . . arises from your own too lenient tolerance of the presence of newspaper reporters within your lines."[17]

Editorials in the Confederate press condemned Johnston's actions. The *Atlanta Southern Confederacy* said that behind the order was a great deal of "criminal folly, official incompetence, shameful shortcomings, and no little rascality." It said the public deserved to know what was taking place. When a group of Southern editors met in the spring to discuss a cooperative newsgathering service, they appointed a committee to draft a series of resolutions protesting Johnston's order.[18]

Confederate censorship was particularly tight during the fighting around New Orleans in the spring of 1862. A correspondent for the *Memphis Appeal* wrote to his newspaper that the press in the city had been "expressly enjoined from publishing or telegraphing any of the movements or occurrences hereabouts." As a result, newsmen had to rely on the official dispatches of the military, which expressed full confidence that the forts protecting New Orleans could repel the Union assault. The Confederate War Department never acknowledged the capture of the South's largest city.[19]

After the battle of Shiloh, Union General Henry W. Halleck took over direction of the campaign. More than 30 correspondents were following the push toward Corinth in anticipation of the next major battle. But the deliberative Halleck—his nickname was "Old Brains"—moved slowly and he became increasingly defensive with reporters who wanted to know why. To stop the reports, he issued Field Order No. 54 expelling all "unauthorized hangers on" from the army. Frank Wilkie of the *New York Times* wrote that he could understand why the general wanted to ban many from his army. "Almost every third man you meet is the "Reporter of the Something Diurnal," Wilkie wrote. "Half of them are individuals who board with some officer, and whose letters invariably inform the world that the gallant Colonel of the regiment preeminently distinguished himself in the late fight." But when it became apparent that Halleck included reporters in his order, they protested loudly.[20]

⚜

On the eve of the Peninsula campaign, correspondents were under strict orders not to reveal the movement of the Union army. Any newspaper publishing military news not expressly authorized would have their privilege of receiving news by telegraph revoked. When correspondents protested, the order was modified to provide the publication of past facts, provided they did not reveal information about the position or strength of the army. Perhaps to show that it meant business, the War Department arrested John Russell Young, editor of the *Morning Chronicle*, for a news items about the movement on one division en route to the Peninsula. The editor of the *Boston Journal* was threatened with court-martial because the newspaper published a letter with information about the Peninsula expedition while it was still in progress. Then the War Department issued another order revoking the passes of all correspondents with the Army of the Potomac. Two days later the order was revoked without explanation. Still unhappy about the way censorship was being handled, the department issued new rules that, in effect, made each correspondent his own censor. The "parole" was a two-page document in which each correspondent was required to give his word of honor that he was a citizen of the United States and that he would not write or transmit any information that would give aid to the enemy. The new order was never enforced.[21]

Meanwhile, General Johnston's order continued throughout the Peninsula campaign and Confederate correspondents found it difficult to report significant news. When Union troops threatened Richmond in mid-May and panic gripped the city, authorities took control of the telegraph lines south of the capital. Correspondents were unable to describe the state of affairs on the Peninsula, leading the editor of the *Richmond Dispatch* to complain that military authorities had erected an "impassible barrier" to gathering news. The restrictions continued even after the Confederate army pushed the Union army back from Richmond. The editorial protests continued loudly, but military authorities did not loosen the restrictions. General Lee complained to the secretary of war that newspapers were providing the location of his divisions. Lee noted that the enemy could easily find the Richmond newspapers and he urged the secretary to take steps to ensure that military secrets were not revealed in the press.[22]

Perhaps no Confederate commander battled the press more than General Braxton Bragg. Starting with his first command in Pensacola, the combative Bragg showed little respect for journalists and their jobs. Before Bragg's army invaded Kentucky in 1862, he issued an order that "no person not connected to this army will be permitted to accompany it—whenever found within the lines, they will be arrested and confined." At the time, Bragg was battling the *Montgomery Advertiser* and correspondent Wallace Screws. Bragg ordered Screws arrested in August for a story that allegedly contained information about the movements of the Army of the Mississippi. The general accused Screws of "gross violation of all known rules in armies—not to declare to the enemy the movement of troops." The letter went on: "As long as you confined yourself to personal abuse and detraction, though false and malignant . . . Gen. Bragg cared nothing for it. But when you assail our cause and expose our plans to the enemy, it becomes his duty to interfere; and you may rest assured he will do it." The newspaper's editor fired back, accusing the general of "petty tyranny and vindictiveness." He said that "no one doubts the correctness of the rule" prohibiting the press from printing military secrets, "but all will question its application to this case." Bragg soon ordered Screws to be released.[23]

Confederate reporters were largely kept away from the vicinity of Fredericksburg in the days before the battle. Peter W. Alexander applied for a pass and was informed that no one not engaged in military business was being permitted to travel. When Alexander told the officer that three reporters already had gotten through, the officer said that should not have been allowed to happen. On the other side, news of the Federal army's disastrous defeat was kept out of newspapers for more than 24 hours. As soon as the extent of the defeat was known, many editors howled. The *New York Times* complained that "every effort was made by the correspondents there to transmit the facts speedily to their respective newspapers; and every effort was made by the Government to prevent them from doing so. The telegraphic wires were forbidden, except to the most meager statements . . . and reporters were compelled to run a blockade more strict than that of Charleston Harbor."[24]

The situation did not improve for correspondents on either side. After assuming command in mid-April, Union General Joseph Hooker had a series of run-ins with the press. He wrote Stanton demanding an investigation of a news leak that appeared in a newspaper about the size and organization of his army. Hooker said the chief of the secret service "would have willingly paid $1,000 for such information in regard to the enemy." Stanton told Hooker that the War Department would support any measure he took to control journalists. That same day, Hooker issued General Order No. 48 requiring all reporters attached to the Army of the Potomac "to publish their communications over their own signatures."[25]

Newsmen on both sides recognized that irresponsible correspondents were writing reckless stories that hurt their side. In a letter to the *Savannah Republican* Alexander, one of the most skillful Southern reporters, wrote:

The truth is there are correspondents who invariably magnify our successes and depreciate our losses, and who when there is a dearth of news will draw upon their imaginations for their facts. The war abounds in more romantic incidents and thrilling adventures than poet ever imagined or novelist described; and it would be well if the writers of fiction from the army, who devote themselves to the marvelous and poetic affairs rather than to the stern realities of the campaign, would remember this fact.

But Alexander also repeatedly argued for the necessity of a free press. "This is the people's war," he wrote. "Their sons and brothers make up the army. . . . And shall they not be allowed to know anything that is transpiring within that army? . . . Is the army to be a sealed book to the country?"[26]

News of the Union loss at Chancellorsville was withheld from the Northern public for several days. Censors in Washington would not allow the news to be sent over the telegraph. Reporters for the New York newspapers left the army quietly and traveled straight to New York with the news. But both the *New York Herald* and *New York Tribune* refused to print the news immediately. The *New York Times* was the first to publish the story on Tuesday. Two days later, the censorship restrictions were withdrawn and the rest of the country learned about the devastating defeat. Confederate newspapers also had trouble getting information about the fighting at Chancellorsville. One editor wrote to the Southern Telegraph Company saying that news of the battle was sent late, a growing problem with telegraphic dispatches. The editor of the *Augusta Constitutionalist* also complained about the "ridiculously and pitifully false accounts" of the fighting he received.[27]

❧⟨∞⟩❧

In the West, General Sherman also was battling the press. The mercurial Sherman had been a target of newspaper criticism since early in the war. He had been called "eccentric," "insane," and a "monomaniac." Sherman responded in kind, calling reporters "spies," "fawning sycophants," "damned mongrels," "sneaking, croaking scoundrels," and "the most contemptible race of men that exists." He declared that lying was a reporter's stock in trade, that newspapers had repeatedly foiled Union moves by revealing secrets, and that Napoleon would have been beaten by a free press.[28]

At the end of 1862, General Grant ordered Sherman to command part of what was to be a three-pronged attack on Vicksburg. Before his expedition departed, Sherman issued General Order No. 8 forbidding civilians from accompanying the army. Anyone on board the transports who wrote anything for publication would be arrested and treated as a spy. Despite the orders, several reporters managed to get on board the transports and filed stories with their newspapers. On December 29, Sherman's army attacked and was badly repulsed, suffering more than 2,500 casualties. Numerous reporters blamed Sherman for the defeat. Even friendly newspapers accused the general of underestimating the Confederates and displaying poor judgment.[29]

Thomas Knox's story, published in the *New York Herald* on January 18, ran more than a full page. Knox began the story by explaining that an officer on Sherman's staff had intercepted his original story. The correspondent acidly noted, "Had they all acted as earnestly and persistently against the rebels as against representatives of the press, there is little doubt that Vicksburg would, ere this, have been in Union hands." Knox was a good reporter and his account provided an outstanding picture of the battle, complete with vivid details including the terrain. He kept his opinion out of the story until the end when he clearly blamed Sherman for the defeat. The general's conduct was "so exceedingly erratic," Knox reported, "that questions about his sanity were being raised by some in the army." He also made it clear that another commanding officer would not have suffered such a loss.[30]

Disappointed over the failure of the attack and furious about the criticism of him, Sherman decided to try to silence the press by taking the unusual step of court-martialing a reporter. Although he could have chosen several Union reporters who had criticized him, the general selected Knox. When Knox learned that Sherman planned to prosecute him, he claimed that his account of the battle was correct, although he admitted it was based on a "narrow channel of information." Since writing his story, he had seen other reports of the fighting and realized that he had "labored under repeated errors." He told Sherman he was now convinced of the "prompt, efficient and judicious management of the troops under your control." However, when Knox was brought before Sherman the correspondent's attitude changed. He told the general he had no personal animosity against him, but that he was regarded as "the enemy of our set, and we must in self-defense write you down."[31]

The court-martial began on February 4. Knox was charged with: "Giving intelligence to the enemy, directly or indirectly"; "Being a spy"; and "Disobedience of orders." The correspondent pleaded not guilty. Sherman was the only prosecution witness and testified for two days. He repeated the charges that Knox had violated orders and, as a result, provided the enemy with information about the army's strength. The false accusations against officers, he claimed, worked to the detriment of the government and gave comfort to its enemies. The defense presented character witnesses who testified to Knox's reliability and loyalty. The defense also argued that his story was written four days after the battle when Sherman's army was safely away. It also claimed that there was no evidence that a copy of the *Herald* with Knox's story had come into the possession of the enemy.[32]

After deliberating for four days, the panel found Knox not guilty of the first and second charges. He was found guilty of the third charge, but the panel attached "no criminality." The correspondent was ordered outside of the army's lines, but Sherman was furious with the ruling. He argued that by finding no criminality with Knox's actions, the panel had inferred that a commanding officer had no right to prohibit citizens from a military expedition and if they should, citizens could not be prosecuted. He also claimed the court was wrong in saying that the correspondent had not provided the enemy with information.[33]

When friends of Knox appealed the ruling to Lincoln, the president's response was characteristically shrewd. He said that Knox could return if Grant gave his consent. The president, of course, knew that Grant would not go against the wishes of a trusted officer. Grant said he would not allow Knox to join the army unless Sherman agreed. Knox wrote to Sherman asking to return and expressing regret at "the want of harmony between portions of the Army and the Press." Sherman rejected Knox's appeal and wrote:

> Come with a sword or musket in your hand, prepared to share with us our fate in sunshine and storm, and I will welcome you as a brother and associate; but come as you do now, expecting me to ally the reputation and honor of my country and my fellow soldiers with you, as the representative of the press, which you yourself say makes so slight a difference between truth and falsehood, and my answer is, Never.[34]

Censorship continued throughout the war. In the North, it was not used as heavily, in part, because starting in the summer the Union army began to fare better on the battlefield. Military officials were glad to permit stories about the victories at Vicksburg, Gettysburg, Chattanooga, and other places. In the field, commanders still battled correspondents who they believed acted irresponsibly. Angered by a story in the *Philadelphia Inquirer,* General George Meade ordered Edward Crapsey drummed out of camp riding backward on a mule with signs saying "Libeler of the Press." Meade later let Crapsey return to reporting from his army and admitted that he had been overly harsh in his treatment of the newsman.[35]

In the South, where the battlefield losses were multiplying, censorship persisted and the complaints of correspondents continued. When Alexander tried to send a story about the fighting at Brandy Station, a battle in which General J.E.B. Stuart was embarrassingly caught by surprise, he discovered that telegraph censors in Richmond had suppressed his report. Alexander sarcastically suggested that "to be consistent the Government should establish a censorship over the mailbags, over the railway trains, and over the minds and tongues of men" because "there was scarcely a letter sent from the army the day after the battle that did not admit the surprise, nor was there an individual, white or black, who left here by the railroad, who had not heard of it, or who would not speak of it."[36]

After repeated instances of censors suppressing dispatches in the spring of 1864, the *Charleston Courier* published an editorial politely asking for a relaxation of rules. The newspaper argued that readers could stand to hear the truth, "even if not up to the most sanguine expectations." By blocking the transmission of unfavorable news, it argued, the military encouraged the exaggeration of unfavorable news. The *Courier* encouraged officials to send a daily news bulletin to the Confederate press. "Must we wait for flags of truce to bring us the earliest reports, true or false, uttered by Yankee journalists?" the newspaper asked. "Give us the news to all completed events—we ask not any premature revelations of plans or purposes or numbers, or any information which the most cautious policy should detain."[37]

The editorial had no effect on the rules because Confederate officials cracked down on the press during the Atlanta campaign that spring. After General's Johnston's troops fell back repeatedly over a period of weeks, telegraphic dispatches from the front were stopped. The general manager of the Confederate Press Association traveled to Johnston's headquarters in an attempt to get the restrictions eased but he was unsuccessful. As a result, the Confederate press had to rely on visits to Atlanta by reporters and the reports of railroad passengers. One disgusted newsman, Samuel Chester Reid, left the army to avoid the restrictions. In a letter to the *Montgomery Advertiser* he explained that the difficulty of finding an officer to approve news dispatches and the irregularity of mail service made reporting difficult, if not impossible. He wrote that the censorship often was a "humbug" and that the inspectors were entirely unpredictable in what they permitted to be sent.[38]

Northern correspondents and generals also continued to clash. William Kent, a reporter for the *New York Tribune,* published a story critical of Union commanders, including Meade, during the siege of Petersburg in the summer of 1864. At the insistence of Meade, General Grant ordered the *Tribune* reporter to be arrested on the charges of "publishing false intelligence for a malicious purpose." Kent did not want to face the possibility of Crapsey's humiliating experience, so he promptly left the army and did not report the war again.[39]

☙❧

The other forms of press suppression during the war were the closing of newspapers considered disloyal, the arrest of editors, and the denial of postal privileges. During the 19th century, it had become fairly routine for newspapers to be banned, their editors threatened, or presses wrecked. But during the war there were more such cases than at any time in American history. One study found that 92 newspapers were subjected to some form of restriction, and 111 were wrecked by mobs. The vast majority of the incidents took place in the North. Military commanders or political leaders, concerned about the effect of virulent editorials by the Democratic press, ordered many of the newspaper closings. But others were the result of angry citizens or soldiers acting on their own and usually with force.[40]

Opposition editors who were arrested or saw their newspapers closed had few avenues for legal redress. Although the First Amendment protected the press, journalists had limited legal defense during the mid-19th century. Judges based their view of press freedom on English judge William Blackstone's opinions written almost 100 years earlier. Blackstone wrote that free citizens had the right to say what they wanted and that any prohibition of opinions would destroy freedom of the press. However, he also noted that if a journalist "publishes what is improper, mischievous, or illegal, he must take the consequences of his own temerity." Blackstone's definition gave judges broad discretionary power to determine the limits of expression.[41]

At the same time, citizen mobs generally were protected by the legal view that communities should have some control over ideas disseminated in their midst in order to protect the citizenry. This common law doctrine for regulating community activities generally placed majority interests over individual rights. Nineteenth-century law also left many regulatory responsibilities to local authorities. The experiences of abolitionist editors in the North and South, who were repeatedly attacked by mobs during the decades before the war, showed that local officials often were willing to let angry crowds largely do what they wanted to silence outspoken editors.[42]

Concern about the effect of a disloyal press began soon after the first shots of the war were fired. Citizen groups in various cities across the North, usually festive, demanded that newspapers demonstrate their fidelity to the Union. In New York, groups paraded through the streets at night and insisted that all publications fly the American flag. But the attack on Federal troops in Baltimore convinced the administration that unprecedented steps were needed, and less than a week later, President Lincoln claimed the power to suspend the writ of habeas corpus. Article 1, Section 9, of the Constitution stipulates that privilege of the writ "shall not be suspended unless when in cases of rebellion or invasion the public safety may require it." When Judge Robert B. Taney denied the president's right to suspend the writ, Lincoln refused to obey it. In a message to a special session of Congress, the president argued that his duty was to put down the rebellion so that the laws of the United States could be executed in the South. Suspension of the writ was a vital weapon against the Confederacy. "Are all the laws *but one* [the right of habeas corpus], to go unexecuted and the Government itself go to pieces, lest that one be violated?" Lincoln asked rhetorically.[43]

The Union army's defeat at First Bull Run provided fodder for opposition editors to attack the administration and call for peace. A Federal grand jury in New York asked the U.S. Circuit Court if five pro-Southern newspapers in the city could be subject to indictment. The grand jury accused the *Daily News, Journal of Commerce, Day Book, Freeman's Journal,* and *Brooklyn Eagle* of "expressing sympathy and agreement" with the rebels. The grand jury acknowledged that "free governments allow liberty of speech and of the press to their utmost limit," but it said, "there is, nevertheless a limit."[44]

None of the editors of the five newspapers were indicted. However, Postmaster General Montgomery Blair issued an order denying postal privileges to the publications. He argued that treason should be stopped by "prompt and direct interference" rather than by "slow judicial prosecution." Blair later defended his action in a letter to the House Judiciary Committee, claiming the authority to prevent hostile materials from reaching the enemy and encouraging others to cooperate. He said that although the post office had no authority to suppress publications, it could prevent them from being distributed. The committee found that the postmaster general had the right during wartime to deny the use of the mails to publications considered treasonous. "The act of the Postmaster General was not only within the scope of his powers, but induced solely by considerations of the public good," the committee said.[45]

With a large and vocal pro-Southern press, it was not surprising that numerous incidents of newspaper suppression took place in Baltimore. Several of the city's newspapers were openly hostile toward the administration. In an editorial the day after Fort Sumter surrendered, the *Daily Exchange* declared:

> We believe that right and justice are with our brethren of the South, and that the cause they represent and are defending is the case of their domestic institutions, their chartered rights and their firesides. We look upon the government which is assailing them as the representative, not of the Union, but of a malignant and sectional fanaticism, which takes the honored name of the Union in vain and has prostrated and is trampling on the Constitution.

A few days later, the *South* was launched to promote the Confederate cause in Maryland, just as the newspaper's name suggested. "It is a righteous and holy cause and we are ready to stand by it to the last," an editorial declared in the first issue. "If it is rebellion we are content to be rebels . . . we are contending for the inviolability of the soil of Maryland and her emancipation from Federal thralldom and sectional domination."[46]

Concerned about the vituperative editorials being published, the post office revoked the mailing privileges of the *Daily Exchange* and *South*. Several days later, the editors of the newspapers were arrested and imprisoned at Fort McHenry. The *Daily Exchange* never published again, but the *South* appeared later with a new editor. When the newspaper renewed its attacks on the Federal government, the new editor was arrested and the office seized by authorities. The *South* did not publish again for the rest of the war.[47]

The secretary of war issued the initial orders against the Democratic press in Baltimore. But starting in early 1862, the city's commanding general was directed to act on his own in suppressing and censoring newspapers considered disloyal. The owners of the *Daily Republican* were arrested in September 1863, sent to the South, and told not to return or they would be treated as spies. The *Evening Post* was closed for posting on its bulletin board an account from the *Cincinnati Enquirer* about police firing upon a mob. The commanding general in Baltimore even went so far as to prohibit newspapers in the city from publishing critical articles from other publications, including the *New York World* and *Chicago Times*.[48]

❧❧

Beginning in 1862, the closing of Democratic newspapers moved from the northeast states to the Midwest. There was considerable Southern sympathy in Illinois, Indiana, Iowa, and Ohio, not to mention the border states of Kentucky and Missouri. The editors of pro-Southern Democratic newspapers in those states had long been critical of the Lincoln administration and repeatedly called for peace. The criticism erupted following the president's order suspending the writ of habeas corpus followed by his issuance of the preliminary Emancipation Proclamation.

State and local officials repeatedly wrote to the administration warning about the opposition press and recommending that forceful action was needed against them. Indiana Governor Oliver P. Morton sent a letter to Stanton saying that conspirators were using newspapers to "manufacture public opinion" against the war effort. Morton said that Democrats were employing "every means in their power" to turn citizens against the war with "treasonous and poisonous" publications and speeches. The Republican governor included an editorial from the Indiana *State Sentinel* and recommended that it be shut down.[49]

Eleven Democratic newspapers were closed in Indiana during a six-week period in 1863. General Milo Hascall, commander of the District of Indiana, had issued an order that any newspaper or public speaker that encouraged resistance to the Enrollment Act "or any other law of Congress passed as a war measure" would be treated as a traitor. Editors reacted angrily to the order including Daniel E. Van Valkenburg, editor of the *Weekly Democrat* in Plymouth. He wrote, "Brig. General Hascall is a donkey, an unmitigated, unqualified donkey, and his bray is long, loud and harmless. . . . Will Brig. Gen. Hascall please inform us why the citizens of Illinois and Kentucky, sister States, are permitted to express their minds freely, and the citizens of Indiana alone are selected for this abject submission." Less than a week later, the editor was awakened when soldiers broke down the door to his room. Van Valkenburg was taken to Indianapolis to appear before Smith and later to Cincinnati where Burnside ordered him released. Burnside told the editor "to be more careful in the future in the manner in which he criticized those in authority."[50]

Numerous Democratic newspapers were closed in Missouri, perhaps the most of any state during the war. As a border state, Missouri had been bitterly divided before the war and that was reflected in its newspapers. General John C. Frémont began a crusade to crush the opposition press almost as soon as he was made commander of the Department of the West in July 1861. Frémont put the state under martial law and used that to close two newspapers considered disloyal. He then barred the five

Democratic New York newspapers charged by the grand jury from being distributed in the state. More newspapers were closed over the next several months, including the *St. Louis News,* whose editor and assistant were arrested and charged with criticizing Fremont's military strategy. The editor of the *State Journal* also was accused of aiding and abetting the enemy for his editorials expressing pro-Southern sympathy. Troops seized the newspaper's office.[51]

Lincoln recalled Frémont from his post before the end of the year, but subsequent military commanders in Missouri continued to suppress opposition newspapers. The editor of the *Boone County Standard* was arrested, convicted, and sent to the Confederate lines. The editor of the *Chillicothe Constitution* was seized by authorities, and when the editor of the *Journal of Commerce* in Kansas demanded an explanation, he too was thrown in jail. At the same time, the provost marshal of St. Louis forbid the circulation of other Democratic newspapers, including the *Chicago Times, New York World, New York Journal,* and the *Crisis.*[52]

While military authorities closed many of the newspapers in Missouri, mobs often did the work in Ohio. One of the first to be wrecked was the *Stark County Democrat* in Canton whose editor, Archibald McGregor, staunchly opposed the war. He demanded that the town reimburse him for his loss and leaders agreed to pay $3,000. The next year McGregor was arrested, and while he spent a month in jail, his wife published the newspaper. A mob of citizens and soldiers also destroyed the *Mahoning Sentinel* in Youngstown. The editor published the news of the attack in an extra printed on the press of his Republican rival in the city. Another group destroyed the office of the *Democrat* in Greenville. But the mob did not stop there and also wrecked the law office of William Allen, a former U.S. senator and a Democrat. In the case of the *Jackson Express,* a friend tipped off the editor that an angry crowd was coming to close the paper. Supporters formed a cordon around the office and the mob was discouraged from attacking it.[53]

The most celebrated newspaper closing involved the *Chicago Times.* Wilbur Storey had made a name for himself as a scurrilous Democratic editor when he directed the *Detroit Free Press* for eight years. In an editorial published early in 1861, the *Free Press* famously declared, "The fanaticism which will have dissolved the Union will not . . . be allowed to convulse the continent with Civil War. Never! It must be stopped. . . . Public opinion commands it to stop, and . . . if it shall attempt war then it will be assailed with a fire in the rear which will compel it to stop." Storey purchased the *Chicago Times* in mid-1861 and initially supported the Lincoln administration. As long as it remained a war to preserve the Union, Storey supported the conflict. But the editor hated abolitionists and would not support a war to end slavery. He believed that abolitionists wanted to destroy the Constitution and had divided the country. He also argued that blacks were "incapable of taking care of themselves . . . and as a population they would be the worse infliction that has ever befallen any country."[54]

Storey called Clement Vallandigham's arrest and conviction "the worst case of illegal and arbitrary proceeding against an individual" in the country's history. He later wrote, "If a terrible retribution does not fall upon the perpetrators of this foul wrong, then God is not just." General Burnside had seen enough. On June 1 the general ordered the *Chicago Times* to cease publishing because of its "repeated expression of disloyal and incendiary statements."[55]

When Storey refused, troops broke into the building, took all issues of the newspaper, and tore them up. Within hours, supporters of the *Times* called for a rally. The angry crowd—one account estimated the number to be 20,000—gathered at Court House Square and officials were concerned a riot would break out. Business and political leaders met to pen a letter "respectfully" asking Lincoln to revoke the order in the interests of "the peace of this City and State, if not the general welfare of the country."[56]

Burnside's order put the president and his cabinet in a difficult position. Secretary of Treasury Gideon Welles wrote that the closing of the *Times* "gave bad men the rights of questions, an advantage of which they avail themselves. Good men, who wish to support the Administration, find it difficult to defend these acts." And Stanton told Burnside that the president believed, "The irritation produced by such acts is . . . likely to do more harm than the publication would do." While the administration "approves of your motives," Stanton told Burnside, the president wanted to be consulted about "the arrest of civilians and the suppression of newspapers not requiring immediate attention." Burnside revoked the order and on June 5 the *Times* began publishing again.[57]

The controversy surrounding Burnside's order gave the *Chicago Times* new attention. Storey seized upon it and stepped up his attacks on Lincoln. He called the president "a mean, wily, illiterate, brutal, unprincipled and utterly vulgar creature" and "a man who jokes while a nation mourns." Burnside hereafter was referred to as "The Beast of Fredericksburg," a reference to his disastrous command.[58]

The accounts of the *Chicago Times* and other newspapers closed were sensationally described in the *Crisis,* one of the most outspoken Democratic newspapers. Samuel Medary launched the *Crisis* in Columbus, Ohio, on January 31, 1861, and named it for the conflict that was enveloping the country. Medary, who was 60 years old at the time, wrote, "I feel it a duty I owe my country and myself, that I should not be a silent spectator of the most dangerous controversy that every impended over the American people." Medary started the *Crisis* as a means to oppose the war, but as opponents sought to silence it and other opposition newspapers, the editor's focus increasingly turned to what he viewed as unconstitutional assaults on press freedom. He deplored the attacks on fellow Democratic publications and argued that the administration had nothing to fear from them. He also argued that the peace press had pure motives but that did not mean it was above the law. "While the law guarantees freedom of the press, it wisely holds every person answerable for the abuse of the privilege," he wrote. As publisher of the *Crisis,* Medary said he stood behind everything printed in his newspaper. "If a man does not write what he feels and feel responsible for what he writes, he abuses his own intellect, and does a gross wrong to the public," he wrote.[59]

Medary increasingly came under criticism, and the *Crisis* became the target of an attack in 1863 when a group of men, mainly soldiers from nearby Camp Chase, wrecked the office. The newspaper did not have a press—it was printed at a local job shop—and published an account of the incident the next week. The *Crisis* charged that its Republican rival organized the attack and supplied liquor to the participants. Medary, who was in Cincinnati when his newspaper was destroyed, returned home to a large crowd that welcomed him with music by a brass band. The commander of the 2nd Ohio Cavalry later admitted that some of his men participated in the attack. He returned four bound volumes of *Crisis* files.[60]

The next year a grand jury in Cincinnati indicted Medary on a charge of conspiracy against the government. The editor appeared before a judge and was released on bond. In the meantime, Medary's friends in the Democratic press rallied to his defense. The *Freeman's Journal* said the charge was "outrageous and preposterous." The *Age* said Medary was arrested because he dealt "heavy blows upon the heads of Lincoln, Seward and Stanton." And the *Iowa Courier* charged that that it "has always been a mania with Lincoln to arrest American citizens without warrant and to suppress American papers without authority." Before he went on trial, Medary collapsed while making a speech. He died several days later.[61]

In some cases, Union troops acted on their own to shut down newspapers considered disloyal. Soldiers were avid newspaper readers and some bitterly denounced the drumbeat of antiwar editorials in the Copperhead press saying they hurt military morale. A captain with the 103rd Illinois complained: "You can imagine how much harm these traitors are doing, not only with their papers, but they are writing letters to the boys which discourage the most loyal of men." An officer with the 8th Connecticut wrote that "the papers published at the North & letters rec[eive]d by the soldiers are doing the Army an immense amount of evil."[62]

Republican editors generally supported the closing of the most virulent Democratic publications. After the suppression of the five New York newspapers in 1861, the *New York Evening Post* argued that those who claimed the closings curtailed personal liberty only shielded "the great northern conspiracy." "How long shall it be before all are made to heed the simple truth that the constitution protects only those who acknowledge and support it?" the newspaper said. And in the midst of crisis surrounding the closing of the *Chicago Times,* the *Chicago Tribune* declared of war critics:

It is license they want, not liberty! License to stab the bosom of the Republic—our beautiful mother! And drag her corpse to be trampled upon by the blaspheming South—to the end that they may set up in her stead the loathsome harlot of the Confederacy. If ruffians like these are not to be arrested and punished with severe penalties, there is no reason in our fighting the rebels at Vicksburg.

But many editors also contended that newspapers had a right to criticize elected officials. After the closing of the *Chicago Times,* a group of New York editors condemned newspapers that "incite, advocate, abet, uphold or justify treason or rebellion." However, they maintained "the right of the press to criticize firmly and fearlessly the acts of those charged with the administration of government" and condemned "the right of any military officer to suppress the issues or forbid the circulation of journals" outside areas of military action.[63]

Numerous Union editors whose newspapers were closed wrote President Lincoln asking that the orders be countermanded. Reverend Stuart Robinson of Louisville claimed that his publication, the *True Presbyterian,* was shut down because of personal enmities. However, Lincoln was told that Robinson was a Southern sympathizer and he did not respond. Robinson, who had fled to Canada, did not resume publishing until after the war. James A. McMaster, editor of the *Freeman's Journal,* was arrested for allegedly publishing treasonous statements in his newspaper. His wife wrote the president to tell him that the incarceration was ruining the newspaper financially. She said that she was operating the newspaper and would not criticize the administration. Lincoln agreed to release McMaster, but only after he took a loyalty oath under protest.[64]

❧❦

Lincoln generally let his commanders and secretary of war shut down newspapers considered disloyal. However, the president took a more active role in the bogus proclamation hoax in 1864. On the morning of May 18, just as the press foreman was completing the typesetting for the morning edition of the *New York Journal of Commerce,* an assistant rushed in with a dispatch from the Associated Press. The dispatch supposedly was a proclamation signed by President Lincoln establishing May 26 as a day of fasting and prayer and calling for up to 400,000 additional men for active military service. The proclamation came in the midst of the spring campaign as hard fighting was taking place at the Wilderness and Spotsylvania Courthouse. The timing seemed to suggest that the fighting was not going well for the Union as the 1864 presidential election was getting underway.[65]

The *New York World, New York Herald, New York Daily News,* and other newspapers in the city also received the dispatch. However, only the *Journal of Commerce* and *World* published it. The other publications had learned that the dispatch was a forgery. When contacted by one paper, a night clerk with the Associated Press said the dispatch was "as false as hell." When the two learned of the mistake, they immediately posted notices on the bulletin boards outside their offices. The *World* also published an extra edition announcing that the proclamation was a hoax.[66]

Knowing the Democratic sympathies of the *Journal of Commerce* and *World,* the Lincoln administration immediately launched an investigation. General John A. Dix met with the *Journal of Commerce*'s editor, William C. Prime, and the *World*'s editor, Manton Marble. At the same time, some officials speculated that the forgery might be a case of financial speculation. Bad military news would drive up the price of gold, and by manufacturing bad news individuals could make a fortune by buying gold before the price shot up. But the administration saw the hoax as more sinister. Lincoln believed the forgery was an act of treason because it gave "aid and comfort to the enemies of the United States and to the rebels now at war against the government, and their aiders and abettors." He ordered the two editors to be arrested and their newspaper offices seized.[67]

Dix delayed following the orders. An angry Stanton telegraphed the general to remind him that the president's message "was an order to you" and it was "your duty to execute [it] immediately." However, just before the editors were put on a steamer for Fort Lafayette, the military prison in New York harbor, administration officials decided to release them. But the *Journal of Commerce* and *World* remained closed until May 22. In the meantime, police arrested the perpetrator of the hoax, Joseph Howard Jr., city editor of the *Brooklyn Eagle* and a staunch Republican. Howard planned the scheme as a way to reap a financial windfall.[68]

In their first issues after being suspended, the *Journal of Commerce* and *World* said printing the bogus proclamation was an honest mistake and insisted they were guilty of no crime. The *Journal of Commerce* claimed that it had printed numerous orders from the administration with "every order coming to us in almost facsimile of this forged dispatch, and with no verification whatsoever." It went on: "There is scarcely a night in the year that the War Department does not send us . . . some such proclamation or order. If we should refuse to publish one of these we should be denounced as Copperheads. If we demanded verification or pay, we should be hooted as traitors." Marble wrote an angry letter to the president, which was published in the *World*. The editor claimed that the troops that seized the newspaper had damaged the office and stolen equipment. Marble also asked Lincoln, "Had the Tribune and the Times published this forgery . . . would you, Sir, have suppressed the Tribune and Times as you suppressed the World and the Journal of Commerce? If not, why not? Is there a different law for your opponents and for your supporters?"[69]

While the suppression of the *Journal of Commerce* and *World* received plenty of attention at the time, less well known was the seizure of the Independent Telegraph

Company in New York. The president's order shutting down the two newspapers also included the Independent, a telegraph network established during the war to compete with the American Telegraph Company. Although the War Department had taken control of the American Telegraph in the early days of the fighting, it had no control over the Independent. Dix was ordered to close the four offices of the Independent in the city, confiscate the equipment and records, and arrest all its personnel. The administration also ordered Washington's provost marshal to seize the office of a wire service that had been started by three war correspondents. Soon after Howard was arrested for the forgery, the offices of the Independent and the news service were reopened and their staffs released.[70]

In the end, the bogus proclamation episode turned out to be a major embarrassment for the Lincoln administration. Although some blamed Stanton for the arrests and seizures, Lincoln assumed responsibility. The administration quickly took steps to mend fences. Within days of the seizure, Stanton invited the Independent Telegraph to connect its lines with the War Department offices, thus giving it a share of the government's lucrative telegraph business. And the wire service operated by Henry Villard and his partners in Washington soon began publishing exclusive stories provided by the White House and War Department. Interestingly, the Associated Press was never touched during the whole bogus proclamation episode, even though the dispatches allegedly came from the wire service.[71]

Confederate officials took far fewer measures against their opponents in the press. In fact, it was a point of pride of the Davis administration, which was critical of the Union's efforts to suppress newspapers. In his inaugural address, President Davis had said that the "malignity and barbarity" in the Union's handling of civil liberties cases showed "the incapacity of our late associates to administer a Government as free, liberal, and humane" as the Confederacy. The president boasted that "through all the necessities of an unequal struggle there has been no act on our part to impair personal liberty or the freedom of speech, of thought, or of the press." Later in an interview, Davis said that his belief in a free press kept him from closing his longtime nemesis, the *Richmond Examiner*. "Better suffer from that evil which is temporary, than to arrest it by still a greater one," the president was quoted as saying. "It is a dangerous thing to interfere with liberty of the press; for what would it avail us if we gain our independence and lost our liberty."[72]

Still, Confederate officials silenced one of the most virulent opposition editors, William Brownlow, who published the *Knoxville Whig* in Knoxville, Tennessee. A Methodist preacher known as "Parson," Brownlow used his newspaper to promote his pet causes: Methodism, temperance, slavery, and the Union. The weekly's masthead carried the slogan: "Cry aloud and spare not." As a steadfast Unionist, Brownlow directed his strongest criticism at those who wanted to break up the country. In one editorial he defended flying the stars and stripes at his home and said that, despite the threats he had received, he would not take down the flag. "Sink or swim, live or die, survive or perish, I am a Union man, and owe my allegiance to the Stars and Stripes of my country," Brownlow wrote. When he was asked to serve in the Confederate army, the editor declared, "When I shall have made up my mind to go to hell, I will cut my throat, and go direct, and not travel round by way of the Southern Confederacy."[73]

During the first year of the war, Brownlow turned out repeated editorials criticizing the Confederacy. By the end of the year, authorities had seen enough and he was jailed on a charge of treason. In the last issue before his arrest, Brownlow wrote that Confederate officials wanted to "dry up, break down, silence, and destroy the last and only Union paper left in the eleven seceded States, and thereby to keep from the people of East Tennessee the facts which are daily transpiring in the country." Brownlow argued that suppressing the *Whig* violated the freedom of the press guaranteed by the Confederate constitution. "I shall in no degree feel humbled by being cast into prison . . . but, on the contrary, I shall feel proud of my confinement," he wrote. "I shall go to jail . . . for my *principles.*"[74]

Brownlow prepared to be hanged, but Confederate officials decided to banish him to the North instead. On March 15, 1862, he was escorted under a flag of truce to the Union army lines. He stayed in Nashville briefly and then went on a speaking tour of Northern cities, including Cincinnati, Indianapolis, Chicago, and Philadelphia. Brownlow eventually settled in New Jersey where he wrote *Parson Brownlow's Book,* which included editorials and correspondence from the *Whig,* as well as a narrative of his time in jail. When Union troops occupied Knoxville, Brownlow returned home. He resurrected his newspaper, renaming it the *Whig and Rebel Ventilator,* and resumed his scorching criticism of the Confederacy.[75]

The peace movement in the South also led to the mobbing of the *North Carolina Standard.* As a staunch Unionist, editor William W. Holden had always been controversial in the state. One of his newspaper rivals even challenged him to a duel. Holden refused the invitation but when another editor called him a "poltroon," Holden assaulted him with a cane. Holden's support for peace starting in 1863 garnered the editor plenty of critics. Opponents claimed that leaders of the peace movement, such as Holden, were demoralizing the army and encouraging desertions. An alarmed Davis warned North Carolina Governor Zebulon Vance of the seriousness of the situation and said that Holden's activities might warrant prosecution. Vance said it would be a mistake to interfere with Holden or his newspaper, and he told Davis he would deal with the leaders of the peace movement in the state.[76]

In the meantime, Confederate army officers became concerned about the effect the *Standard's* calls for peace negotiations were having on morale. They sought unsuccessfully to stop the newspaper from circulating in camp. At regimental meetings, officers secured the passage of resolutions condemning Holden and the peace movement. A group of North Carolina troops, mainly officers, demanded that the *Standard* be suppressed and the peace movement dissolved. Holden charged that the resolutions were the product of a few officers who wanted to "prostrate our people at the feet of central power." He also claimed that the criticism of him in the army "has the implied if not direct sanction of the President and the Secretary of War." Ratcheting up the hysteria, he argued that if authorities tried to carry out the resolutions, the worst days of the French Revolution would be reenacted. "Civil Liberty will expire in the blood of our own people, and we shall have a reign of terror such as the world has never witnessed," Holden proclaimed.[77]

Georgia troops passing through Raleigh decided to take matters into their own hands. On the evening of September 9, a group of soldiers broke into the *Standard*'s office and scattered ink, paper, and type. Vance arrived and persuaded the troops to return to camp, probably preventing more destruction. But upon hearing the news, supporters of Holden retaliated against the *Standard*'s rival in the city, the *State Journal*, which had called for the newspaper to be suppressed. A worried Vance wired the president and threatened to recall North Carolina troops unless Confederate soldiers traveling through the state were ordered to not enter Raleigh. Less than a month after the violence, the *Standard* resumed publication; the *State Journal* never published again.[78]

An undaunted Holden continued his calls for peace. Then Davis suspended the writ of habeas corpus in the case of citizens resisting Confederate authority or "inciting others to abandon the Confederate cause." To demonstrate his outrage, Holden suspended publication of the *Standard*. He told a friend "that if I could not continue to print as a freeman I would not print at all, and I could not bear the idea of lowering and changing my tone." When the *Standard* resumed three months later, it was largely to promote Holden's campaign for governor of North Carolina. Holden had decided to run against Vance. However, his controversial calls for peace cost the editor and he was resoundingly defeated.[79]

FIVE

IMPACT OF THE WAR

The Civil War took a devastating toll on the South's press. No sooner had the fighting started, then newspapers and magazines in the 11 Confederate states experienced shortages of materials and staff that made publishing difficult, and, in many cases, impossible. As more and more areas of the Confederacy fell, newspapers in the captured cities and towns were taken over by Federal troops or wrecked. The shortages and closings continued to the point where less than half of the South's newspapers and magazines still were publishing at the end of the war.

At the same time, the war had a positive impact on numerous journalistic practices in the North and South. Reporting methods and writing styles employed by the press changed to better cover a war of great complexity and a vast scale. Newspapers also took advantage of 19th-century technological developments to get news of the fighting into the hands of more readers and far faster.

The war also had a major effect on the readership habits of many Americans. More than they had ever done before, citizens of the North and South turned to the press for news. With Americans fighting against Americans, the war was the biggest event in people's lives, and they could not get enough information about what was taking place. The war helped make the United States a nation of newspaper and magazine readers.

In the best of times, getting out a newspaper in the 19th century had never been easy. In the words of the *Carolina Spartan,* a good journalist needed "the constitution of a horse, obstinancy of a mule, independence of a wood-sawyer, pertinacity of a dun, endurance of a starving anaconda, impudence of a beggar . . . he must be a moving target for everybody to shout at, and is expected to know everything, and to assist busybodies, to pry into the business of his neighbors." The war made the task that much harder.[1]

The conditions under which the press of the South published had a great impact on the reporting and editorializing it could do. Like the rest of Southern society, newspapers and magazines dealt with continual material and manpower shortages, not to mention financial problems and the devastating effect of the fighting. At no time in American history had the press faced so many prolonged challenges in simply publishing.[2]

❧   ❧

Business in the South was hurt as soon as the war began, and newspapers felt the effect in the loss of advertising and circulation almost immediately. Advertising in many publications dropped off by a third or more. In the fall, the *Charleston Mercury* said it was reducing the size of the newspaper as a "measure of economy" and added, "In the present stagnation of trade, the advertising business, which is the sustaining element of newspaper incomes, has, in great measure, been cut off."[3]

The Confederate press also experienced shortages of materials and manpower starting in the early months of the war. The lack of suitable paper on which to print was particularly acute. Publishers published regular appeals for readers to save cotton rags and bring them to the newspaper offices to be made into paper. The *Augusta Chronicle & Sentinel* even put its appeal to verse, a portion of which read, "Save your rags, and save your tags, Save your good-for-nothing bags—Bring them to this office, soon. Bring them morning, evening or noon." Beginning in mid-1862, many publications began publishing half-sheets; by the following year, it was a common practice throughout the South. Editors also were forced to reduce the size of the paper they printed on to the point where, by the end of the war, some newspapers published on mere slips of paper.[4]

When regular paper was not available, editors printed on whatever paper they could find, including colored paper, brown wrapping paper, and, in a few cases, the back of wallpaper. The *Memphis Appeal* said newspapers never appeared in "so much variety as now . . . they are of all sizes and colors, and sometimes contain four pages, and sometimes two. They are short enough for a pocket handkerchief one day, and big enough for a table cloth another. They assume as many hues as Niagara in the sunshine, and are by turns blue, yellow, green, red, purple, grey, and common brown packing paper."[5]

One of the reasons for the shortage of paper was the small number of mills in the South. The exact number of paper mills is not certain, but one count noted that there were twelve mills in Virginia, five in Tennessee, four in South Carolina, two in North Carolina, and two in Georgia. The number dwindled during the war, and an especially damaging blow came in 1863 when a fire destroyed the Bath Paper Mills in South Carolina, at the time the largest in the South. The impact was felt almost immediately. The price of paper jumped $3 a ream and many newspapers were forced to cut their size. Others announced they were suspending publication of the afternoon edition.[6]

Scarcity of ink and type with which to print also was a problem for the Confederate press. Editors regularly complained about the quality of ink they were forced to use and some appealed to inventive members of the public to devise new sources. The *Atlanta Southern Confederacy* printed an appeal for help:

Printer's News Ink.
Who has any for sale?
Where is it?
What is the price?
Why don't somebody make it?
Nothing would pay better.
Where is ink made?
Address us immediately.

Near the end of 1864, *Savannah Republican* editor James Sneed wrote to President Davis complaining that the supply of type and nearly every other kind of material had been depleted "until we are now reduced to the necessity of printing a paper which, half the time, nobody can read." Sneed asked Davis for permission to ship 10 bales of cotton from Wilmington, North Carolina, to Nassau in a blockade runner. The editor promised to use the proceeds from the sale of the cotton to purchase materials for his newspaper. There is no record of Davis's response to the request or if Sneed followed through with his plan.[7]

Editors also faced the problem of finding enough skilled employees to get their newspaper out. When the war began, printers, clerks, correspondents, and editors joined the Confederate army in large numbers. The Macon *Telegraph* reported that less than a week after the attack on Fort Sumter, 9 of its 20 employees had enlisted. Ten members of the *Memphis Appeal*'s printing staff resigned to join a company in the city. Editors were among those who enlisted. According to the *Abbeville Press,* by the end of April 1861, at least 14 South Carolina editors had left their newspapers to join the military, including its own editor. Of the approximately 800 printers in the Confederacy in 1863, 75 percent had been or were in the army by June 1864, one newspaper estimated.[8]

Editors and publishers regularly appealed for anyone who knew how to operate printing equipment to join their staff. The *Atlanta Daily Intelligencer* carried the following advertisement in 1863: "A good Compositor, one who does not keep 'fashionable hours', can find a permanent 'sit' in this office. Those that are in the habit of getting intoxicated need not apply." By the end of the war, most editors were using all the resources at their disposal to publish. The staff of one Savannah newspaper included two disabled war veterans, two soldiers detailed by the government to work in the office because of their printing skills, and two women.[9]

Shortages of material and personnel—along with inflation of the Confederate currency—sent prices skyrocketing. In 1860 the *North Carolina Standard* said it was paying 10 cents per pound for paper and 25 cents per pound for ink. Printers were being paid $9 per week. Four years later, the *Standard* said it was paying $2 per pound for paper and $2 per pound for ink. Printers were being paid $60 per week.[10]

Demanding higher wages, printers in Atlanta went on strike in April 1864. For a week, the city's two major dailies, the *Daily Intelligencer* and the *Southern Confederacy,* were silenced. In their place, printers published their own daily publication, the *Atlanta Reveille. Daily Intelligencer* publisher Jared I. Whitaker complained that printers, who were demanding a 50 percent increase in wages, had given no warning that they might strike. "We will not dispute the necessity that prompted this act of theirs," he wrote. "But we did, and do now protest against the manner, the abruptness, the want of courtesy, that characterized the act—the denial of time to consider what they conceived to be a just demand, and the time selected for it." What prompted the strike to end, and whether the printers received an increase in wages, was never made clear, although it appears that few, if any, of the demands were met. In an editorial after the strike was over, Whitaker wrote that he was struggling simply to keep the *Daily Intelligencer* publishing and it would not be his fault if printers went on strike again. The *Columbus Times* sympathized with the plight of Atlanta's newspapers:

> There is one thing that seems certain, and that is that the face of the Atlanta press will be the fate of the Southern press if matters get much worse, or a cheaper system of labor cannot be devised. There are comparatively few Southern journals that are even now self-sustaining. The difficulties in the way of procuring printers will doubtless force upon publishers the necessity of employing girls and boys to do the work heretofore done by men.[11]

⤜∾⤛

Newspapers bore much of the higher costs for labor and materials, but they also passed some along to their readers and advertisers. The average annual subscription price of Confederate dailies at the beginning of the war was $5. By the spring of

1865, the price had risen to $120. Prices were rising so rapidly by this point, however, that most newspapers were taking subscriptions for only three months at a time, and some were quoting prices only for a month. In explaining the need to increase the subscription price of the *North Carolina Standard,* the editor said that in 1860 an annual subscription to the newspaper would buy "two bushels of corn, twenty pounds of bacon, twenty dozen of eggs, ten pounds of butter, a four-horse load of wood, a pair of servant's shoes, [and] twenty yards of cotton cloth." Four years later, he said, an annual subscription would only buy "a half bushel of corn, a pound and half of bacon, four dozen of eggs, two pounds of butter, a one-horse load of wood, [and] two yards and half of cotton cloth."[12]

Still another problem for the Confederate press was subscribers not paying their bills. The problem was not new and, in fact, had plagued newspapers in the North and South for years. But it became more pressing during the war. "Few there are on our books who do not owe us for one or more year's subscription," the *Southern Federal Union* announced. "Send us $2, $4, or $5, just [as close as] you think you can come to the nearest amount." Another newspaper said that on May 1 it had 1,300 subscribers. Since then, it had ceased sending the newspaper to 300 subscribers who were in arrears from two to seven years. Of 1,000 subscribers remaining, 700 were arrears from one to two years. Some newspapers used collection agents to track down delinquent subscribers, but the practice was never very effective. One collection agent noted that after making 117 calls, he had netted only $3.12. He noted that he had thrashed a few of the delinquents, but also admitted that on occasion, he " 'got licked like thunder' himself."[13]

With increasingly fewer subscribers able or willing to pay their bills, many editors, especially in rural areas, began accepting produce and other items in lieu of money. The practice of readers in Athens, Georgia, to pay for their newspaper with produce had become so popular by 1864 that the *Southern Watchman* began publishing a list of the prices it would allow in exchange for the paper. According to the list, corn, rye, peas and beans fetched $1 per bushel, butter and lard went for 15 cents per pound, and chickens got 15 cents each. The list concluded: "Thus, it will be seen, that a bushel and half of wheat, two bushels of corn or peas, or four gallons of sorghum syrup . . . will pay one year's subscription to the Southern Watchman."[14]

Advertisers also paid some of their bills by bartering. When one Confederate newspaper was captured at the end of the war, Federal troops found 37 boxes of tobacco, most likely received in trade. Many newspapers advertised their job-printing operations, which provided various amounts of income. Among the job printing done by the *Memphis Appeal* during the war were the minutes of the Alabama Baptist Association and the Confederate Press Association.[15]

Newspaper delivery had always been unreliable and the problems became worse during the war. In large cities, most newspapers were delivered by carriers but editors regularly published apologies to subscribers who did not get their paper the previous day. The post office delivered newspapers to readers living out of town. However, postal service in the Confederacy was notoriously poor. As early as 1862, one editor declared that the postal service was "the worst ever imposed upon patient and suffering people." The problems only got worse as the war continued. Editors, who relied on the mail for stories from correspondents and their newspaper exchanges, complained constantly and called for changes in the post office. The *Charleston Mercury* became so outraged at the poor mail service that the paper investigated the problem. It found that there was a two-in-one chance that mail transported by trains would not reach its destination in a timely manner.[16]

Bowing to the pressures, many Confederate editors sold, merged, or closed their publications. Because the record of Southern newspapers that published during the war is incomplete, it is impossible to give precise figures. Yet it is clear that during the first three years of fighting there was a steady attrition in the number of newspapers publishing. So many publications closed in Texas that the *Red Land Express* in San Augustine, mordantly joked about the situation:

> The days of the "Chronicles" are past; the shrill notes of the "Clarion" no more are heard; the stalwart strokes of the "Pioneer" have ceased to greet our ears; the "Banners" no longer unfurl their bright folds to the sun; the "Times" gave place to revolution; the "Enquirer" long ceased questioning; the "Printer" has yielded up the ghost, and there is not even an "Echo" to tell us where they have gone. We can but "Express" our deep grief at the early loss of our boon companions, and pray that our fate be not soon like theirs.[17]

The fate of the *Upson Pilot* in Thomasville, Georgia, was characteristic of many Southern newspapers, especially rural weeklies. The *Pilot*'s editor, G. A. Miller, joined the Confederate army after First Bull Run and was sent to Savannah. An associate took over operation of the newspaper, but he struggled in the face of limited circulation and a declining advertising base to get it out on a regular basis. By the end of the year, the *Pilot* was making desperate appeals for subscribers to pay their overdue bills, accepting everything from "firewood" to "goobers" in the place of cash. In the end it was not enough. Less than a year after the war started, the *Pilot* ceased publishing.[18]

Shortages of staff and materials also had an impact on Southern magazines. In just its second issue, the *Southern Illustrated News* ran an advertisement that said: "Wanted Immediately: Two competent wood engravers. The highest price ever paid in this country will be given to good artists." Apparently, few engravers applied because the magazine soon published another plea: "Wanted—Two Apprentices, to learn the Wood Engraving Business. Apply to the proprietors of the 'News'." The *Southern Illustrated News* repeatedly missed issues because of material shortages and equipment problems. The editors apologized for one missed issue saying that machinery had broken and they were unable to have any repairs made during the Christmas holidays.[19]

The loss of newspapers and magazines was a hardship for Southerners, many of whom had come to count on them for news of the war. Cornelia Phillips Spencer wrote in her diary that many people who had never before subscribed to more than their country weekly, considered the Richmond dailies a necessity during the war. She said there was "general anxiety to have the latest news . . . above all from the army." People besieged the post office wanting the "dingy half sheets." Newspapers from the North were even harder to come by. Spencer wrote that it was rare when a newspaper from New York made its way to her hometown of Chapel Hill, North Carolina. When one did appear, the newspaper "was sent from house to house until utterly worn out."[20]

❧

Another blow to the Southern press was the Union army. Starting in the summer of 1861, town and cities in the Confederacy began falling to Federal forces. Prominent citizens in the communities often fled, fearing their fate in the hands of the enemy. Because they had been among the most outspoken supporters of secession, newspaper editors believed they would be targeted for reprisals and many left just ahead of the Union troops. But others, either unwilling to face the hardships of refugee life or determined to protect their property, decided to stay and face the enemy.[21]

More than 100 Southern towns and cities were occupied as Federal army posts at one time or another during the war. They included New Orleans, Memphis, Nashville, Norfolk, Portsmouth, Alexandria, Jacksonville, Little Rock, Savannah, Charleston, and Wilmington. The Northern authorities that took control of cities often had stereotypes and preconceptions of the South. They also assumed that a large proportion of the people were loyal citizens subjugated by the slave interests, while the rest were ignorant pawns manipulated by secessionists. The first group must be freed from oppression and protected by Federal troops; the others must be enlightened and brought back to the Union. Authorities believed that newspapers could help achieve these goals, so they found Unionist editors to publish them, often Northern newsmen.[22]

The "Yankee" newspapers usually were printed from the offices of the old Confederate press. Many of the publications used names reflecting the fact they now served a community under Union control. The newspaper in Key West, Florida, was named the *New Era;* the one in Little Rock, the *Unconditional Unionist;* the one in Norfolk' the *New Regime;* the one in Wilmington the *Herald of the Union;* and the one in Beaufort, South Carolina, the *Free South.*[23]

Military authorities usually issued strict orders guiding the publishing of newspapers in occupied areas. Editors were ordered to expunge rebel sentiment from their newspapers and avoid any criticism of the Federal government or the military authorities. When the *Memphis Avalanche* implied that the rights of citizens had suffered under Union occupation, the provost marshal called the story "exceedingly objectionable" and ordered the paper suspended. It was only allowed to resume when the writer of the story resigned. After the capture of Savannah, General William T. Sherman permitted only two newspapers to be published in the city. He also declared that editors would "be held to the strictest accountability, and will be punished severely in person and property for any libelous publications, mischievous matter, premature news, exaggerated statements, or any comments whatever upon the acts of the constituted authorities."[24]

Even if no orders were issued, the new editors invariably declared their intent to publish only "loyal" sentiment. "We shall strive to do what we can for the Union, and for those who have left home and friends to serve and protect it," declared the editors of the *New Era.* "Our aim is to be useful to our country and to our fellow man." In their first issue, the Unionist editors of the *Charleston Courier* wrote that they intended to make it a "thoroughly loyal Union newspaper." The *Courier* would not avoid "a fair and candid" discussion of events, they announced but it would "henceforth be enlisted in the service of the Union Government and the advocacy of Union sentiments."[25]

The Federal army and War Department helped sustain many Unionist newspapers. With their pro-Union sentiment, the publications could not count on many local readers or advertisers. But local commanders bought space for military notices and advertisements. Federal soldiers often bought copies. The War Department also paid for the printing of general orders, government broadsides, and other documents.[26]

To their credit, the best Unionist newspapers tried to cover the news in their communities. That was the case in Savannah where little happening in the city seemed to escape the notice of the *Herald* and *Republican.* They announced ships arriving at the city's docks and new guests staying at the Pulaski House, Savannah's finest hotel. They reported the election of officers for the fire department's Ax, Hook, and Ladder Company. Court and crime news appeared regularly in the *Herald* and *Republican.* Virtually every day, the newspapers reported cases heard by the city's two provost courts. The *Republican* published the news that an army guard shot another Union soldier who had refused his order to stop and present his pass. The *Herald* also reported the escape of three prisoners who removed the wooden planks from their cell, tunneled out, and then climbed over the jail wall.

But many Unionist editors could not resist occasionally taking swipes at the South and the old Confederate press. Editors enjoyed printing jokes and puns that poked fun at the Confederacy. "A new State has been added to the Southern Confederacy," the *Examiner* in St. Augustine, Florida, told readers. "It is a doleful state." In Savannah, the *Herald* rarely missed the chance to insult the city's old Confederate newspapers, as well as the newspapers still publishing in the South. In its first issue, the *Herald* announced that it had been established on "the ruins of the old Savannah News, a fire-eating sheet with a worm-eaten office." In another issue, the editor bragged that for several days the *Herald* had been printed using fine new ink imported from the North. It was a big improvement over the "vile compound the rebels used," he wrote. The *Herald* described Southern newspapers as nothing more than a "hireling press," which had been under the thumb of the Confederate government since the beginning of the war. It claimed the South's press had purposely misrepresented the Union army as, "a horde of barbarians who have respected neither tottering age nor lisping childhood—who violated person and property with a savage wantonness that would shame Atilla and his savage horde." He said the kind treatment shown Savannah residents by Federal troops since the capture of the city showed how wrong the press had been about the North.[27]

In some cases, fleeing editors had to leave their newspapers behind and deal with the consequences of Union occupation. Editor Melvin Dwinell returned to Rome, Georgia, after the war to find the *Courier's* office wrecked and the presses stolen by Federal troops. Dwinell, who had been an officer in the Confederate army, wrote that he found, "[s]tands, tables, cases, presses, stores and stove pipe, imposing stone, cabinets, racks and everything else all turned topsy-turvey." The office had been "beaten to pieces with sledge hammers and crow-bars until [it] looked like the Demons from the Infernal Region had been holding high carnival in there," he wrote. After capturing Columbus, Georgia, in the final weeks of the war, Federal troops wrecked two of the city's newspapers, the *Sun* and the *Times.* For unknown reasons, the office of their competitor, escaped unharmed. In Richmond, the *Dispatch, Enquirer,* and *Examiner* were burned in the fire that destroyed a significant portion of the city. Only the *Whig* survived the blaze.[28]

In other cases, newspaper staffs managed to escape ahead of the Union forces, often with at least some of their presses and supplies. The staffs of Milledgeville's two newspapers, the *Confederate Union* and *Southern Recorder,* hid their presses and equipment before Union forces captured Georgia's capital in 1864. The editor and nine employees of the *Mobile Register and Advertiser* were among a group of residents that fled just ahead of the Union army's occupation of Mobile. They took with them four power presses and all the ink and paper they could carry. The *Charleston Mercury* was not as lucky. The newspaper suspended publication in early 1865 and moved out of the city before it fell. The staff considered resuming the *Mercury* in Augusta, Georgia, but the press and other equipment were destroyed at the railroad junction in Charleston.[29]

Refugee newspapers in Knoxville, Tennessee; Huntsville, Alabama; Galveston, Texas, and other cities managed to escape and resume publishing in other locations, often doing so from train boxcars or abandoned buildings. As Chattanooga, Tennessee, was being shelled in 1863, the editors of the *Chattanooga Rebel* put the newspaper's presses and equipment on a train and sent them south to Marietta, Georgia, where the newspaper was published for several months. When Union forces threatened Marietta in the spring of 1864, the *Rebel* moved south to Griffin, Georgia, where it resumed publishing. And when Griffin was in danger of being captured, the *Rebel* moved one more time, this time to Selma, Alabama. There it was captured by Union troops in the closing weeks of the war. The soldiers used the *Rebel*'s press to print several issues of the *Yankee Cavalier*. Then before leaving Selma, soldiers wrecked the press and burned three files of the *Rebel*.[30]

The *Memphis Appeal* moved so many times that it became known as the "Moving Appeal." Benjamin F. Dill and John R. McClanahan, the editors and owners of the *Appeal*, were prepared for the fall of their city and were determined to escape rather than face the censorship that newspapers in other captured cities endured. On the evening of June 5, 1862, as the Federal fleet assembled to sail into the almost defenseless city, the staff published the last edition of the *Appeal* to appear in Memphis. Then they loaded their press and other equipment on a train bound for Grenada, Mississippi. Three days later, a two-page edition of the *Appeal* appeared bearing a Granada dateline. An editorial explained the newspaper's reason for leaving Memphis: "Our fate is indissolubly connected with that of the Confederacy. . . . The Appeal will not swerve from its course, come what will, no matter how great the sacrifices we may find it necessary to make."[31]

For five months, the *Appeal* published from Grenada. Only one member of the staff, a native of the North without strong ties to Confederacy, refused to flee with the newspaper. The *Appeal* had always been read in Grenada. It continued publishing news of the war, including news from Memphis copied from the papers still publishing in the city. But when Union advances threatened northern Mississippi in November, the *Appeal* packed up and moved south again, this time to Jackson.[32]

In their third home, Dill and McClanahan promised to "remain at our posts until hope is gone—until we know our foes will triumph." After hearing of the newspaper's new home, other editors expressed their delight. "[T]he best newspaper in the Confederate states, re-appears from Jackson, and it does us good to see its sparkling face again," said the *Houston Telegraph*. The *Appeal* kept its promise and continued publishing until May 14, 1863, the same day Federal troops entered the Mississippi capital. Once again, the *Appeal* managed to escape just ahead of the "disappointed Yankees," as the editors bragged. They were also proud to report that "as was anticipated, early inquiries were made by the enemy as to our whereabouts, and they were not slow in expressing their rage at our escape."[33]

The *Appeal*'s staff made a circuitous journey via Mobile and Montgomery to Atlanta. The staff was now calling themselves "citizens of the Confederacy," and in the first edition from Atlanta the newspaper declared, "Whatever of service to the general cause we might be able to render, could be accomplished here as well as elsewhere."

The *Appeal* published from Atlanta for more than a year. Dill and McClanahan remained in charge. Most of the printing staff were former pressmen from New Orleans who joined after the *Appeal* fled from Memphis. Some of the staff stayed at hotels in Atlanta while others stayed at the *Appeal*'s office on Whitehall Street.[34]

Like all newspapers in the South, the *Appeal* dealt with shortages of paper and ink. But the newspaper had bought a new press and type before the war, so it was in better shape than many other papers. Even so, the *Appeal* had little advertising and depended mainly on circulation for its revenue. In Atlanta, the newspaper had a daily press run of 8,000 to 14,000 in the morning and 6,000 in the afternoon. When Federal troops reached the outskirts of Atlanta in the summer of 1864, the *Appeal*'s staff shipped most of their equipment to Montgomery. Some of the staff remained behind to publish daily bulletins from a small press, but in early September they too left Atlanta. By September 20, the *Appeal*'s staff had reassembled in Montgomery and was publishing again.[35]

The *Appeal* limped along in the final months of the war. Then in April, Dill and McClanahan made one last attempt to keep the newspaper from being captured. Shortly before Montgomery fell to Union troops, the staff scattered. A small press and most of the type went to Columbus, Georgia, and the large press and a small amount of type went to Macon. When a cavalry regiment found the *Appeal*'s equipment in a Columbus warehouse, they took it into the street and burned it. General James H. Wilson, who commanded the troops that captured Columbus and Montgomery, later recalled that "one of the most gratifying incidents" of the campaign was "the capture of a notorious Southern newspaper, known as The Memphis Appeal."[36]

⸙⸙⸙

On the other side, the Northern press did not suffer appreciably from the war. Newspapers and magazines lost hundreds of employees to the military, but with a far larger population, Union publications could more easily replace them. Shortages of paper and other printing materials were not a problem, except in the West, where some newspapers occasionally resorted to printing on whatever paper they could find. And while the newspapers in some communities in the North were disrupted by the fighting, particularly in the border states, it generally was short lived.[37]

In many respects the war was a boon to the Northern press. Across the Union, the circulation of newspapers and magazines increased as people sought news of the fighting. Numerous newspapers added afternoon editions to keep up with the demand for news. The *New York Herald* even published three afternoon editions at 1:30, 3:00, and 4:30. Sunday editions, which had been rare before the war because of long-standing practices about the Sabbath, were added in many cities. Extra editions also became commonplace during the war. On one newsworthy day during the Peninsula campaign, the *New York Tribune* published three "extras" in less than two hours.[38]

To meet the growth in circulation, some newspapers purchased new high-speed cylinder presses. The *Baltimore American* bragged about its "magnificent" new press, purchased in 1864, and the additional room built to accommodate the larger machine. "This new press has been running only for a few weeks, and already our circulation has so largely increased that it would have been utterly impossible for us to supply the present demand with our old press, which had outlived its usefulness in three years of service," the *American* said.[39]

Newspapers were sold everywhere during the war, including army camps. A Federal brigade commander in the Shenandoah Valley wrote, "In the messiest business one could hear the squeaking voice of the 'news boy' over the fusillade, crying 'New York Herald, New York Tribune.'" Many soldiers on both sides were avid newspaper readers, eager to get the latest news. A private with the 17th Mississippi wrote in his diary: "Spend much time in reading the daily papers & discussing the war question in general. We always close by coming to the conclusion that we will after much hard fighting succeed in establishing our independence." A Union officer described the popularity of newspapers when items were exchanged between the two sides during periods of truce. "[W]e sent sugar and old newspapers to them; they tobacco and newspapers to us," he wrote.[40]

The standards for reporting and writing generally rose during the war. The best editors in the North and South set high expectations for their correspondents. They wanted stories to be accurate, complete, and sent in a timely fashion. Reporters for the *New York Herald* were instructed: "In no instance, and under no circumstances, must you be beaten. . . . You will have energetic and watchful men to compete with. Eternal industry is the price of success. . . . Remember that your correspondence is seen by half a million personal daily and the readers of the Herald must have the latest news." And *New York Tribune* managing editor Sydney Gay reminded one correspondent that the *Tribune* was "a daily newspaper—or meant to be—& not a historical record of past events. Correspondents to be of any value must be prompt, fresh & full of facts."[41]

In terms of writing, the language used by the most talented correspondents on both sides generally was more direct and concise than earlier times. Certainly some newsmen resorted to stock phrases, including "eager for the fray" and "spoiling for a fight." But whereas many newsmen before the war wrote in a leisurely narrative style and often saved the most important information for the end, correspondents increasingly wrote in a more straightforward manner and often used leads that summarized the essential news. Some of the most effective writing during the war also had an outstanding descriptive quality.[42]

Reporters on both sides learned to evaluate news sources and depend on those who could be considered reliable. They also kept informed by making regular visits to key offices and developing relationships with sources inside the government and military. Correspondents learned that they could get news tips at a variety of places, including the telegraph office, restaurants, and railroad stations.

Certainly, unscrupulous and less-skilled correspondents on both sides produced numerous stories that were exaggerated, sensationalized, or simply incorrect. The result of conjecture, sloppy reporting, unfounded rumors, or downright lying, news stories claimed that General Stonewall Jackson was killed at Fredericksburg and accused General Irwin McDowell of being drunk at Bull Run, among many other things. Other stories incorrectly stated at various times that Vicksburg, Atlanta, Petersburg, Richmond, and other cities had fallen. Soldiers recognized the mistakes in many stories. "We have learned not to swallow anything that we see in the papers," a Union sergeant noted in his diary. "If half the victories we read of were true the Rebellion wouldn't have a leg to stand on." And General George Meade wrote to his wife: "Do not be deceived about the situation of affairs by the foolish dispatches of the papers. Be not over-elated by reported success, nor over-depressed by exaggerated rumors of failures."[43]

To their credit, the best correspondents corrected their mistakes in later stories or acknowledged what they had missed. After First Bull Run, correspondent Peter W. Alexander admitted that "no full, fair, and satisfactory account" of the battle had yet been written. Alexander then went on to list more than a dozen items that should have been included in his report, including "the brigade that first encountered the enemy . . . the position of the several batteries . . . [and] where the commanding generals were during the fight."[44]

The best newsmen for the North and South showed considerable enterprise in providing interesting, informative, and insightful stories during the long periods when the two armies were not fighting, what one editor called "the inner life of the army." The stories gave readers revealing pictures of entertainment, camp life, and religious ceremonies, as well as picket duty, military punishments, and executions. A Union correspondent described what soldiers did at night at camp: reading, playing cards, writing letters home, playing musical instruments, cooking food, and washing their clothes. He also told of the sounds heard: "Up through the night wails the bugle; along the valley rolls the beat of drums; down from the crags float, 'When this cruel war is over'." And a Confederate correspondent told how it was possible to tell from the dialect, mannerisms, and appearance of the troops in camp what state they were from. Virginians "are sure to use to use the word *indeed* unnecessarily," he wrote. "They . . . almost invariably respond 'yes *indeed*' or 'no *indeed*', as the case may be." On the other hand, he wrote, "soldiers from North Carolina say 'weins' or 'youins', instead of *we* or *our,* and *you* or *yours.*" The troops from Louisiana "are rather cosmopolitish [*sic*] in their manners, have a tinge of French friskiness and politeness, and are merry under all circumstances." And Texans, he wrote, have "a 'rough and ready' air of recklessness, and seem to really enjoy the excitement of fighting."[45]

Journalists during the war were in no way objective. Moreover, in an era when news and opinion often mixed, correspondents on both sides regularly injected their personal views, prejudices, and patriotic sentiments into stories. After the Union defeat at Fredericksburg, Murat Halstead of the *Cincinnati Commercial* wrote: "It can hardly be in human nature for men to show more valor, or Generals to manifest less judgment, than were perceptible on our side that day. . . . We did not take a battery or silence a gun. We did not reach the crest of the hights [*sic*] held by the enemy in a single place. . . . The occupation of Fredericksburg was a blunder." And a report in the *New York Tribune* declared that the enemy "has outgeneraled us." "This is the plain unvarnished truth; we have been whipped by an inferior forces of inferior men, better handled than our own."[46]

However, the most honest reporters on both sides did not ignore problems with the military or the administration of the war when they became apparent. Alexander wrote several blistering accounts of the poor treatment of wounded Confederate soldiers. He reported that many field surgeons performed their work sloppily, with seemingly little concern for the soldiers. "While engaged at the amputation table, many of them feel it to be their solemn duty, every time they administer brandy to the patient, to take a drink themselves," he wrote. Alexander also described the poor condition of hospitals in towns near the battlefields. "Invariably," he wrote, the hospitals were located in "the most noisy, dusty and dirty parts of town," while officers occupied fine homes in quiet areas. Whitelaw Reid described the issue of Union army officers who were political appointees. "The honest truth is that not one half of our volunteer officers in this department have any adequate conception whatever of the nature and responsibilities of their duties," Reid wrote in the fall of 1861. "The men are brave enough . . . but I believe also that there have been times within the last thirty-six hours, when five hundred regulars, properly handled, would have stampeded our whole force." Felix Gregory de Fontaine wrote about the lack of shoes and clothing for many Confederate soldiers. "There has been a criminal neglect somewhere in not supplying the army with shoes and clothing," he wrote in 1862. "At least a fourth of the troops are destitute of shoes. . . . If the General Government fails to take this matter in hand, let the noble women of the land do so and promptly. . . . Winter is approaching rapidly and a movement of this kind cannot take place too soon."[47]

The sheer volume of reporting impressed observers. "Every morning the latest intelligence streams forth—fresh, strong, and rather coarsely flavored—like new whiskey from a still," wrote a correspondent with London's *Morning Herald*. That attention to providing news of the war in all its many facets, albeit with numerous problems, made the press essential reading for Americans, both in the North and South. Oliver Wendell Holmes no doubt spoke for many when he wrote, "We must have something to eat, and the papers to read. Everything else we can do without.[48]

EPILOGUE

The assassination of President Lincoln at Ford's Theater on the evening of April 14, 1865, ended the celebrations over the Confederacy's surrender, and journalists rushed to report the shocking news. Newspapers across the country printed the initial dispatches from Secretary of War Stanton about the president's grave condition, many rushing out extra editions. Big multiple-deck headlines such as the one published by the *New York Times* summarized what was known:

AWFUL EVENT.

———

PRESIDENT LINCOLN SHOT BY AN ASSASSIN.

———

The Deed Done at Ford's Theatre Last Night.

———

THE ACT OF A DESPERATE REBEL.

———

The President Still Alive at Last Accounts.

———

No Hopes Entertained of His Recovery.

———

Attempted Assassination of Secretary Seward.

———

DETAILS OF THE DREADFUL TRAGEDY.

———

When Lincoln died the next day, newspapers printed the news and dressed their columns with thick black rules, in a sign of mourning. Some printed woodcut portraits of the president. The focus of news coverage quickly turned to actor John Wilkes Booth and his co-conspirators who had also planned to kill Vice President Andrew Johnson and Secretary of State Seward but only succeeded in wounding Seward. Booth had prepared a letter for publication in the *National Intelligencer* explaining the motives for the elaborate plot, but a friend to whom he entrusted the letter destroyed it.[1]

The assassination of the president challenged editorial writers to express in words the calamitous event. "Our heart stands almost still as we take our pen in hand to speak of the tragedy of last night," said the *National Intelligencer*. "We have no words at command." The *Burlington Free Press* remarked on how "an unseen Providence" had protected the president until the war ended. "Surely this is a day of grief such as this nation never saw before," the newspaper declared. Some publications in the North were quick to blame the Confederacy. "The death of the President must not be merely charged to the mad impulse of an infuriated assassin," said the *Harrisburg Telegraph*. "Booth is not the only man with blood on his hands." But others argued that the South should not be held responsible. "The thoughtless and the vicious may affect to derive satisfaction from the sudden and tragic close of the President's career, but every reflecting person will deplore the awful event," the *Richmond Whig* said. "God grant that it may not rekindle excitement or inflame passion again!"[2]

Editorial cartoonists for the illustrated weeklies were unable to capture the grief over Lincoln's assassination—or perhaps the magazines thought they were not the right venue to mourn the slain president. However, a two-page illustration in *Harper's Weekly* showed a grief-stricken Columbia weeping over the casket of Lincoln. Two small pictures on either side of the main illustration showed a Union soldier and sailor mourning.[3]

During the next several weeks, reporters, artists, and photographers recorded the rush of events. Artists recreated the assassination scene and the house across the street where the president died. They made illustrations of the farmhouse where Booth was killed by Union soldiers and portraits of the co-conspirators after they were captured. Artists also sketched the funeral in Washington and the trip across the country to the interment in Springfield. Cameramen made pictures of Ford's Theater, including the president's box and chair. They photographed several of the co-conspirators.

They also photographed Lincoln's funeral parade in Washington before it set off for Illinois, stopping at every city the president visited on his trip to the capital in 1861.[4]

Censorship continued during the funeral events. Photographer Jeremiah Gurney got permission to make pictures of the president's coffin in the New York City Hall. Gurney made a tasteful photograph of the open coffin with two officers standing at the head and foot. He was more than 40 feet from the casket and did not interfere with the solemnity of the occasion. However, when Stanton learned about the pictures he was furious and ordered the plates destroyed. The officer in charge of the events appealed to the secretary saying the photograph "did not strike me as objectionable under the circumstances it was done." Stanton was unmoved and the plates were destroyed, except for a single print that was hidden for decades.[5]

On the day Lincoln was buried, newspapers published more editorial tributes. The *Baltimore American* said the beloved president would remain in the country's memory forever. "He has exchanged the laurel wreath of time for the crown of immortality," it declared. And the *New York Tribune* was prophetic in declaring that Lincoln's grave would become a national shrine. "[H]e sleeps the sleep of the honored and just," the newspaper said, "and there are few graves which will be more extensively, persistently visited or bedewed with the tears of a people's prouder, fonder affection, that that of Abraham Lincoln."[6]

The coverage of the remarkable events reflected how the American press had evolved during the four years of the war. Newspapers reported the assassination news as quickly as possible. Illustrations and photographs provided a visual record of the events and key figures. Editorials sought to capture the grief and outrage about what happened. And the administration got out its own messages while putting restriction on some coverage. Meanwhile, a badly hobbled Southern press tried to keep up with the events, but most newspapers had only the space and ability to print the most important news. Even then, it was usually days late.

The American press came of age during the Civil War. Already popular before the fighting began, newspapers became essential reading for many citizens. Magazines also saw the foothold they had begun to establish grow during the war, thanks in large part to the popularity of the illustrated weeklies. At the same time, journalistic practices became more sophisticated to cover fighting on such a vast scale. Reporting and editing increasingly became a profession with its own set of standards. The editorial page remained popular to voice opinions and editorial cartoons earned a prominent place. Finally, photography emerged as an important tool in recording many news events.

The press would become even more essential, influential, and, sometimes, controversial throughout the rest of the 19th century. Newspapers, especially daily publications, continued to grow in number and size. Much of the growth took place in the West, which was becoming increasingly settled. The first newspaper chain was launched after the war, ushering in an important new era in press ownership. In the South, newspapers struggled to rebuild from the devastation of the fighting. While some publications eventually reopened, others never did. At the same time, a growing number of newspapers owned by blacks began to emerge after the war, serving the group of Americans perhaps in greatest need of a strong press and a group largely ignored by the mainstream press. By the end of the century, there were more than 100 black-owned publications.

After the war, the country's newspapers continued to distance themselves from political parties in order to serve the broader interests of an increasingly urbanized and industrialized society. A more profit-oriented press emphasized circulation and advertising. Newspapers provided more diverse content to appeal to a wider audience, putting a major emphasis on local news. They made even greater use of the telegraph to report the news faster. They also published more illustrations and experimented with page design that appealed visually to readers. With professional standards developing, newspapers increasingly emphasized balance and objectivity in reporting the news. And some publications took their watchdog role more seriously than ever.

The number of magazines also grew in size and number, thanks in part to more national advertising. The illustrated weeklies remained popular with readers as they continued to emphasize pictures and cartoons. But hundreds of new publications joined the lineup of magazines, many of them emphasizing illustrations. Some of the magazines were innovators in applying photographic processes to wood engravings. Additionally, a new group of talented writers, some of whom would go on to careers in literature, provided magazine content that was more relevant, interesting, and readable. More than 3,000 magazines were published in the United States by the end of the century.

Photographers recorded many of the major news events of the late 1800s, including the settlement of the West and the Plains Wars. Their vivid images remained popular with a public that more and more expected to see pictures of the news that they read about. The development of the halftone process at the end of the century finally permitted photographs to be published in newspapers and magazines, although it would be years before that was done extensively.

As with so many aspects of American life, journalism had been unalterably and forever changed by the Civil War. With the country embarking on a new era in its history, the press was in a better position to cover it.

NOTES

INTRODUCTION

1. Frank Luther Mott, *American Journalism: A History, 1690–1960* (New York: Macmillan, 1950), 283.

2. Quoted in Joyce Appleby, *Inheriting the Revolution: The First Generation of Americans* (Cambridge: Harvard University Press, 2000), 102–103.

3. Joseph C. G. Kennedy, *Preliminary Report on the Eighth Census, 1860* (Washington, D.C.: Government Printing Office), 101–102.

4. Allan Pred, *Urban Growth and City-Systems in the United States, 1840–1860* (Cambridge: Harvard University Press, 1968), 222.

5. Gerald J. Baldasty, *The Commercialization of News in the Nineteenth Century* (Madison: University of Wisconsin Press, 1992), 46–48; Michael Schudson, *Discovering the News: A Social History of American Newspapers* (New York: Basic Books, 1978), 14–31.

6. *Philadelphia North American,* March 1, 1847; *Springfield Republican,* July 17, 1844.

7. Thomas Kiernan, *The Road to Colossus: A Celebration of American Ingenuity* (New York: William Morrow, 1985), 120.

8. Frank Presbey, *The History and Development of Advertising* (Garden City, NY: Doubleday, 1929), 227–243.

9. Donald E. Reynolds, *Editors Make War: Southern Newspapers in the Secession Crisis* (Nashville: Vanderbilt University Press, 1966), 8.

10. Kennedy, *Preliminary Report on the Eighth Census,* 211–213.

11. Hazel Dicken-Garcia, *Journalistic Standards in Nineteenth-Century America* (Madison: University of Wisconsin Press, 1989), 106–115.

12. Lorman A. Ratner and Dwight L. Teeter Jr., *Fanatics & Fire-Eaters: Newspapers and the Coming of the Civil War* (Urbana: University of Illinois Press, 2003), 19–20, 32–33.

13. Quoted in Reynolds, *Editors Make War,* 216; Ratner and Teeter, *Fanatics & Fire-Eaters,* 89.

CHAPTER 1

1. J. Cutler Andrews, *The North Reports the Civil War* (Pittsburgh: University of Pittsburgh Press, 1955), 60–61; J. Cutler Andrews, *The South Reports the Civil War* (Princeton: Princeton University Press, 1970), 48–49.

2. *New York Times,* April 30, 1862.

3. *Columbus Enquirer,* September 8, 1863; quoted in Andrews, *The North Reports the Civil War,* 192; *Atlanta Southern Confederacy,* March 12, 1862.

4. Quoted in Patricia G. McNeely, Debra van Tuyll, and Henry H. Schulte, *Knights of the Quill: Confederate Correspondents and Their Civil War Reporting* (West Lafayette: Purdue University Press, 2010), 63; *Columbus Enquirer,* September 8, 1863.

5. *Charleston Courier,* May 20, 1862.

6. Bernard A. Weisberger, *Reporters for the Union* (Boston: Little, Brown, 1953), 288.

7. *Atlanta Southern Confederacy,* April 8, 1864.

8. Louis M. Starr, *Bohemian Brigade: Civil War Newsmen in Action* (New York: Alfred A. Knopf, 1954), 101; Andrews, *The North Reports the Civil War,* 73.

9. Weisberger, *Reporters for the Union,* 100.

10. Starr, *Bohemian Brigade,* 182–193.

11. Andrews, *The North Reports the Civil War,* 429, 539.

12. Weisberger, *Reporters for the Union,* 96; *New York Herald,* November 17, 1862.

13. McNeely, van Tuyll, and Schulte, *Knights of the Quill,* 238–246.

14. Justin E. Walsh, *To Print the News and Raise Hell! A Biography of Wilbur F. Storey* (Chapel Hill: University of North Carolina Press, 1968), 177–178.

15. Ford Risley, "Bombastic Yet Insightful: Georgia's Civil War Soldier Correspondents," *Journalism History* 24 (Autumn 1998): 104–111.

16. Ibid.

17. *Southern Banner,* May 27, 1863; *Atlanta Southern Confederacy,* January 24, 1862.

18. *Boston Herald; Philadelphia Inquirer,* July 18, 1862; *Atlanta Daily Intelligencer,* December 12, 1862; *Savannah Republican,* October 6, 1863.

19. Robert Luther Thompson, *Wiring a Continent: The History of the Telegraph in the United States, 1832–1866* (Princeton: Princeton University Press, 1947), 217–239; Richard Schwarzlose, *The Nation's Newsbrokers,* Vol. 1 (Evanston: Northwestern University Press, 1989), 79–121; Menahem Blondheim, *News over the Wires: The Telegraph and the Flow of Public Information in America, 1844–1897* (Cambridge: Harvard University Press, 1994), 11–67.

20. Victor Rosewater, *History of Cooperative News-Gathering in the United States* (New York: Appleton, 1936), 99–106; Schwarzlose, *The Nation's Newsbrokers,* 254–258; Starr, *Bohemian Brigade,* 336.

21. Blondheim, *News over the Wires,* 133–137; Schwarzlose, *The Nation's Newsbrokers,* 242–249.

22. *The Press Association of the Confederate States of America* (Griffin, GA: Hill & Swayze's Printing House, 1863), 29, 41; Ford Risley, "The Confederate Press Association: Cooperative News Reporting of the War," *Civil War History* 47 (September 2001): 222–239.

23. *The Press Association of the Confederate States of America,* 54.

24. Ibid., 9–10.

25. Andrews, *The North Reports the Civil War,* 1–5; Andrews, *The South Reports the Civil War,* 14–18; *Philadelphia Inquirer,* April 13, 1861.

26. *Richmond Dispatch,* April 16, 1861; *Columbus Times,* April 18, 1861.

27. McNeely, van Tuyll, and Schulte, *Knights of the Quill,* 46–50.

28. Andrews, *The North Reports the Civil War,* 80–81.

29. Andrews, *The South Reports the Civil War,* 81–87; Andrews, *The North Reports the Civil War,* 87–92.

30. Starr, *Bohemian Brigade,* 43–51; Andrews, *The North Reports the Civil War,* 94–96.

31. *Savannah Republican,* July 23, 1861.

32. Quoted in Andrews, *The North Reports the Civil War,* 97.

33. *Charleston Courier,* July 29, 1861 *Rome Courier,* August 13, 1861.

34. *New York Times,* September 30, 1861.

35. *New York Herald,* November 14, 1861.

36. Andrews, *The North Reports the Civil War,* 227; Starr, *Bohemian Brigade,* 90–93.

37. *New York Times,* March 14, 1862; quoted in Andrews, *The North Reports the Civil War,* 230–231.

38. Andrews, *The North Reports the Civil War,* 179–180; Andrews, *The South Reports the Civil War,* 145–147.

39. Bingham Duncan, *Whitelaw Reid: Journalist, Politician, Diplomat* (Athens: University of Georgia Press, 1975), 1–19; *Cincinnati Gazette,* April 14, 1862; Starr, *Bohemian Brigade,* 101–103.

40. *Savannah Republican,* April 14, 1862.

41. Andrews, *The South Reports the Civil War,* 149–151.

42. *New York Herald,* May 10, 1862; *New York Times,* May 8, 1862; Andrews, *The North Reports the Civil War,* 242.

43. Starr, *Bohemian Brigade,* 106.

44. Ibid., 113–114; *Philadelphia Inquirer,* July 19, 1862.

45. *Mobile Register and Advertiser,* May 22, 1862; *Memphis Appeal,* May 22, 1862.

46. *Rome Courier,* May 3, 1862.

47. Andrews, *The South Reports the Civil War,* 267–270; Starr, *Bohemian Brigade,* 129–132.

48. *Charleston Courier,* September 11, 1862.

49. *Augusta Chronicle & Sentinel,* September 9, 1862.

50. *Savannah Republican,* August 26, 186; *Mobile Register and Advertiser,* September 10, 1862.

51. Andrews, *The North Reports the Civil War,* 276–282; Starr, *Bohemian Brigade,* 142–148.

52. *Savannah Republican,* September 10, 1862.

53. Andrews, *The North Reports the Civil War,* 35–40.

54. Roy Basler, ed., *The Collected Works of Abraham Lincoln,* Vol. 3 (New Brunswick: Rutgers University Press, 1955), 27; William Henry Herndon and Jessie W. Weik, *Herndon's Lincoln: The True Story of a Great Life* (Chicago: Belford, Clarke & Co., 1889), 304; James E. Pollard, *The Presidents and the Press* (New York: Macmillan, 1947), 312–313; Robert S. Harper, *Lincoln and the Press* (New York: McGraw-Hill, 1951), 1–7; Allen Thorndike Rice, ed., *Reminiscences of Abraham Lincoln by the Distinguished Men of His Time* (New York: North American Review, 1888), 436.

55. Andrews, *The North Reports the Civil War,* 54–55; Starr, *Bohemian Brigade,* 152–158; Charles A. Dana, *Lincoln and His Cabinet* (Cleveland: De Vinne Press, 1896).

56. Andrews, *The North Reports the Civil War,* 40–49; Michael Burlingame, ed., *Lincoln Observed: Civil War Dispatches of Noah Brooks* (Baltimore: Johns Hopkins Press, 1998), 1–11.

57. David B. Sachsman, S. Kittrell Rushing, and Roy Morris Jr., eds., *Words at War: The Civil War and American Journalism* (West Lafayette: Purdue University Press, 2008), 293–305; Starr, *Bohemian Brigade,* 250.

58. Andrews, *The South Reports the Civil War,* 54–55.

59. Quoted in Andrews, *The South Reports the Civil War,* 287–288; Clement Eaton, *Jefferson Davis* (New York: Free Press, 1977), 234–235.

60. McNeely, van Tuyll, and Schulte, *Knights of the Quill,* 104–126.

61. *Mobile Register and Advertiser,* December 5, 1862.

62. *Richmond Enquirer,* December 15, 17, 1862.

63. *Mobile Register and Advertiser,* December 25, 1862.

64. *War of the Rebellion,* Series 1, 25 (Pt. 2): 300–301; Starr, *Bohemian Brigade,* 195–196.

65. Andrews, *The North Reports the Civil War,* 368–370; *New York Herald,* May 7, 9, 1863.

66. Quoted in Andrews, *The North Reports the Civil War,* 370.

67. Andrews, *The South Reports the Civil War,* 297–299; Augusta *Daily Constitutionalist,* May 14, 1863.

68. *Augusta Constitutionalist,* May 12, 1863; *Atlanta Daily Intelligencer,* May 12, 1863.

69. *Chicago Tribune,* June 23, 1863.

70. *Augusta Constitutionalist,* July 26, 1863.

71. *Savannah Republican,* July 10, 1863.

72. Andrews, *The South Reports the Civil War,* 309; Andrews, *The North Reports the Civil War,* 414–416.

73. *Augusta Constitutionalist,* July 23, 1863.

74. *Richmond Enquirer,* July 22, 1863; *New York Times,* July 8, 1863.

75. Andrews, *The North Reports the Civil War,* 429–430.

76. *Savannah Morning News,* July 8, 9, 1863; *Atlanta Daily Intelligencer,* July 9, 1863.

77. *Savannah Republican,* July 19, 1863.

78. Harper, *Lincoln and the Press,* 282–289.

79. Ibid.

80. Andrews, *The North Reports the Civil War,* 531; Starr, *Bohemian Brigade,* 297; *New York Tribune,* May 9, 1864.

81. *Richmond Dispatch,* May 19, 1864.

82. *Savannah Republican,* May 25, 1864; *New York Times,* May 18, 1864; Andrews, *The North Reports the Civil War,* 539.

83. John F. Marszalek, *Sherman's Other War* (Memphis: Memphis State University Press, 1981), 145, 163–165.

84. Andrews, *The North Reports the Civil War,* 553.

85. Ibid., 562–563.

86. *Atlanta Daily Intelligencer,* June 10, 1864; *Atlanta Southern Confederacy,* June 18, 1864.

87. *Columbus Times,* August 27, 1864.

88. *Augusta Chronicle & Sentinel,* September 6, 1864.

89. Marszalek, *Sherman's Other War,* 174–175; *Atlanta Daily Intelligencer,* November 18, 1864; *New York Herald,* December 28, 1864.

90. *Macon Telegraph and Confederate,* December 1, 1864.

91. Marszalek, *Sherman's Other War,* 176–177; *New York Herald,* March 18, 1865.

92. *Boston Journal,* March 3, 1865; *New York Tribune,* March 2, 1865.

93. Quoted in McNeely, van Tuyll, and Schulte, *Knights of the Quill,* 538; *Philadelphia Inquirer,* January 20, 1865.

94. Quoted in Doris Kearns Goodwin, *Team of Rivals: The Political Genius of Abraham Lincoln* (New York: Simon & Schuster, 2005), 717.

95. *Philadelphia Press,* April 6, 1865.

96. *New York Herald,* April 14, 1865.

97. Ida M. Tarbell, *A Reporter for Lincoln: The Story of Henry E. Wing, Soldier and Newspaperman* (New York: Book League of America, 1929), 76–77.

CHAPTER 2

1. Frank Luther Mott, *A History of American Magazines, 1850–1865* (Cambridge, MA: Harvard University Press, 1957), 43–45, 452–460, 469–476; W. Fletcher Thompson Jr., *The Image of War: The Pictorial Reporting of the American Civil War* (New York: Thomas Yoseloff, 1959), 19–24.

2. Joshua Brown, *Pictorial Reporting, Everyday Life, and the Crisis of Everyday America* (Berkeley: University of California Press, 2002), 35–40; Frederick E. Ray, *"Our Special Artist": Alfred R. Waud's Civil War* (Mechanicsburg: Stackpole, 1994), 27–28.

3. Thompson, *The Image of War,* 74–76.

4. Quoted in Judith Bookbinder and Sheila Gallagher, *First Hand: Civil War Drawings from the Becker Collection* (Chicago: University of Chicago Press, 2009), 47.

5. Thompson, *The Image of War,* 81–82; Bookbinder and Gallagher, *First Hand,* 29–31.

6. Brown, *Beyond the Lines,* 53–54.

7. Bob Zeller, *The Blue and Gray in Black and White: A History of Civil War Photography* (Westport, CT: Praeger), 4–5.

8. Martha A. Sandweiss, ed., *Photography in Nineteenth-Century America* (New York: Harry N. Abrams, 1991), 135–137.

9. Zeller, *Blue and Gray in Black and White*, 75–76.

10. Quoted in James D. Horan, *Mathew Brady: Historian with a Camera* (New York: Crown Publishers, 1955), 41.

11. *War of the Rebellion,* Series 2, 2 (Pt. 2): 286; J. Cutler Andrews, *The North Reports the Civil War* (Pittsburgh: University of Pittsburgh Press, 1955), 198.

12. *Harper's Weekly,* October 3, 1863.

13. Brown, *Beyond the Lines,* 53.

14. *Leslie's Illustrated,* January 5, 26, February 2, 9, March 9, 16, 30, 1861; *Harper's Weekly,* January 19, 26, February 16, 23, March 9, 16, 23, 1861.

15. *Leslie's Illustrated,* April 27, May 11, 1861; *Harper's Weekly,* April 27, May 4, 1861; *New York Illustrated News,* April 27, May 4, 1861.

16. Zeller, *Blue and Gray in Black and White,* 31–37; *Harper's Weekly,* March 23, 1861.

17. Ibid., 42–46.

18. Michael L. Carlebach, *The Origins of Photojournalism in America* (Washington, D.C.: Smithsonian Institution Press, 1972), 70–72; quoted in Sandweiss, *Photography in Nineteenth-Century America,* 143; William C. Davis, ed., *Touched by Fire: A Photographic Portrait of the Civil War,* vol. 1 (Boston: Little, Brown, 1985), 165–191; William C. Davis, ed., *Touched by Fire: A Photographic Portrait of the Civil War,* vol. 2 (Boston: Little, Brown, 1986), 159–198.

19. Mary Panzer, *Mathew Brady and the Image of History* (Washington, D.C.: Smithsonian Institution Press, 1997), 9–21.

20. Thompson, *The Image of War,* 31–34; Panzer, *Mathew Brady,* 102–103.

21. D. Mark Katz, *Witness to an Era: The Life and Photographs of Alexander Gardner* (New York: Viking, 1991), 3–7, 14–18.

22. Carlebach, *Origins of Photojournalism,* 72.

23. *Harper's Weekly,* April 27, May 4, 11, 1861.

24. Thompson, *The Image of War,* 35–36; *Harper's Weekly,* May 18, 25, June 8, 15, 1861.

25. Thompson, *The Image of War,* 30.

26. Ray, *Our Special Artist,* 11–14.

27. *Illustrated News,* July 29, August 5, 1861; *Harper's Weekly,* August 3, 10, 17, 1861, *Leslie's Illustrated,* July 27, August 3, 1861.

28. Carlebach, *Origins of Photojournalism,* 77; Sandweiss, *Photography in Nineteenth-Century America,* 139.

29. Zeller, *Blue and Gray in Black and White,* 58–62.

30. *Harper's Weekly,* October 5, 12, November 2, 1861; *Leslie's Illustrated,* September 14, October 5, 1861.

31. *Illustrated News,* October 2, 1861; Ray, *Our Special Artist,* 27.

32. *Harper's Weekly,* October 12, 19, 26, November 9, 1861.

33. Brown, *Beyond the Lines,* 50; Thompson, *The Image of War,* 23.

34. Starr, *Bohemian Brigade,* 242; Thompson, *The Image of War,* 23.

35. Thompson, *The Image of War*, 62–63; *Harper's Weekly*, June 22, 1861, August 31, 1861, February 1, March 1, 1862.

36. Thompson, *The Image of War*, 66–68; *Leslie's Illustrated*, March 1, 8, 15, 1862; *Harper's Weekly*, March 1, 8, 15, 22, 1862.

37. Thompson, *The Image of War*, 70–73; *Leslie's Illustrated*, May 3, 10, 17, 1862; *Harper's Weekly*, May 3, 1862.

38. Thompson, *The Image of War*, 69; *Harper's Weekly*, May 24, 1862.

39. James D. Horan, *Mathew Brady: Historian with a Camera* (New York: Crown Publishers, 1955), 40.

40. Zeller, *Blue and Gray in Black and White*, 67–69.

41. Ibid., 68.

42. *New York Times*, July 21, 1862.

43. William A. Frassanito, *Antietam: The Photographic Legacy of America's Bloodiest Day* (New York: Charles Scribner's, 1978); Zeller, *Blue and Gray in Black and White*, 72–77.

44. *Harper's Weekly*, October 18, 1862; *New York Times*, October 20, 1862; *Atlantic Monthly*, July 1863.

45. Katz, *Witness to an Era*, 50–51; Zeller, *Blue and Gray in Black and White*, 101–102.

46. Forbes quoted in Zeller, *Blue and Gray in Black and White*, 72–73; *Harper's Weekly*, October 11, 18, 1862; *Leslie's Illustrated*, October 18, 1862.

47. *Harper's Weekly*, August 26, 1862, June 13, 1863.

48. *Harper's Weekly*, December 13, 20, 27, 1862.

49. Thompson, *The Image of War*, 127–128; See, for example, *Harper's Weekly*, July 20, August 31, December 28, 1861, January 4, August 16, 1862, January 3, September 26, November 7, 1863.

50. Philip C. Beam, *Winslow Homer's Magazine Engravings* (New York: Harper & Row, 1979); Lloyd Goodrich, *Winslow Homer* (New York: Macmillan, 1944); David Tatham, *Winslow Homer and the Pictorial Press* (Syracuse: Syracuse University Press, 2003); *Harper's Weekly*, December 21, 1861, January 24, July 12, November 29, 1862, February 28, 1863.

51. *Harper's Weekly*, December 21, 1861; Hermann Warner Williams Jr., *The Civil War: The Artist's Record* (Boston: Beacon Press, 1961), 17–18.

52. Thompson, *The Image of War*, 153–155; *Harper's Weekly*, February 14, 1863, January 30, February 6, 27, 1864.

53. Bookbinder and Gallagher, *First Hand*, 75–106; *Harper's Weekly*, December 21, 1861, January 18, 1862, January 23, March 12, 1864.

54. *Harper's Weekly*, January 31, February 21, 1863.

55. *Leslie's Illustrated*, May 21, 1863.

56. Charles Hamilton and Lloyd Hostendorf, *Lincoln in Photographs: An Album of Every Known Pose* (Norman: University of Oklahoma Press, 1963), ix–x.

57. Katz, *Witness to an Era*, 107–116.

58. Ibid., 116–129.

59. Zeller, *Blue and Gray in Black and White*, 144–147.

60. Thompson, *The Image of War,* 115–120; *Harper's Weekly,* June 20, 27, July 4, 11, 18, 25, 1863.

61. Andrews, *The North Reports the Civil War,* 413; Thompson, *The Image of War,* 122.

62. Ray, *Our Special Artist,* 42–43; *Harper's Weekly,* July 25, August 8, 15, 22, 1863; *Leslie's Illustrated,* July 18, 25, 1863.

63. Katz, *Witness to an Era,* 61–69; Zeller, *The Blue and Gray in Black and White,* 106–108.

64. William A. Frassanito, *Gettysburg, A Journey in Time* (New York: Scribner's, 1975), 24–34; Katz, *Witness to an Era,* 64–71.

65. Frassanito, *Gettysburg,* 35–40; Zeller, *Blue and Gray in Black and White,* 110–112.

66. Frassanito, *Gettysburg,* 41–48.

67. Zeller, *Blue and Gray in Black and White,* 88–99.

68. Ibid.

69. Ibid., 120–121.

70. Ibid., 125–128, 131–133.

71. Sandweiss, *Photography in Nineteenth-Century America,* 139.

72. Horan, *Timothy O'Sullivan,* 22; William A. Frassanito, *Grant and Lee: The Virginia Campaigns* (New York: Scribner's 1983), 78–79, 113–114.

73. Frassanito, *Grant and Lee,* 116–121.

74. Thompson, *The Image of War,* 142–147; Ray, *Our Special Artist,* 47–48; *Harper's Weekly,* June 4, 11, 18, 25, July 9, 16, August 6, 13, 1864.

75. Frassanito, *Grant and Lee,* 172–175.

76. Ibid., 258–259, 282–287, 307–311.

77. Zeller, *Blue and Gray in Black and White,* 144–147.

78. Ibid., 148–149.

79. Bookbinder and Gallagher, *First Hand,* 56–57.

80. *Harper's Weekly,* July 2, August 27, September 3, January 7, 14, 21, 1865.

81. *Harper's Weekly,* March 4, 11, 18, 25, April 1, 8, 1865.

82. Zeller, *Blue and Gray in Black and White,* 173–174; Thompson, *The Image of War,* 179–181.

83. Thompson, *The Image of War,* 181–182; *Harper's Weekly,* April 22, 1865; *Leslie's Illustrated,* April 22, 29, 1865.

84. Frassanito, *Grant and Lee,* 388–410.

85. Horan, *Timothy O'Sullivan,* 54; Thompson, *The Image of War,* 225.

86. Frassanito, *Grant and Lee,* 416–418.

CHAPTER 3

1. *New York Times,* June 9, 1863.

2. Culver H. Smith, *The Press, Politics, and Patronage: The Government's Use of Newspapers, 1789–1875* (Athens: University of Georgia Press, 1975); Hazel Dicken-Garcia, *Journalistic Standards in Nineteenth-Century America* (Madison: University of Wisconsin Press, 1989).

3. Allan Nevins and Frank Weitnkampf, *A Century of Political Cartoons: Caricature in the United States from 1800 to 1900* (New York: Octagon Books, 1975), 9–18; J. G. Lewin and

P. J. Huff, *Lines of Contention: Political Cartoons of the Civil War* (Washington: HarperCollins, 2007), vii–xi.

4. *Boston Advertiser,* April 15, 1861; *Montgomery Advertiser,* April 13, 1861; *Memphis Appeal,* April 14, 1861.

5. *Daily Times,* April 13, 1861; *Knoxville Whig,* April 27, 1861.

6. *New York Times,* April 16, 1861, *Augusta Chronicle & Sentinel,* April 18, 1861.

7. *Philadelphia Public Ledger,* June 7, 1861; *National Anti-Slavery Standard,* April 27, 1861.

8. *Charleston Mercury,* April 19, 1861; *New Orleans Daily Picayune,* July 4, 1861.

9. *Daily Palladium,* April 29, 1861; *New Orleans Bee,* May 1, 1861.

10. *North Carolina Standard,* April 24, 1861; Donald E. Reynolds, *Editors Make War: Southern Newspapers in the Secession Crisis* (Nashville: Vanderbilt University Press, 1966), 205–206.

11. Joel H. Sibley, *A Respectable Minority: The Democratic Party in the Civil War Era, 1860–1868* (New York: Norton, 1977); quoted in Robert S. Harper, *Lincoln and the Press* (New York: McGraw-Hill, 1951), 195.

12. *New York Tribune,* June 26, 1861; Ralph Ray Fahrney, *Horace Greeley and the Tribune in the Civil War* (Cedar Rapids: Torch Press, 1936), 80–84; *Charleston Mercury,* June 1, 1861.

13. *Philadelphia Inquirer,* July 25, 1861; *Baltimore American,* July 22, 1861, *New York Tribune,* July 25, 1861; quoted in Gilbert H. Muller, *William Cullen Bryant: Author of America* (Albany: State University of New York Press, 2008), 265; Fahrney, *Horace Greeley and the Tribune in the Civil War,* 85–90.

14. *Memphis Appeal,* July 23, 1863; *Richmond Examiner,* July 26, 1861.

15. Ford Risley, *Abolition and the Press: The Moral Struggle against Slavery* (Evanston: Northwestern University Press, 2008), 160–162; *Douglass' Monthly,* July 1861.

16. *Liberator,* December 6, 1861; *Douglass' Monthly,* October 1861.

17. *New York Tribune,* August 20, 1862; *National Intelligencer,* August 23, 1862; Allen C. Guelzo, *Lincoln's Emancipation Proclamation: The End of Slavery in America* (New York: Simon and Schuster, 2004), 130–137.

18. *New York Tribune,* September 23, 1862; *Chicago Tribune,* September 23, 1862; *Douglass' Monthly,* October 1862.

19. *Chicago Times,* September 24, 1862; *New York World,* September 24, 1862.

20. *Augusta Chronicle & Sentinel,* October 3, 1862.

21. Carl R. Osthaus, *Partisans of the Southern Press: Editorial Spokesman of the Nineteenth Century* (Lexington: University Press of Kentucky), 76–94, 101–117.

22. *Augusta Chronicle & Sentinel,* September 9, 1862; *World* and *Tribune* quoted in Fahrney, *Horace Greeley and the Tribune in the Civil War,* 103–104.

23. Harry J. Carmann and Reinhard H. Luthin, *Lincoln and the Patronage* (New York: Columbia University Press, 1943), 118–129; Harper, *Lincoln and the Press,* 77.

24. *Morning Chronicle,* December 7, 1864; Harper, *Lincoln and the Press,* 181–182.

25. *Sunday Morning Chronicle,* March 31, 1861, February 2, June 22, 1862; Ford Risley, "The President's Editor: John W. Forney of the *Press* and *Morning Chronicle,*" *American Journalism* 26 (Fall 2009): 63–85.

26. Clement Eaton, *Jefferson Davis* (New York: Free Press, 1977), 234–235.

27. *North Carolina Standard,* November 5, 1862.

28. *Dubuque Herald,* October 8, 1862; *Jonesboro Gazette,* September 27, 1862.

29. *Chicago Tribune,* November 10, 1862; *New York Times,* November 7, 1862.

30. *Richmond Examiner,* November 15, 1862; *Charleston Mercury,* November 10, 1862.

31. *War of the Rebellion,* Series 1, 23 (Pt. 2): 237; Frank L. Klement, *The Limits of Dissent: Clement L. Vallandigham and the Civil War* (Lexington: University Press of Kentucky, 1970), 87–95.

32. *Dubuque Herald,* May 10, 1863; *Chicago Times,* May 27, 1863; *Chicago Tribune,* March 7, 1863; *New York Times,* May 13, 1863.

33. Quoted in Sachsman, Rushing, and Morris, *Words at War,* 198.

34. William C. Harris, *William Woods Holden: Firebrand of North Carolina Politics* (Baton Rouge: Louisiana State University Press, 1987), 127–155; *North Carolina Standard,* June 19, 1863; *Augusta Chronicle & Sentinel,* November 8, 1864.

35. Quoted in Harris, *William Woods Holden,* 131–132; *Augusta Chronicle & Sentinel,* November 8, 1864; *Southern Recorder,* October 4, 1864; *New York Herald,* November 4, 1864.

36. Quoted in Bell I. Wiley, "Soldier Newspapers of the Civil War," *Civil War Times Illustrated* 16 (July 1977): 22–23; quoted in Chandra Manning, *What this Cruel War was Over: Soldiers, Slavery, and the Civil War* (New York: Alfred A. Knopf, 2007), 124.

37. Wiley, "Soldier Newspapers of the Civil War," 25–26; Manning, *What this Cruel War was Over,* 114, 42.

38. Wiley, "Soldier Newspapers of the Civil War," 24–25.

39. Ibid., 27–29.

40. *New York Times,* July 7, 1863.

41. *Charleston Courier,* July 14, 1863; *Augusta Chronicle & Sentinel,* July 15, 1863.

42. *North Carolina Standard,* April 9, 1862; *Atlanta Daily Intelligencer,* March 15, 1864.

43. *Chicago Tribune,* May 16, 1863; *Cleveland Plain Dealer,* February 19, 1863.

44. Adrian Cook, *The Armies of the Night: The New York City Draft Riots of 1863* (Lexington: University Press of Kentucky, 1974).

45. *New York World,* July 14, 1863; *New York Tribune,* July 14, 1863; *Richmond Examiner,* July 18, 1863.

46. *Atlanta Daily Intelligencer,* March 15, 1864.

47. Dudley Taylor Cornish, *The Sable Arm: Negro Troops in the Union Army, 1861–1865* (New York: W. W. Norton, 1966); *Douglass' Monthly,* March 1863; *Democratic Watchman,* March 6, 1863.

48. *National Anti-Slavery Standard,* August 8, 1863; *New York Tribune,* September 8, 1863.

49. John C. Waugh, *Reelecting Lincoln: The Battle for the 1864 Presidency* (New York: Crown, 1997).

50. *Philadelphia Inquirer,* June 9, 1864; *Cleveland Plain Dealer,* September 8, 1864.

51. *Chicago Times,* July 4, 1864; reprinted in *Crisis,* February 17, 1864.

52. *Augusta Chronicle & Sentinel,* September 18, 1864; *Mobile Register and Advertiser,* March 11, 1864.

53. *Springfield Republican,* November 10, 1864; *Richmond Examiner,* November 11, 1864.

54. *Morning Chronicle,* October 5, 1862; *Albany Patriot,* June 9, July 13, 1864; *Atlanta Daily Intelligencer,* May 19, 1864; see generally, Alan Bussel, "The Atlanta Daily Intelligencer Covers Sherman's March," *Journalism Quarterly* 51 (1974): 405–410.

55. *Baltimore American,* September 8, 1864, *Columbus Times,* September 9, 1864.

56. *Southern Federal Union,* September 3, 1861; *Confederate Union,* December 6, 1864.

57. *New York Tribune,* December 26, 1864; *Richmond Examiner,* December 27, 1864.

58. *Daily Sun,* December 31, 1864; quoted in William Warren Rogers Jr. *Confederate Home Front: Montgomery during the Civil War* (Tuscaloosa: University of Alabama Press, 1999), 126; *Augusta Constitutionalist,* December 30, 1864.

59. Robert F. Durden, *The Gray and the Black: The Confederate Debate on Emancipation* (Baton Rouge: Louisiana State University Press, 1972); *Richmond Enquirer,* October 6, 1864; *Richmond Examiner,* November 8, 1864.

60. *Atlanta Daily Intelligencer,* September 29, 30, 1864.

61. *Philadelphia Inquirer,* November 11, 1864; *New York Herald,* March 1, 1865.

62. *Boston Advertiser,* May 4, 1865; *New York Herald,* April 5, 1865.

63. *New York Times,* April 10, 1865.

64. *National Intelligencer,* April 12, 1865; *Albany Patriot,* April 27, 1865.

65. *North Carolina Standard,* April 17, 1865; *Augusta Chronicle & Sentinel,* April 20, 1865.

66. *Harper's Weekly,* May 4, 1861.

67. Kristen Smith, ed., *The Lines are Drawn: Political Cartoons of the Civil War* (Athens: Hill Press, 1999), xi–xii; Nevins and Weitnkampf, *A Century of Political Cartoons,* 12–18.

68. *Harper's Weekly,* June 8, 1861.

69. *Harper's Weekly,* September 14, 1861, November 8, 1862.

70. Smith, ed., *The Lines are Drawn,* 35; *Southern Illustrated News,* September 19, 1863, April 23, 1864.

71. *Harper's Weekly,* October 26, 1861, March 15, June 7, 1862.

72. *Harper's Weekly,* September 7, 1861, August 30, 1862.

73. *Harper's Weekly,* April 19, 1862.

74. Morton Keller, *The Art and Politics of Thomas Nast* (New York: Oxford University Press), 3–13.

75. *Harper's Weekly,* January 24, February 7, December 5, 1863, January 2, 1864.

76. *Harpers' Weekly,* September 3, 1864.

77. *Leslie's Illustrated,* February 1, 22, 1862; *New York Illustrated News,* September 13, 1862; December 20, 1862.

78. *Southern Illustrated News,* January 31, February 28, 1863; February 27, 1864.

79. *Harper's Weekly,* January 3, December 7, 1863.

80. *New York Illustrated News,* July 15, 1861; *Leslie's Illustrated,* December 6, 1862, April 1, 1865.

81. *Leslie's Illustrated,* October 25, 1862, December 5, 1863; *Harper's Weekly,* July 18, August 22, 1863.

82. *Southern Illustrated News,* November 8, 1862, March 14, 1863; Smith, ed., *The Lines are Drawn,* 103.

83. *Harper's Weekly,* February 28, August 1, 1863; *Leslie Illustrated,* June 20, August 29, 1863.

84. *Harper's Weekly,* September 17, November 12, 26, 1864; *Leslie's Illustrated,* October 29, 1864.

85. *Harper's Weekly,* February 18, 1865; *Leslie's Illustrated,* January 14, April 22, 1865.

86. *Harper's Weekly,* April 22, 1865; *Leslie's Illustrated,* June 3, 1865.

87. *Harper's Weekly,* May 27, 1865.

CHAPTER 4

1. *Harper's Weekly,* August 3, 1861.

2. Tom Reilly, "Newspaper Suppression during the Mexican War," *Journalism Quarterly* 54 (Summer 1977): 262–270.

3. Jeffery A. Smith, *War & Press Freedom: The Problem of Prerogative Power* (New York: Oxford Press, 1999), 99–100.

4. *War of the Rebellion,* Series 3, 1: 324; J. Cutler Andrews, *The North Reports the Civil War* (Pittsburgh: University of Pittsburgh Press, 1955), 95.

5. J. Cutler Andrews, *The South Reports the Civil War* (Princeton: Princeton University Press, 1970), 529.

6. *Richmond Enquirer,* July 1, 1861.

7. *Mobile Register and Advertiser,* July 7, 1861.

8. Quoted in Andrews, *The South Reports the Civil War,* 79.

9. *New York Times,* July 24, 1861.

10. Andrews, *The North Reports the Civil War,* 151.

11. Richard Kielbowicz, "The Telegraph, Censorship, and Politics at the Outset of the Civil War," *Civil War History* 35 (1994): 95–118.

12. Ibid.

13. March 20, 1862, 37th Congress, 2nd. Session, House Reports, vol. 3, no. 64, 1–8, 13; Smith, *War and Press Freedom,* 100–101.

14. *War of the Rebellion,* Series 3, 1: 879, 899.

15. Quoted in Andrews, *The South Reports the Civil War,* 103.

16. Quoted in Donna Lee Dickerson, *The Course of Tolerance: Freedom of the Press in Nineteenth-Century America* (Westport, CT: Greenwood Press, 1990), 158.

17. *Richmond Dispatch,* December 30, 1861; Andrews, *The South Reports the Civil War,* 162.

18. Andrews, *The South Reports the Civil War,* 162–163.

19. *Memphis Appeal,* April 27, 1862; Andrews, *The South Reports the Civil War,* 149–150.

20. Andrews, *The North Reports the Civil War,* 182–188.

21. Ibid., 194–195.

22. *Atlanta Southern Confederacy,* March 1, 1862; *Richmond Dispatch,* May 29, 1862; *War of the Rebellion,* Series 1, 11 (Pt. 3): 635–636.

23. *New York Tribune,* September 1, 1862; Patricia G. McNeely, Debra van Tuyll, and Henry H. Schulte, *Knights of the Quill: Confederate Correspondents and Their Civil War Reporting* (West Lafayette: Purdue University Press, 2010), 265–267.

24. Andrews, *The South Reports the Civil War,* 223–234; Andrews, *The North Reports the Civil War,* 330–336; *New York Times,* December 27, 1862.

25. *War of the Rebellion,* Series 1, 25 (Pt. 2): 239, 300–301.

26. *Savannah Republican,* June 16, 1862.

27. Andrews, *The North Reports the Civil War,* 368–370; Andrews, *The South Reports the Civil War,* 297–298.

28. John F. Marszalek, *Sherman's Other War* (Memphis: Memphis State University Press, 1981), 49–93.

29. Ibid., 117–153; Andrews, *The North Reports the Civil War,* 377–379.

30. *New York Herald,* January 18, 1862; Marszalek, *Sherman's Other War,* 123–125.

31. Marszalek, *Sherman's Other War,* 126–129.

32. Ibid., 130–137; Andrews, *The North Reports the Civil War,* 381.

33. Ibid., 138–141.

34. Ibid., 142–144.

35. Andrews, *The North Reports the Civil War,* 546–548.

36. *Mobile Register and Advertiser,* June 19, 1863.

37. *Charleston Courier,* May 21, 1864.

38. *Montgomery Advertiser,* May 27, 1864.

39. *War of the Rebellion,* Series 1, 11 (Pt. 2): 567, 583, 593; Andrews, *The North Reports the Civil War,* 550–551.

40. John Nerone, *Violence Against the Press* (New York: Oxford University Press), 117–120; Reed W. Smith, *Samuel Medary & the Crisis: Testing the Limits of Personal Freedom* (Columbus: Ohio State University Press, 1995), 10.

41. Timothy W. Gleason, *The Watchdog Concept: The Press and the Courts in Nineteenth Century America* (Ames: Iowa State Press, 1990), 4, 48.

42. Michael Kent Curtis, *Free Speech, "The People's Darling Privilege": Struggles for Freedom of Expression in American History* (Durham: Duke University Press, 2000); Richard B. Kielbowicz, "The Law and Mob Law in Attacks on Antislavery Newspapers, 1833–1860," *Law and History Review* 24 (Fall 2006): 559–600.

43. James M. McPherson, *Battle Cry of Freedom: The Civil War Era* (New York: Ballantine Books, 1988), 287–289; William F. Duker, *A Constitutional History of Habeas Corpus* (Westport, CT: Greenwood Press, 1980), 143–149.

44. Robert S. Harper, *Lincoln and the Press* (New York: McGraw-Hill, 1951), 113–125.

45. Dickerson, *The Course of Tolerance,* 167–168.

46. Sidney T. Matthews, "Control of the Baltimore Press during the Civil War," *Maryland Historical Magazine* 47 (June 1941): 50–152.

47. Ibid., 153–157.

48. Ibid., 158–170.

49. Jeffery A. Smith, "Lincoln's Other War: Public Opinion, Press Issues, and Personal Pleas," *American Journalism* 26 (2009): 98–99.

50. David Bulla, *Lincoln's Censor: Milo Hascall and Freedom of the Press in Civil War Indiana* (West Lafayette: Purdue University Press, 2009), 1–3.

51. Harper, *Lincoln and the Press,* 141–144.

52. Ibid., 145–148.

53. Ibid., 195–207.

54. Justin E. Walsh, *To Print the News and Raise Hell! A Biography of Wilbur F. Storey* (Chapel Hill: University of North Carolina Press, 1963), 145–165; *Detroit Free Press,* February 6, 1861; *Chicago Times,* October 8, 1861.

55. *Chicago Times,* May 7, 27, 30, 1863; *War of the Rebellion,* Series 1, 23 (Pt. 2): 381.

56. Walsh, *To Print the News and Raise Hell!* 174–175; *Chicago Times,* June 3, 5, 1863; *War of the Rebellion,* Series 1, 23 (Pt. 2): 385.

57. Welles quoted in Walsh, *The Print the News and Raise Hell!* 175; *War of the Rebelion,* Series 2, 5: 723–724; *War of the Rebellion,* Series 3, 3: 252; *War of the Rebellion,* Series 1, 23 (Pt. 2): 386.

58. Quoted in Walsh, *To Print the News and Raise Hell!* 183–184.

59. Smith, *Samuel Medary,* 63–65, 89–91.

60. Ibid., 106–108.

61. Ibid., 136–145.

62. Letters quoted in James M. McPherson, *This Mighty Scourge: Perspectives on the Civil War* (Oxford: Oxford University Press, 2007), 164.

63. Quoted in Gilbert Muller, *William Cullen Bryant* (2004), 273; *Chicago Tribune,* June 12, 1863; Mark E. Neely Jr., *The Union Divided: Party Conflict in the Civil War North* (Cambridge: Harvard University Press, 2002), 90–111.

64. Quoted in Smith, *Lincoln's Other War,* 98–99.

65. Menahem Blondheim, " 'Public Sentiment is Everything': The Union's Public Communication's Strategy and the Bogus Proclamation of 1864," *Journal of American History* (December 2002), 869–898, Harper, *Lincoln and the Press,* 289–303; Neely, *The Union Divided,* 111–117.

66. *New York Journal of Commerce,* May 18, 1864; *New York World,* May 18, 1864; Blondehim, "Public Sentiment is Everything," 882–883, Harper, *Lincoln and the Press,* 292–293.

67. Blondheim, "Public Sentiment is Everything," 869–898; Harper, *Lincoln and the Press,* 293–294.

68. Blondheim, "Public Sentiment is Everything," 869–898; Harper, *Lincoln and the Press,* 294–297.

69. *New York Journal of Commerce,* May 23, 1864, *New York World,* May 23, 1864.

70. Blondheim, "Public Sentiment is Everything," 890–893.

71. Harper, *Lincoln and the Press,* 301–302; Neely, *The Union Divided,* 111–113.

72. Quoted in McNeely, van Tuyll and Schulte, *Knights of the Quill,* 12–13.

73. E. Merton Coulter, *William G. Brownlow: Fighting Parson of the Southern Highlands* (Chapel Hill: University of North Carolina Press, 1937), 35–52; Stephen V. Ash, ed.,

Secessionists and Other Scoundrels: Selection from Parson Brownlow's Book (Baton Rouge: Louisiana State University Press, 1999), 2–4, 61–63.

74. Ash, *Secessionists and Other Scoundrels,* 74–78.

75. Ibid., 5–8.

76. Harris, *William Woods Holden,* 108–109, 131–135.

77. Ibid., 135–139.

78. Ibid., 139–140.

79. Ibid., 142–152.

CHAPTER 5

1. Quoted in David B. Sachsman, S. Kittrell Rushing, and Roy Morris Jr., eds., *Words at War: The Civil War and American Journalism* (West Lafayette: Purdue University Press, 2008), 100.

2. Charles W. Ramsdell, *Behind the Lines in the Southern Confederacy* (Baton Rouge: Louisiana State University Press, 1944), 48.

3. *Charleston Mercury,* October 7, 1861.

4. *Augusta Chronicle & Sentinel,* August 30, 1863; Mary Elizabeth Massey, *Ersatz in the Confederacy* (Columbia: University of South Carolina Press, 1952), 139–147.

5. Frank Luther Mott, *American Journalism: A History, 1690–1960,* 3rd ed. (New York: Macmillan, 1962), 363; Henry T. Malone, "Atlanta Journalism during the Confederacy," *Georgia Historical Quarterly* 37 (September 1953): 216; as quoted in J. Cutler Andrews, *The South Reports the Civil War* (Princeton: Princeton University Press, 1970), 42.

6. Mott, *American Journalism,* 310; *New Orleans Daily Picayune,* December 18, 1861.

7. Quoted in Andrews, *The South Reports the Civil War,* 47.

8. *Abbeville Press,* April 26, 1861.

9. *Atlanta Daily Intelligencer,* December 3, 1863; *Savannah Republican,* September 17, 1864.

10. *North Carolina Standard,* September 14, 1864.

11. *Atlanta Daily Intelligencer,* April 19, 1864; Malone, "Atlanta Journalism during the Confederacy," 217–218; *Columbus Times,* April 13, 1864.

12. *North Carolina Standard,* September 14, 1864.

13. John Nerone, *Culture of the Press in the Early Republic* (New York: Garland, 1989), 47; *Southern Federal Union,* April 16, 1861; *Sandersville Central Georgian,* July 3, 1861; Louis Turner Griffith and John Erwin Talmadge, *Georgia Journalism, 1763–1950* (Athens: University of Georgia Press), 57.

14. *Southern Watchman,* June 1, 1864.

15. Thomas H. Baker, "Refugee Newspaper: The Memphis Daily Appeal, 1862–1865." *Journal of Southern History* 29 (February 1963): 332, 344.

16. *Augusta Chronicle & Sentinel,* August 27, 1862; *Memphis Appeal,* July 19, 1862; *Charleston Mercury,* June 6, 1862.

17. Quoted in *Memphis Appeal,* April 30, 1862.

18. *Upson Pilot,* December 14, 1861.

19. Mott, *The History of Magazines,* 100.

20. Cornelia Phillips Spencer, *The Last Ninety Days of the War in North Carolina* (n.p.: Watchman Publishing, 1866), 244, 249.

21. Stephen V. Ash, *When the Yankees Came: Conflict and Chaos in the Occupied South, 1861–1865* (Chapel Hill: University of North Carolina Press, 1995), 44–45; Mary Elizabeth Massey, *Refugee Life in the Confederacy* (Baton Rouge: Louisiana State University Press, 1964), 41.

22. Ash, *When the Yankees Came,* 170–177.

23. Richard H. Abbott, *For Free Press and Equal Rights: Republican Newspapers in the Reconstruction South* (Athens: University of Georgia Press, 2004), 7–23; Lester J. Cappon, "The Yankee Press in Virginia, 1861–1865," *William and Mary Quarterly Historical Magazine* 15 (January 1935): 81–88.

24. Ash, *When the Yankees Came,* 58; *War of the Rebellion,* Series 1, 44: 813.

25. *New Era,* May 17, 1862; *Charleston Courier,* February 21, 1865.

26. Abbott, *For Free Press and Equal Rights,* 8–9.

27. *St. Augustine Examiner,* May 8, 1862; *Savannah Daily Herald,* January 24, February 1, 1865.

28. Andrews, *The South Reports the Civil War,* 496–500.

29. *Atlanta Southern Confederacy,* May 24, 1864; *Mobile Register and Advertiser,* October 10, 1865; Andrews, *The South Reports the Civil War,* 496.

30. Massey, *Refugee Life in the Confederacy,* 165–167.

31. B.G. Ellis, *The Moving Appeal: Mr. McClanahan, Mrs. Dill, and the Civil War's Great Newspaper Run* (Macon: Mercer University Press, 2003), 153–182; Baker, "Refugee Newspaper," 326–327; *Memphis Appeal,* June 6, 1862.

32. Ellis, *The Moving Appeal,* 160–187; Baker, "Refugee Newspaper," 327–328; *Memphis Appeal,* June 13, 1862.

33. Ellis, *The Moving Appeal,* 188–221; Baker, "Refugee Newspaper," 328–329; *Memphis Appeal,* May 12, 1863.

34. Baker, "Refugee Newspaper," 328–329; *Memphis Appeal,* June 6, 1863.

35. Baker, "Refugee Newspaper," 330–333; Ellis, *The Moving Appeal,* 318–347.

36. Ellis, *The Moving Appeal,* 348–353; Baker, "Refugee Newspaper," 42–44.

37. James Melvin Lee, *History of American Journalism* (Garden City: Garden City Publishing, 1917), 310.

38. Ibid., 309; Starr, *Bohemian Brigade,* 31, 105.

39. *Baltimore American,* November 10, 1864.

40. Quoted in McPherson, *This Mighty Scourge,* 156–157; Jerome Mushkat, ed. *A Citizen-Soldier's Civil War: The Letters of Brevet Major General Alvin C. Voris* (DeKalb: Northern Illinois University Press, 2002), 125.

41. Starr, *Bohemian Brigade,* 233; J. Cutler Andrews, *The North Reports the Civil War* (Pittsburgh: University of Pittsburgh Press, 1955), 403.

42. Starr, *Bohemian Brigade,* 266–271; Andrews, *The North Reports the Civil War,* 646–647.

43. Quoted in Starr, *Bohemian Brigade,* 247–248.

44. *Savannah Republican,* August 27, 1861.

45. *New York Herald,* March 19, 1865; quoted in Andrews, *The North Reports the Civil War,* 447–448; *Rome Courier,* January 15, 1863.

46. Andrews, *The North Reports the Civil War,* 331; *New York Tribune,* September 8, 1862.

47. *Mobile Register and Advertiser,* October 24, 1862; quoted in Andrews, *The North Reports the Civil War,* 109; *Charleston Courier,* September 25, 1862.

48. Quoted in Starr, *Bohemian Brigade,* 255; *Atlantic Monthly,* September 8, 1861.

EPILOGUE

1. *New York Times,* April 16, 1865; David T. Z. Mindich. "Edwin M. Stanton, the Inverted Pyramid, and Information Control." *Journalism Monographs* 140 (1993): 1–31; David Herbert Donald, *Lincoln* (New York: Simon & Schuster, 1995), 596.

2. *National Intelligencer,* April 15, 1865; *Burlington Free Press,* April 15, 1865; *Harrisburg Telegraph,* April 20, 1865; *Richmond Whig* (as quoted in *National Intelligencer*), April 19, 1865.

3. *Harper's Weekly,* April 29, 1865.

4. *Harper's Weekly,* May 6, 13, 20, 27, 1865; *Leslie's Illustrated,* April 29, May 6, 13, 20, 1865.

5. Bob Zeller, *The Blue and Gray in Black and White: A History of Civil War Photography* (Westport, CT: Praeger, 2005), 166–170.

6. *Baltimore American,* April 18, 1865; *New York Tribune,* April 19, 1865.

BIBLIOGRAPHICAL ESSAY

No topic in American history has such a vast literature as the Civil War. Within this tremendous body of work are numerous studies on the journalism of the war, particularly the reporting, editorializing, photography, and illustrations.

The most valuable works on reporting of the war are two books by J. Cutler Andrews, *The North Reports the Civil War* (1955) and *The South Reports the Civil War* (1970). Other useful works include Bernard A. Weisberger, *Reporters for the Union* (1953); Emmet Crozier, *Yankee Reporters, 1861–1865* (1956); *Louis M. Starr, Bohemian Brigade: Civil War Newsmen in Action* (1954); James M. Perry, *A Bohemian Brigade: The Civil War Correspondents—Mostly Rough, Sometimes Ready* (2000); and Patricia G. McNeely, Debra Reddin van Tuyll, and Henry H. Schulte, eds., *Knights of the Quill: Confederate Correspondents and Their Civil War Reporting* (2010).

Nineteenth-century newspaper editors were a colorful and, often controversial group. As such, they have been the subjects of numerous biographies. The best are Ralph R. Fahrney, *Horace Greeley and the Tribune in the Civil War* (1936); E. Merton Coulter, *William G. Brownlow: Fighting Parson of the Southern Highlands* (1937); Wilbur F. Storey, *To Print the News and Raise Hell! A Biography of Wilbur F. Storey* (1963); Laura A. White, *Robert Barnwell Rhett: Father of Secession* (1965); William C. Harris, *William Woods Holden: Firebrand of North Carolina Politics* (1987); William S. McFeely, *Frederick Douglass* (1991); Reed Smith, *Samuel Medary & the Crisis:*

Testing the Limits of Press Freedom (1995); Henry Mayer, *All on Fire: William Lloyd Garrison and the Abolition of Slavery* (1998); Gilbert Muller, *William Cullen Bryant* (2004); and Lonnie A. Burnett, *The Pen Makes a Good Sword: John Forsyth of the Mobile Register* (2006).

There are few biographies of newspaper correspondents. But Ida M. Tarbell, *A Reporter for Lincoln: The Story of Henry M. Wing, Soldier and Newspaperman* (1927); Joseph J. Matthews, *George W. Smalley: Forty Years a Foreign Correspondent* (1973); and Bingham Duncan, *Whitelaw Reid: Journalist, Politician, Diplomat* (1975) have sections on the newsmen's war reporting. After the war, some journalists wrote about their work or their stories have been compiled. The best memoirs and compilations include Felix Gregory de Fontaine, *Marganalia, or Gleanings from an Army Notebook* (1864); Lawrence Augustus Gobright, *Recollections of Men and Things at Washington during the Third of a Century* (1869); Charles Carleton Coffin, *My Days and Nights on the Battlefield* (1887); Francis Bangs Wilkie, *Pen and Powder* (1988); Thomas Morris Chester, *Thomas Morris Chester, Black Civil War Correspondent: His Dispatches from the Virginia Front* (1989); Michael Burlingame, ed. *Lincoln Observed: Civil War Dispatches of Noah Brooks* (1998); and Richard N. Griffin, ed., *Three Years a Soldier: The Diary and Newspaper Correspondence of Private George Perkins, Sixth New York Independent Battery, 1861–1864* (2006).

There are numerous histories of newspapers that played a significant role during the war. They include Alan Nevins, *The Evening Post: A Century of Journalism* (1922); Archer H. Shaw, *The Plain Dealer: One Hundred Years in Cleveland* (1942); Thomas E. Dabney, *One Hundred Great Years: The Story of the Times-Picayune from Its Founding to 1940* (1944); Meyer Berger, *The Story of the New York Times, 1851–1951* (1951); Herbert Ravenel Sass, *Outspoken: 150 Years of the News and Courier* (1953); Thomas Harrison Baker, *The Memphis Commercial Appeal: The History of a Southern Newspapers* (1971); and William E. Ames, *A History of the National Intelligencer* (1972).

Several valuable compendiums contain stories, editorials, cartoons, illustrations, and photographs from the war. They include Herbert Mitgang, *Lincoln as the Saw Him* (1956); Charles Hamilton and Lloyd Hostendorf, *Lincoln in Photographs: An Album of Every Known Pose* (1963); Kristen Smith, ed., *The Lines are Drawn: Political Cartoons of the Civil War* (1999); Ford Risley, *The Civil War: Primary Documents on Events from 1860–1865* (2004); David A. Copeland, ed., *The Greenwood Library of American War Reporting: The Civil War, North and South* (2005); J. G. Lewin and P. J. Huff, eds., *Witness to the Civil War: First-Hand Accounts from Frank Leslie's Illustrated Newspaper* (2006); J. G. Lewin and P. J. Huff, *Lines of Contention: Political Cartoons of the Civil War* (2007); and Harold Holzer and Craig L. Symonds, eds., *The New York Times Complete Civil War, 1861–1865* (2010).

W. Fletcher Thompson Jr., *The Image of War: The Pictorial Reporting of the American Civil War* (1959) is an excellent overview of magazine illustrations during the war. Bob Zeller, *The Blue and Gray in Black and White: A History of Civil War Photography* (2005) is the best single source on the role of photography. Michael L. Carlebach, *The Origins of Photojournalism in America* (1992) is a good synopsis of photojournalism in the 19th century. Three valuable books by William A. Frassanito, *Gettysburg, A Journey in Time* (1975), *Antietam: The Photographic Legacy of America's Bloodiest Day* (1978), and *Grant and Lee: The Virginia Campaigns* (1983), examine the photographs made of major battles and campaigns.

There are several good biographies of war artists and photographers. They include Lloyd Goodrich, *Winslow Homer* (1944); James D. Horan, *Mathew Brady: Historian with a Camera* (1955); James D. Horan, *Timothy O'Sullivan: America's Forgotten Photographer* (1966); Morton Keller, *The Art and Politics of Thomas Nast* (1968); Frederick E. Ray, *"Our Special Artist": Alfred R. Waud's Civil War* (1994); Mary Panzer. *Mathew Brady and the Image of History* (1997); and Mark D. Katz, *Witness to an Era: The Life and Photography of Alexander Gardner* (1999).

A number of important works examine press freedom during the war, usually as part of larger studies. They include James G. Randall, *Constitutional Problems Under Lincoln* (1926); Donna Lee Dickerson, *Freedom of the Press in Nineteenth-Century America* (1990); Timothy W. Gleason, *The Watchdog Concept: The Press and the Courts in Nineteenth-Century America* (1990); Mark A. Neeley, *The Fate of Liberty: Abraham Lincoln and Civil Liberties* (1991); Jeffery A. Smith, *War and Press Freedom: The Problem of Prerogative Power* (1999); Michael Kent Curtis, *Free Speech, "The People's Darling Privilege": Struggles for Freedom of Expression in American History* (2000); and David Bulla, *Lincoln's Censor: Milo Hascall and Freedom of the Press in Civil War Indiana* (2009).

Among the most valuable works on other topics, Victor Rosewater, *History of News-Gathering in the United States* (1930) includes information about the Associated Press during the war. James E. Pollard, *The Presidents and the Press* (1947) has a chapter on Lincoln's relationship with journalists. Robert S. Harper, *Lincoln and the Press* (1951) is an anecdotally rich study of the relationship between the president and the press. Donald E. Reynolds, *Editors Make War: Southern Newspapers in the Secession Crisis* (1966) deals primarily with events before the war, but provides an excellent overview of where newspapers of the South stood editorially. John F. Marszalek, *Sherman's Other War: The General and the Civil War Press* (1981) examines the general's combative relationship with the press. Hazel Dicken-Garcia, *Journalistic Standards in Nineteenth-Century America* (1989) is a valuable synopsis of the state of journalism. Menahem Blondheim, *News over the Wires: The Telegraph and the Flow of Public Information, 1844–1897* (1994) is a helpful work on the critical role of the telegraph.

B. G. Ellis, *The Moving Appeal: Mr. McClanahan, Mrs. Dill, and the Civil War's Great Newspaper Run* (2003) is a lively account of the South's best-known refugee newspaper. Ford Risley, *Abolition and the Press: The Moral Struggle against Slavery* (2008) is an overview of antislavery newspapers with a chapter on their role during the war.

Other useful works on various include subjects include Harry J. Carmann and Reinhard H. Luthin, *Lincoln and the Patronage* (1943); Mary Elizabeth Massey, *Refugee Life in the Confederacy* (1964); Hodding Carter Jr., *Their Words Were Bullets* (1969); Robert F. Durden, *The Gray and the Black: The Confederate Debate on Emancipation* (1972); Martha A. Sandweiss, ed., *Photography in Nineteenth-Century America* (1991); Gerald J. Baldasty, *The Commercialization of News in the Nineteenth Century* (1992); John Nerone, *Violence Against the Press: Policing the Public Sphere in U.S. History* (1994); Stephen V. Ash, *When the Yankees Came: Conflict and Chaos in the Occupied South, 1861–1865* (1995); David T.D.Z. Mindich, *Just the Facts: How "Objectivity" Came to Define American Journalism* (1998); William E. Huntzicker, *The Popular Press, 1833–1865* (1999); Henry J. Maihafer, *War of Words: Abraham Lincoln and the Civil War Press* (2001); Richard H. Abbott, *For Free Press and Equal Rights: Republican Newspapers in the Reconstruction South* (2004); Chandra Manning, *What this Cruel War was Over: Soldiers, Slavery, and the Civil War* (2007); James M. McPherson, *This Mighty Scourge: Perspectives on the Civil War* (2007); Hazel Dicken-Garcia and Giovanna Dell' Orto, *Hated Ideas and the American Civil War Press* (2008); David B. Sachsman, S. Kittrell Rushing, and Roy Morris Jr., eds., *Words at War: The Civil War and America Journalism* (2008); and David W. Bulla and Gregory A. Borchard, *Journalism in the Civil War Era* (2010).

Several surveys of journalism and news history include sections on the war press. Among the standard works are Frederick Hudson, *Journalism in the United States, from 1690–1872* (1873); James Melvin Lee, *History of American Journalism* (1917); Frank Luther Mott, *American Journalism: A History of Newspapers in the United States: 1690–1950* (1950); Michael Schudson, *Discovering the News: A Social History of American Newspapers* (1978); Michael Emery and Edwin Emery, *The Press and America: An Interpretive History* (1988); and Wm. David Sloan, *The Media in America, A History* (2011).

There has been a resurgence of interest in Civil War journalism scholarship in the last decade and a number of valuable scholarly articles on various subjects have been published, joining older studies. They include Lester J. Cappon, "The Yankee Press in Virginia, 1861–1865," *William and Mary Quarterly Historical Magazine* 15 (1935): 81–88; Sidney T. Matthews, "Control of the Baltimore Press during the Civil War," *Maryland Historical Magazine* 36 (June 1941), 50–152; James W. Silver, "Propaganda in the Confederacy," *Journal of Southern History* 11 (November 1945): 487–503; Henry T. Malone. "Atlanta Journalism during the Confederacy," *Georgia*

Historical Quarterly 37 (September 1953): 210–219; J. Cutler Andrews, "The Confederate Press and Public Morale," *Journal of Southern History* 32 (November 1966): 445–465; Thomas A. Baker, "A Refugee Newspaper: The Memphis Daily Appeal, 1862–1865," *Journal of Southern History* 29 (February 1973): 326–344; Richard B. Kielbowicz, "The Telegraph, Censorship, and Politics at the Outset of the Civil War," *Civil War History* 35 (1994): 95–118; Ford Risley, "Bombastic Yet Insightful: Georgia's Civil War Soldier Correspondents," *Journalism History* 24 (Autumn 1998): 104–111; Debra Reddin van Tuyll, "The Rebels Yell: Conscription and Freedom of Expression in the Civil War South," *American Journalism* (Spring 2000): 15–29; Ford Risley, "The Confederate Press Association: Cooperative News Reporting of the War," *Civil War History* 47 (September 2001): 222–239; Menahem Blondheim, " 'Public Sentiment is Everything': The Union's Public Communications Strategy and the Bogus Proclamation of 1864," *Journal of American History* (December 2002): 869–899; Ford Risley, " 'Dear Courier': The Civil War Correspondence of Editor Melvin Dwinell," *Journalism History* 31 (Fall 2005): 162–170; David W. Bulla, "Abraham Lincoln and Press Suppression Reconsidered," *American Journalism* 26 (Fall 2009): 11–33; Mary M. Cronin, "Fiend, Coward, Monster, or King: Southern Press Views of Abraham Lincoln," *American Journalism* 26 (Fall 2009): 35–61; Ford Risley, "The President's Editor: John Forney of the *Press* and *Morning Chronicle*," *American Journalism* 26 (Fall 2009): 63–85; and Jeffery A. Smith, "Lincoln's Other War: Public Opinion, Press Issues, and Personal Pleas," *American Journalism* 26 (Fall 2009): 87–117.

INDEX

ABOUT THE AUTHOR

FORD RISLEY is a professor of communications and head of the Department of Journalism at Penn State University. He is the author of *Abolition and the Press: The Moral Struggle against Slavery* (Northwestern University Press, 2008) and articles on Civil War–era journalism. He lives in State College, Pennsylvania, with his wife and two daughters.